Enter St

Also by Feisal Alkazi

Exploring an Environment
(First edition, INTACH, 1990; second edition, Orient Longman, 2001)

Rang Biranga Rangmanch
(First edition National Book Trust, 2000; twelfth edition 2019)

Forever Friends
(First edition, Pratham Books, 2008; fourth edition 2015)

Srinagar: An Architectural Legacy
(First edition Roli Books with INTACH, 2014; second edition 2015)

Enter
Stage Right

The Alkazi/Padamsee Family Memoir

Feisal Alkazi

SPEAKING
TIGER

SPEAKING TIGER BOOKS LLP
4381/4, Ansari Road, Daryaganj
New Delhi 110002

First published by Speaking Tiger Books in hardback in 2020

ISBN: 978-93-90477-07-4
eISBN: 978-93-91477-04-3

10 9 8 7 6 5 4 3 2 1

Typeset in EB Garamond by SÜRYA, New Delhi
Printed at Sanat Printers, Kundli

For Roshen and Radhika, Zaen and Armaan
for being who they are

Contents

Prologue

Around the Horseshoe-Shaped Table

Enlish theatre in Bombay was born on my grandmother's horseshoe-shaped dining table in 1943. Literally. A group of young college students, among them my father, Ebrahim Alkazi, listened wide-eyed as my uncle, Sultan Padamsee, spoke of how they intended to form their own group, simply called the Theatre Group.

Sultan Padamsee's infamous production of Oscar Wilde's *Salome* had recently been refused permission to perform at St Xavier's College as the ideas in the play were seen as being too 'salacious'. In Oscar Wilde's inimitable style and with his fantastic use of language, *Salome* is based on the Biblical tale in which Salome demands the head of John the Baptist from King Herod. A key turning point in the script is the Dance of the Seven Veils in which the tempestuous Salome performs a Biblical striptease. With great difficulty and after much persuasion, the young Parsi woman who played Salome agreed to act, but she drew the line at doing the dance. So my mother, Roshen Padamsee, stepped in, a young nineteen, willing to do all for her beloved brother's production.

That's how my parents met. The intense and handsome young Arab with the mellifluous voice, and the young, pert and pretty Roshen. My father was eighteen, a junior of Sultan Padamsee at St Xavier's College, and had just relocated from Pune. My mother had recently returned from her schooling in England because of the outbreak of World War II. They were part of a large group of amateur actors drawn together by a love of theatre.

Moving out of the college auditorium and looking for an alternative performance space wasn't easy, but the Sir Cowasjee Jehangir Hall opposite the Prince of Wales Museum was selected and booked. With its grand colonnaded entrance, this hall was largely only rented out for wedding receptions, but Sultan decided to mount his play there. Today this building houses the Mumbai chapter of the National Gallery of Modern Art and the museum is now known as Chhatrapati Shivaji Vastu Sangrahalaya!

Salome was one of several plays that Sultan Padamsee was to direct, drawing talent to himself by his charismatic personality. With bravado and full confidence in his abilities, Sultan went easily where no one had been before him. He was a flamboyant personality, tall, well-built, diamond studs in his ears, often dressed in a coloured kurta and pyjamas. Or even in an achkan with one of his mother's pearl chokers around his throat!

And now to return to that legendary horseshoe-shaped dining table that still holds pride of place in my grandmother's flat on Colaba Causeway, and that often still has a pile of scripts on it, and a bunch of eager new-generation actors grouped around it.

The design of the table had been taken from a Hollywood film. On seeing it, my grandmother decided this was what she needed to host her growing family and their constantly expanding group of friends. She had it immediately constructed in the furniture shop the family owned, named Shiraz.

She was a wealthy woman who had, along with her husband,

built eight buildings in south Bombay, each named after one of her children. Four boys and four girls survived out of the fourteen pregnancies she had.

Looking back, my mother recalls: 'She came from an educated background. She possibly saw the difference between her family and my father's family, who were just one removed from villagers and their way of life. Mummy didn't want us to become like that. She had a vision of how she would like her children to be. In those days of colonial rule, the vision was that you should have a very good English education, to help you get into good positions. Being well-educated meant that rather than just going into the family business, you had a choice. Mummy wanted something more which she tried to give us.'

Born in 1922 in Bombay, Bobby (as Sultan was known to all) was sent at the age of five to board and study with two Irish ladies who ran a private school in Bombay; they gave him his idealistic turn of mind and an early love for dramatics. Six of his siblings followed him there. At twelve, he moved to a Jesuit school in Nainital in the Himalayas, where he first began writing poetry and learnt Latin which led him to later study the Greek language and its thought and philosophy. This was, perhaps, the strongest influence felt in his writing. At the age of fourteen, with a brilliant scholastic record, he left for England.

But it was already 1938 and the world was on the verge of war. Bobby had been at Christ Church College, Oxford, only six months when the war broke out. He sought refuge in a little village in Wales along with his mother, later returning to an India then in the last throes of the national movement. This was to affect Bobby deeply, for in his search for his own identity, which led him to express himself in painting, poetry and the theatre, there is also a struggle to find his own roots as an Indian. This is the dilemma of every Indian intellectual brought up solely on Western thought and ideas.

It was April 1942, and Bobby was nineteen years old. In the next three and half years he lived the most intensely creative period possible for an artist. He wrote more than a hundred poems, most of which are in Cycles, he turned out artworks in watercolours, oils and crayons, and his biggest achievement was founding the Theatre Group, bringing a new meaning to theatre, by making it an integral part of our contemporary lives.

Bombay at the time had a very affluent, English-speaking, Westward-seeking elite, up with the 'latest' gossip from Hollywood and the latest novels from Europe. Pastries were available at Ferlettis on Colaba or at Bombellis at Breach Candy, steaks at Gurdons at Churchgate. Parties were held at the Taj Mahal Hotel, then in its heyday, and clubs like the Princess Victoria Gymkhana, the Bombay Gym and Willingdon were where you could spend an evening playing cards, dancing to a jazz band, swimming or just adorning the bar.

The outbreak of World War II in Europe in the spring of 1939 played a key role in shaping the Indian cultural scene of the time. Set against the backdrop of the Indian National Movement, now in its final phase, and the aggression of the Japanese who had reached the very borders of British India, coming as far as Assam, gave a tremendous psychological boost to the whole issue of Asian identity.

The presence of hundreds and thousands of foreign troops in India meant that two entirely different sets of young people met and interacted face to face for the first time. The restrictions imposed by the war changed the Indian economy, ways of doing business and the entire educational system. As art critic Richard Bartholomew wrote, 'While practically the whole of Europe and two of the major countries of the East, Japan and China, were at war, when it seemed that spiritual values were being challenged all around him, the Indian artist, perhaps unconsciously, felt the need to preserve at home the humanistic values of a rich heritage in the arts.'

In 1926, Aldous Huxley had described Bombay as 'one of the most appalling cities of either hemisphere. It had the misfortune to develop during what was, perhaps, the darkest period of all architectural history.'

Though this is a sharp criticism, for many at the time, the growing skyline of Bombay with its distinctive hybrid architecture symbolized the power of money and enterprise. Private entrepreneurs and the government had come together to create the iconic buildings of this port city over the previous fifty years. The Rajabai Clock Tower, reminiscent in its own way of the Big Ben in London and as much a symbol of that city, was said to be inspired by Giotto's Campanile in Florence. Other parts of the University buildings were designed using elements of Venetian Gothic and fifteenth-century French Gothic architecture. Victoria Terminus, the train station, was definitely the most outrageous and spectacular example of the Indo-Gothic style.

Decorative work on several of these public buildings was undertaken by the staff and students of the J.J. School of Art under Lockwood Kipling's (Rudyard's father) direction. The Victoria Terminus, Crawford Market, Rajabai Clock Tower and other landmark structures were also embellished with murals painted by them.

In 1900, a new style of architecture, the Indo-Saracenic style, had replaced the old. The Prince of Wales Museum in Bombay brought together a Mughal dome and carved screen arches with elements of European classicism. The Taj Mahal Hotel overlooking the Gateway of India (which itself was based on sixteenth-century Gujarati architecture) with its characteristic ribbed dome was ready by 1904.

By the 1930s the two sides of the Oval Maidan were in a kind of 'face off': modern Art Deco architecture facing the now moribund, dated Victorian and Indo-Saracenic styles. The Bombay of the time was very different to the city of Mumbai as we know it today. From 1928 to 1942, a huge Backbay Reclamation Scheme was underway, creating 'land' out of the sea, to house the ever-expanding upper middle class. First Churchgate, then Marine Drive and Chowpatty and finally Malabar Hill, Cumballa Hill and beyond, began to be built in the prevailing 'cool' style of Art Deco.

Not only was land being reclaimed from the sea, a country was also being reclaimed from the colonizer. A new wave of modernism was creeping across Bombay, not only in the architecture being practiced but also in the ideas and thinking that came with it. The arts—painting, drama, literature, cinema—were all transforming themselves.

Art Deco is a blanket term for the new style of design that emerged across the world between the wars. Attempting to 'fashion the future' or 'turn life into art', it influenced architecture and interiors, jewellery and ceramic ware. Simplified form, rounded corners, sleek lines highlighted by paint, stylized new age lettering and above all a focus on light and space characterized Art Deco architecture. Zest, colour, playfulness were the key concepts. In Bombay the decorative details of frozen waterfalls in ironwork grills, stylized foliage in building details, sunburst designs and wild colourful terrazzo flooring that can be seen till today, are a homage to the building frenzy the city went through in the 1930s and 40s.

Most prominent among the buildings that came up was the Eros Theatre, even now a wonderfully conserved Art Deco property. At the time it was built, besides the movie theatre, it also housed a ballroom and restaurant that could seat 500 people, an ice-skating rink, luxury offices and swanky retail stores. Money had poured into Bombay.

In such an atmosphere of ferment and flux the Theatre Group served as the perfect training ground for a bunch of young people, many still in their late teens, to learn the art of theatre together. As my father put it, 'Bobby combined in himself the creative talents of Orson Welles and the majestic impressario faculties of a Sergei Diaghilev.' Orson Welles was the larger than life actor and director, equally at home in cinema (*Citizen Kane*), radio, and on the stage; Diaghilev was one of the most accomplished artists, who called himself 'a cheeky charlatan with a dash'. A true patron of the arts who courted Picasso, Matisse, Nijinsky, Pavlova, Stravinsky and other geniuses to create a completely new stage presentation, with outstanding choreography, original music and avant-garde sets and costumes.

'Bobby had curly hair, he was well-built, and his voice was beautiful. He spoke English beautifully, and he had this deep voice which used to resonate on the stage. He could also speak poetry very well,' is how my mother remembers her brother.

'Plus, he was an intellectual of a very high order and his problem was that he didn't have peers of his own level. There must have been hundreds as brilliant as him. If he had stayed on in Oxford, I'm sure he would have met people of his own level of thinking.'

A country, a city, a society, an individual, all at a time of churning and becoming. There was a widespread questioning of the past, of social structures and relationships, of the freedom of the individual. There was also a collective envisioning of the future.

Nurtured in excellent educational institutions in Bombay

and Nainital, Shropshire and finally at Oxford and with an extremely supportive family behind him, Sultan Padamsee was one among many at the time who was forging a new path, showing a possible way ahead in the arts. The birth of the Theatre Group was imminent.

One

Kulsumbai of Kulsum Terrace

My maternal grandparents belonged to neighbouring towns in Saurashtra and had shifted to Bombay in the early decades of the twentieth century. Over fifteen years ago three of my cousins and I decided to travel back to our ancestral villages and spend five days getting to know something of our past. None of the immediate family had been back for over sixty years. But even as we entered our grandfather's village and identified ourselves as being from the Padamsee clan, we were welcomed and shown around, for our family had been responsible for bringing piped water to the village eighty years ago! A few kilometres down the road was the town of Talaja where my grandmother had grown up. Her stock were opium farmers, commonplace in the last years of the nineteenth century as much of the opium that was exported to China was grown in Gujarat.

From the late eighteenth century till 1947, opium was the third most important source of revenue for the British Indian government after land revenue and the draconian salt tax. My grandmother's family rented out small plots to cultivators to grow their opium crop.

But poppies are temperamental plants, and the harvesting of them is complex, as thousands of small incisions need to be made in the seed heads every two or three days over a four-week period. Whole families would work together but if the crop failed and they were unable to pay, the head of the family would be hanged to death from a huge banyan tree in my grandmother's family farm to serve as a warning against the non-payment of rental.

Of course there were other stories too. How one of my maternal grand uncles had left home early and returned years later as a holy man with a young gay partner. Even as the holy man cured people and wrought miracles, his handsome partner realized he was really bi-sexual and impregnated many of the women in the village!

Khojas of my grandmother's generation strongly believed in the Aga Khan, their spiritual leader. His debonair, larger than life, Westernized image hangs in many Khoja homes. The word 'Khoja' itself, comes from Khwaja (meaning respectable person) and connotes those from present-day India and Pakistan who converted to Nizari Ismaili Islam from the thirteenth century onwards. This small well-knit community hails originally from Kutch and Saurashtra in Gujarat. Many wedding customs clearly link this community to its Hindu ancestry like the use of the swastika, the haldi ceremony of the groom, the significance of a diya and of a coconut. This is a congregational religion, praying together every Friday in a 'Jammat Khana' after which a lavish feast is held with food brought by the believers. However, my grandmother rarely attended any of these events.

Married at a young age, my grandmother moved to Bombay with her husband, Jaffer Ali Padamsee, who joined the family business, Saleh Mohamed Padamsee, that dealt with exclusive glass imported from Czechoslovakia among other places. Till today some of the windows of my grandmother's flat have her initials KJP etched on them in an elaborate arabesque design. This is only an indication of the kind of affluent lifestyle the

Padamsee family could afford. The Khoja community in Bombay to which they belonged was wealthy, progressive and liberal.

This was my grandfather's second marriage. His first wife had died early after giving birth to five children who had all passed away in infancy. The second time round he would ensure that his children would survive.

And Kulsumbai, my grandmother, was determined to give her children the best possible English education. As each child reached the age of four they were sent off to an exclusive, elitist residential school in Bombay itself. Here they rubbed shoulders with royalty: the Scindia boys, Princess Diamond and Princess Pearl of the Rajpipla family, among others. For their summer holidays they were whisked away to cooler climes like Nainital, travelling in a large railway compartment that was cooled by melting blocks of ice!

The Padamsee residence is a flat on the fourth floor of a building built in 1936 with shops on the ground floor and residences above. It overlooks the wide arterial road, Colaba Causeway, known as a 'shoppers' paradise'. The building is simply called 'Kulsum Terrace'. Directly opposite is the Parsi colony of Cusrow Baug. Its identical flats are occupied by Parsis often seen on their balconies in their traditional 'sadra' and 'kasti' with their prayer caps on their heads. Some balconies hold a parrot in a cage, others a few wilted plants that need to be watered morning and evening. Close enough is the BEST office with its characteristic Art Deco architecture rendered in black stone.

The Padamsee flat is accessed by a slow-moving lift with an open plan design. As a result, you can see every floor as you ascend. My grandmother's flat is on the top floor and needless to say, the lift only travels from ground to fourth floor, not stopping anywhere in between. Talk of privilege!

What on other floors are eight tiny flats is here just one big flat with a huge terrace surrounded by water tanks that service the entire building. The floors of the flat are laid out in wild Art Deco designs that swirl across the surface in oranges, yellows and maroons, while the terrace has the same motifs rendered in tiny mosaic tiles.

You enter the flat directly into the drawing room, a huge space which has larger-than-lifesize portraits of family members adorning all the walls. These are suspended on chains at an angle that allows them to look down on you. The faces are blank, neutral. In one Bobby sits in a formal suit on the arm of his mother's chair, his arm protectively cradling her back. She wears round gold-rimmed glasses and is dressed in a heavy pale georgette sari with an elaborate gold-embroidered border. In another portrait my grandparents pose awkwardly together. These are all studio portraits, and as was usual at the time, they are tinted and painted over. A grandfather clock sounds the hour.

The drawing room is decorated in the prevailing style of the early twentieth century. The space is formal and cool, not overcrowded, but neither is it welcoming. A big Persian carpet spreads across the floor with four sofas and two armchairs upholstered in a deep maroony pink formally placed on its edges. Lining the walls are glass cabinets with small objects collected from around the world. But the fun piece of furniture for us children was the 'love seat' on wheels. Occasionally we would disrupt this formality by setting up a table tennis table right in the middle and run around it screaming and laughing as we played rounders. My grandmother would smile benignly, never stopping us. On one side of the drawing room is the dining room and kitchen, on the other two bedrooms that were occupied by my grandmother and all the children. My grandfather's bedroom was located in another part of the house.

I remember her always in a long floor-length dress usually of dark blue cotton with a small print in white. The neck is round, the sleeves are short. Her bunch of keys, for she is constantly locking and unlocking everything, are in her pocket. Her hair is cut short in what we today call a 'boy cut', and she washes it with aretha, a nut with a strange smell that she soaks in a brass vessel that lies on the bathroom floor. The bathroom is all in pinks: floor, walls, washbasin, tub, bidet. There is no actual toilet, for that is in an outhouse on the terrace. My nani's morning starts with opening out her large airing cupboard full of all kinds of groceries and doling out spoons of sugar and tea on a thali. Then she uses a cup to measure out the rations for the day as well, rice and dal. She is beyond thrifty, she is positively parsimonious!

I remember one instance when I locked horns with her— over the money she owed one of the servants she had dismissed. She asked him to return three days later for the meagre sum of three rupees twelve annas that she owed him. This injustice was too much for me to bear and in her presence I pulled out my wallet and paid the man. Those were my 'socialist' teenage years and I must have been one of the few grandchildren who battled with her—and won!

Each floor of Kulsum Terrace told its own story...

On the ground floor, the sole flat was occupied by Miss Hurley, an ancient ballet dancer from Soviet Russia, who was said to have escaped the revolution by walking to India! She was at least eighty, and yet, so the story goes, walked daily for a swim to the American Club at Breach Candy. It was at least five kilometres away and for much of my childhood, the swimming pool there was closed to Indians.

On the first floor a ladies' tailor, Sherbanu, a distant relative of my grandmother, ran a small dress-making business. We children made fun of her behind her back because of her untrimmed facial hair. I recall accompanying my mother on many afternoons to Sherbanu as she designed clothes for herself. Her room was always bathed in light, there would be several women there in various stages of undress, fascinating for a teenage boy, and because the flat was on the first floor, the sound of traffic was frighteningly loud.

Diagonally opposite her flat there hung a dusty blue and white signboard, bearing the letters 'Marge's Bargain Sale'. Run by Marge, a large rundown Anglo-Indian lady, the store had rows of secondhand clothes and heavy coats on sale, good for a bargain when one was travelling abroad and needed outerwear. The tiny flat reeked of musty clothes smelling of mothballs, all in need of an airing, but for us, when we were children, it was almost like the treasures of Aladdin's cave.

The second floor for the longest time operated as a high-class brothel, with the staircase often resounding to the full-throated laughter of Arabs and the clickety-clack of the high-heeled call girls who accompanied them. My grandmother found them easy to deal with as they paid the rent on time and kept the police away by doling out the regular hafta.

People from the building, her tenants, occasionally dropped in for a cup of tea, a word of advice, wanting to delay paying their paltry monthly rentals. At regular intervals another stock character of my childhood, Freny Lala, would come by, with a big bundle of cut pieces of cloth that she peddled from door to door, displaying and selling them with the panache of a Kashmiri shawl seller. My grandmother usually met these uninvited guests while she sat on her rocking chair, a supari cutter in hand, constantly cutting pieces of supari.

After breakfast, which she ate at a small square marble-topped table near the big horseshoe-shaped one, she would spend the day ordering around Nicholas, her Man Friday. A tall weedy man with glasses that were forever smudged and hair that stood on end, Nicholas only dressed in shorts, shirts and sandals even though he was well into his fifties. He was sent on numerous errands across Bombay, pedalling furiously on his cycle, sweating profusely, collecting masalas here, payments there, dropping pastries or dry fruits off at my grandmother's three daughters' houses.

Many years after he passed away, the family would regale itself with yet another 'Nicholas' story. With his acerbic, mean sense of humour, Uncle Alyque often mimicked Nicholas stuttering, 'But m-m-madam', as he faced abuse from the stern matriarch daily.

Her children's friends and even her grandchildren's friends often came around at lunch or dinner time, because she was known to be a superb cook and a generous hostess. Delectable mutton curries, her signature keema potato curry, a sour and sweet dal, paya (trotter) curry... Her flavours and recipes were legendary. The smell of onions being fried till they turned a dark brown (bresta), the melting mouthwatering excellently cut pieces of mutton without a trace of fat, thin delicious rotis with a generous layer of oil on them, fish fried to perfection with a tangy covering of green masala... Khoja cuisine contains elements of both Iranian and Gujarati cuisine but it is uniquely its own, not to be mistaken for Bohri or Memon food.

She often stood over the stove herself, frequently drinking cups of tea, pouring it directly from a boiling saucepan into a cup and drinking it while it was still scalding hot. For many years of my childhood, the cook referred to as 'lame boy' by us, because he had lost his toes in frostbite in the ocean during the battles of World War II, churned out these signature dishes. But even when cooks changed, her food tasted remarkably the same, for she supervised the making of every dish closely.

My grandmother would read late into the night, her gold-framed spectacles perched on her nose, a reading lamp poised over her head, deliciously enjoying the very 'British' characters of an Agatha Christie novel. Occasionally she stretched out a hand to drink water from a matka resting on a metal stand with a ladle precariously poised on the lid. Exactly how it would be in a Gujarati village. How this woman had grown from her early years on a farm in Saurashtra. She was an amazing contradiction, as were many others of her generation, completely liberal and accepting of the many affairs her sons had, and relating easily to their stay-over girlfriends of all religious backgrounds, and yet turning completely intolerant when her sons married these very women! She then debarred their entry to the family home and refused to meet her grandchildren. Though her house reverberated many evenings to rehearsals, parties and dancing, Kulsumbai was rarely seen at a performance.

On every birthday of her children and grandchildren she would be ready with an envelope with the person's name on it, written in the spidery scrawl of her handwriting. Within it, the princely sum of a hundred rupees which was a vast amount of money in the 1950s and 60s.

And for her own birthday my grandmother took us to the same restaurant every year, Coronation Darbar. On one occasion, I remember her ability to pull off the whackiest of jokes with a completely straight face. The government had recently imposed a service charge on bills in restaurants and this appeared at the bottom of a bill presented to my grandmother. 'What is this?' she asked imperiously, her index finger with its five diamond rings twinkling in the light. The waiter sheepishly pointed with a vague gesture to the table and everything on it: dishes, cutlery *et al*. 'Fine,' she said grimly and opening her large handbag, began to put the unused cutlery into it. Seeing the alarmed look on the waiter's face, she burst out laughing.

My childhood in Bombay till I was nine years old, meant that I spent every Sunday at my grandparents, as did all my aunts and cousins.

Summer meant packing up the entire kitchen and moving to a hill station near Bombay with my grandmother. There were usually thirteen of us in all, plus or minus a few. My grandmother would hire a cottage in the hills, never a hotel. A large bungalow with three or four bedrooms (but usually only two bathrooms) situated in a large garden full of trees. Trunks of household goods would be packed and on the appointed day all five of the Jefferies family, two of the Sayani family (except the father, Hamid, and my cousin Alan, who was born much later) and three of us Alkazis (except Dad) would meet up at the railway station with my youngest aunt Dilshad, or Candy as she was always known, and my grandmother. My grandfather never accompanied us on these summer holidays.

This was our one-month-long break from the humid searing heat of Bombay. Mahabaleshwar, Matheran, Panchgani were the hill stations in the Western Ghats we frequented. Once, as a concession to the Alkazis who lived in 'far away' Delhi, everyone trooped up to stay for a month in a cottage on the grounds of Wildflower Hall near Shimla. I suppose for all of my parents' generation, and for my grandmother, this annual holiday reminded them of their childhood spent in the cooler climes of Shropshire in England.

Excitement ran high. Who would sleep where? Would the cousins camp out in a room by themselves having midnight feasts every week, or would everyone be allotted rooms family-wise? Who headed the bathroom roster? What was the day's menu? And most importantly, what would we do all day? Candy often, or rather always, took change of us and much of our day was spent outdoors, running around, playing games, picnicking, sitting on a setrangi (durrie) in the garden playing yet another game of cards, organizing our teams for 'dumb charades' or going for a long walk. At meal times we would gather together to enjoy the sumptuous spread my grandmother and her four daughters had cooked. Evening meant a game of scrabble and reading books.

All in all an idyllic set of summer holidays stretching from childhood well into my adolescence and beyond.

Two

An Anglicized Childhood

M y grandmother's tough and tenacious personality developed over the years. She realized early in her marriage, that despite the beatings her body was taking from her non-stop pregnancies (fourteen in all, like the Mughal empress Mumtaz Mahal) the responsibility of providing her children the best deal in life by giving them an English education, would mainly be hers.

So, after each pregnancy she only kept the child she was breastfeeding at home, packing off the older children to live at Miss Murphy's School at Peddar Road, less than four kilometres away. Six of the Padamsee children studied here. The three brothers: Bobby, the eldest, Alyque, ten years his junior, and Chhotu (Ahmed). The three sisters: Roshen, my mother, two years younger than Bobby, Zarina and Shiraz. The school was run by the elder Miss Murphy, in her early sixties, and the younger Miss Murphy, her niece.

'There was a Dr Delany, who courted and married the young Miss Murphy. He was quite a presence. In the evening they used to have their chhota peg of whiskey. He knew we were Muslims and not supposed to drink but even then he'd take the ice out of his glass and give it to us to suck! There was another strange thing he used to do, when he had a backache, he used to ask us to walk up and down his back,' my mother recounts. At school, Barbara was their nanny. She was a short and stocky cross-looking woman, who dragged my sister Amal and me to midnight mass every Christmas thirty years later. I can still recall her firm grip on my wrist as we made our way through the milling crowds. She would be dressed in a new 'frock' that reached halfway down to her ankles, her thin hair pulled back into a small bun and her face would have a tight smile that verged on a grimace.

Barbara handled all the chores of bathing and dressing the young children in school, looking after their clothes, seeing that the beds were done. There were quite a few boarders, besides the Padamsees, my mother recalls. 'There was the Rajpipla family, who were quite small, while the Gwalior boys were a little older. There was a very interesting Jewish family. A Jewish lady had come, bringing her son, daughter and nephew and put them into the boarding school. The parents lived in Basra and in the beginning they paid the fees regularly but later they stopped sending the money or contacting their children at all. And so Miss Murphy kind of adopted these children.' It only struck the Padamsee family years later that perhaps their parents had disappeared in the Holocaust.

The boarding was on the second floor, while on the ground floor was the day school. In all there were about fifty pupils. Dressed neatly in their uniforms, the boarders trooped down to school every morning. 'There was a very Victorian drawing room with little brass elephants, ivory leg tables with all that carving, little knick-knacks and bric-a-brac and a piano, and this is where we had our singing lessons. All the songs were about Ireland because Miss Murphy was from there,' my mother fondly remembers her schooldays, while her younger brother

Alyque added in an interview years later: 'I remember having to write lines. In those days, writing lines, like "I will never be naughty again", was the norm. And rulers were the rule. If you did something wrong, it would crack across your knuckles, you could be sure...'

But it was here that the Padamsee children had their first lessons in theatre. 'We learnt theatre by doing some acting before an audience down in the courtyard. The rest of the kids would sit on the stairs, and we would act in this little open space,' Alyque shared with me.

I learnt more about these theatre lessons from my mother. 'On Saturdays, we were allowed to take out all the sheets, pillowcases and towels from the dirty clothes' basket before the dhobi arrived to take them away, and dress up in them and do plays. We would leave the door open between Barbara's room and our bedroom and people sat in the bedroom, that is, the others who were not in the play, and we would go behind the curtain and dress up and perform our plays.'

Was it these childhood improvised games that turned the Padamsees into 'theatre zealots'? Wrapping a towel around the head as a turban, dressing in a sheet draped as a Roman toga, enacting stories like 'Blue Beard' and growing maudlin while singing, 'My Bonny Lies over the Ocean' or 'Danny Boy' were perhaps their baby steps towards developing a lifelong interest in the theatre.

Every Saturday, my grandfather's wonderful seven-seater Packard, the Rolls Royce of those times, would arrive at the school to pick up all the Padamsee children and drive them home, to have a sumptuous tea.

'And we'd always go to the 3:30 movie at the Metro Cinema. No change, always the Metro Cinema, and always the 3:30 movie. Daddy, Jafferbhai, would come in the interval with huge bundles of bhel puri. And because there were so many of us, and we'd invite our friends, my dad would shout from the back of the hall to us who were sitting in front—"Alyque, help me, help me!" Everyone would turn around, asking, "What's happened?" I'd rush there quickly, blushing, with my younger brother Chhotu, and we would all help with the bhel puri. Then we'd sit back and watch the movie, *Laurel and Hardy* or *Gone with the Wind*, whatever it was, and we'd thoroughly enjoy it because we'd be talking and eating bhel puri right through!' Alyque recalls.

But despite the nostalgia and fuzzy warmth that colours all their memories of school, my mother had this to say of her childhood: 'It was great fun but at the same time I think that we were all a little frozen because that warmth that you get from parents, you can never get in school. However kind Miss Murphy was, it was not that she used to dandle us in her lap or stroke our hair, the kind of things mothers normally do with their children.'

The huge gulf between their colonial existence and a Bombay increasingly involved in the freedom movement grew. While the ripples of the Dandi March and the Salt March had reached the sands of Chowpatty beach in the 1930s, and while my grandfather was ferrying workers from the shop to their homes during the curfew imposed because of communal violence, the Padamsee children remained far away, ensconced in their cottonwool world.

In my mother's words: 'We had all the mannerisms of English people, all our table manners and everything. We wore these European Swiss dresses all the time and stockings and shoes and hats and all the rest of it, but with no contact at all with other Indians. It was as if we were remote from the rest. Once a month, we were allowed to go for a tram ride, Gowallia Tank to Byculla. That was considered to be a little outing for us and we were always told—"Don't touch the natives, you may pick up something, be careful because we are going to sit in a tram now, and there will be lots of other people."'

As the children grew older, Kulsumbai felt it was the right time for the family to move to England and be admitted to a boarding school there. My grandparents set sail together to make the long sea voyage to England with their children, but within weeks of their arrival my grandfather found it 'too cold' and returned to India.

Two anecdotes often repeated by my mother capture the spirit of innocent adventure that marked their childhood. In fact, they sound like they are straight out of an Enid Blyton book. One relates to when she, Bobby and Zarina heard they were going abroad and in sheer joy, tore up sheets of paper and threw them over the balcony, littering the ground below with 'snow'. Of course their hard taskmaster of a mother sent them down to pick up every last scrap! The second story is of Chhotu and Alyque eating every bit of the large martban of mango pickle that my grandmother had lovingly prepared to see her through her days in England. By the end of the sea journey she found it mysteriously empty!

In England, the Padamsee boys and girls were sent to separate schools. My ever resourceful and resilient grandmother rented a cottage in Shropshire equidistant from the two schools. She spent her days baking and cooking and enhancing her English language skills.

Another story we often heard in our growing-up years was of the weekly baths in the girls' school. How the three sisters (Candy was yet to be born) were allowed into the tub full of tepid, soapy water only after the 'white girls' had finished their baths. The school was worried that some of the 'darkness' from their skins would wash off and taint the other 'white' students! Racism was very much a part of their schooling. In Alyque's words: 'In Ellesmere College (where the boys studied), Bobby got into the top class. He was just waiting to turn sixteen, so he could go to Oxford. We were not in the boys' dormitory, thank God, because a lot of ragging went on there. And because we were a different colour, they'd always make fun of us, whenever they saw us. They used to call us "Golliwogs", a derogatory term for Negros. We had a little studio apartment, and we had a governess, Miss Williamson, in the school. We never went to the classes in the school. Miss Williamson taught us. She was both our governess and our teacher. We'd do lessons with her every day. And then she'd take us on walks and show us the beautiful countryside, and the cows in the fields. She was very pleasant, not at all strict.

'I began my acting career with Bobby when he was cast in the school production of *The Merchant of Venice*. Portia has these three suitors, and one of them is the Prince of Morocco, so obviously the dark guy, Bobby, played the Prince of Morocco. And the two fair guys played the Duke of this and that. Bobby had this lovely idea. He painted Chhotu and me black, like Moors and made us wear big turbans. We were tiny, I was only seven, and Chhotu was six, and we appeared on stage. We didn't say a word, just carried a present for Portia. That was my first proper stage appearance.'

And then it was 1938, the world was on the brink of war, and Kulsumbai hurried them all back to India, except Sultan, who had recently gained admission to Christ Church in Oxford. They had been in England for barely two years.

Once back in Bombay news and rumours made the threat of aerial bombing by the Axis powers very real, and so Kulsumbai carted all her children off to the ancestral home, Padamsee Wadi, in their village near Talaja, mimicking the movement of women and children to rural areas in England, to get away from the bombing of London during the Blitz. Here they stayed with fourteen of their cousins who had grown up in a conservative joint family set-up in Dongri in Bombay.

In 2005, when my three cousins and I made a trip to our ancestral village to get to know our roots, we visited this ramshackle property surrounded by a stone wall. A small door of wood, cut into the large wooden antique door decorated with brass studs, opens into an overgrown courtyard. The walls are mildewed and dark now, covered with fungus. The building is a single-storeyed structure with a tiled roof. A jhoola hangs forlornly on the broad verandah from which a staircase ascends. The walls are painted a pale green. On one of them we recognized a large black-and-white portrait of one of our ancestors. Water is drawn from a tubewell even today.

It was difficult to imagine how our parents would have adjusted to moving from their comfortable luxurious existence in Bombay and England to this old family building in Gujarat. 'English' kids confronting the 'natives'.

Even as the landscape outside had dramatically changed for them from the rolling hills of Devon to the moist and hot vegetation of Saurashtra, they, perhaps, held onto their 'interior' landscape. In a world so 'foreign' to them they still had the comfort of their siblings, with whom they had shared a very special childhood. And encountering their 'country cousins' who had grown up in Dongri and could only speak 'pidgin' English must have pulled them even closer together. It was a family that delighted in ridiculing others. So my grandmother's sisters Hoorubai and Noorubai were nicknamed 'Horror' and 'Norror'. To be able to speak perfect English, boast of an education abroad, set them apart and above their cousins in their view. Throughout their lives the Padamsees saw themselves as being superior to those around them, always speaking in English, never ever attempting to speak any 'vernacular' language. This bond of exclusivity held them in good stead and kept them tightly bound by the iron hoops of family even in their most difficult adult years.

On their return to Bombay from Talaja, my mother recalls: 'Mummy wanted to put me and Zarina in school. But Daddy put his foot down, something he very seldom did. He said "No one will marry our daughters if we are going to make them highly educated, because in our community the boys are not educated, they don't want girls who have gone to college. Do you want to keep them at home, don't you want to get them married?" At that time it was very important for a girl to get married and he really fought with Mummy on this issue. He didn't allow us to continue our studies. I never even completed my Senior Cambridge.'

The family settled into a routine at Kulsum Terrace. My mother was given charge of bringing up her youngest sister Candy (Dilshad), fourteen years her junior. Zarina was put in charge of cooking. Kulsumbai decided to single-handedly brave the long two-week journey by ship to England, despite the possibility of German torpedo attacks, to bring back Sultan who was studying at Oxford. Nothing was denied to this blue-eyed boy. On her return, my grandmother involved herself in running the family furniture store, Shiraz, while Sultan joined St Xavier's College.

So in the initial years, and for some of them throughout their lives, the Padamsee family restricted itself to the southernmost tip of Bombay, barely two or three kilometres wide and not even six kilometres long. South Bombay is recognized even today as being very distinctive, the old British City, a world unto itself.

With parents who had had a very basic education in Gujarat, all the young people in the family were dependant on stimulus from Miss Murphy's boarding school and their briefest of brief exposures to schools in Shropshire, England. Irish folk songs, Shakespeare's plays, novels by Charles Dickens and Thomas Hardy were their world. Sultan's experience as a young man in England before the war had opened up new horizons to him. The Theatre Group's moment had arrived.

Three

Theatre Group Beginnings

Oscar Wilde's *Salome* is a bold choice for any director at any point of time, and certainly in India in 1943 it was extremely bold. Conceived by Oscar Wilde as a 'symbolist' play, it was originally written in French and subsequently translated. The 'symbolists' were a small group in the late nineteenth and early twentieth centuries who strove to break away from 'naturalism', using poetic language and pictorial settings to invoke the inner lives of the characters.

This play is completely different in tone to those brittle comedies by Oscar Wilde that we are more familiar with, like *The Importance of Being Earnest*, with their wonderful one-liners. This script is more in keeping with his powerful fairytale-like stories for young people, gripping tales with a fine sense of drama, atmosphere, foreshadowing and gloom. As in the *Fisherman and his Soul* or *Starchild*.

There are three major conflicts in the play: between Salome and John the Baptist, known as Iokanan in this script, between Herod and his wife Herodias, and between Salome and Herod, the king. Each character's view of the others in a moonlit setting, both sinister and sensual, creates much of the dramatic tension.

Desire and deception, attraction and repulsion, revenge, loss, loneliness, freedom and captivity are the major themes.

Wilde in this script is reaching out to a concept of 'total theatre' where colour and design, the spatial relationship of the actors within the performance arena, music and movement are all intrinsic to expressing the theme of the piece. For the very first production of the play in London, Wilde worked closely with the designer, and it is said that 'he wanted every costume to be of some shade of yellow from clearest lemon to deep orange, with here and there a hint of black'.

To what extent my mother adhered to this colour scheme in Sultan's production is not known, but she and others in the Theatre Group tailored every garment. For all of Sultan's plays and later for all of my father's productions, my mother was the sole designer from the age of seventeen till when she was seventy-seven!

'I had my costume group who used to meet. We used to stitch our own costumes, we didn't have tailors. For the first play I remember, we got out all of Mummy's saris and I did it all in drapes because it was set in older times, I didn't know exactly what it was like. So I experimented with different drapes of these expensive saris and we must have spoilt quite a few with all my safety pins. It looked very glamorous though.'

'I used to watch the rehearsals. Chhotu and I loved to listen to rehearsals, but we also wanted to see them,' recalls Alyque. 'There was a little trellis in our bedroom, the roshendaan. We used to climb up on stools and peek through that window to watch what was going on in the drawing room. Bobby reciting Shakespeare, Roshen stitching costumes, Zarina painting posters, Shiraz making some props. It was like a cottage industry, and it was so thrilling to be in a family that had something so exciting to do!'

Before *Salome*, Bobby had already directed Shakespeare's *Macbeth* and *Twelfth Night* for the St Xavier's College Shakespeare Society in 1943. Khorshed Ezekiel who produced all of Bobby's plays at the time, said in an interview many years later, 'We did *Twelfth Night* and it was amazing, I'd never seen anybody whose mind worked so quickly as Bobby's. He was so agile in that way. He had everything kind of planned out. The sets were in white with a red bougainvillea creeper, we'd never seen anything like it before. Deryck [later to marry Shiraz] must have done a whole lot of work at the back, but the ideas were all Bobby's.

'There was a Baghdadi Jewish girl in college, and she did the lead role of Viola. It was at that time that Ebrahim, who was playing Malvolio, lost his voice, and somebody suggested that he should swallow raw egg yolk. So there I was in the wings, waiting with a cupful of raw egg yolk which he would dutifully swallow after every scene to get his voice back.'

Gods and Kings by Lajos Biro followed, and created its own controversy. Here my father played Napoleon in a sequence with Josephine. Cedric Santos, another early group member recalls, 'I remember the thing that caused a scandal was when one of the lead girls appeared on stage in a bathing suit!'

For *Othello*, which he directed next, Sultan Padamsee decided to restructure the play, opening with the bedchamber scene in which Othello comes to kill Desdemona. Gerson da Cunha, who was a prominent Theatre Group actor, recalls, 'I had not read *Othello* before seeing the production and I wondered how the Shakespeare version of *Othello* could really be an improvement on what I saw, because it seemed so logical. Othello strangles Desdemona and then you go into a flashback to why it happened. Why not? It's only after I read the original version that I began to see how revolutionary and perhaps sensational Bobby's adaptation was. But then there is no doubt that it was great.'

While Bobby played Othello in his production, Hamid Sayani (later to marry Zarina) played Iago. My father appeared in the cameo role of Roderigo.

'When he did *Othello*, he did it from two points of view, Othello's on the one hand and Iago's on the other. I took my British school teacher to see it. I thought she would be thrilled. She was so upset, she said, "What does this young man think he is doing, changing Shakespeare!" Now of course everyone changes Shakespeare, plays around with it, reinterprets it. Even Bollywood directors are making movies inspired by Shakespearean stories. But in those days, we were taught Shakespeare in a specific quasi-religious way in school. Next to the Bible was Shakespeare and our teachers couldn't imagine that anyone would want to tinker with him. I found it fascinating that in 1943 a man could experiment so much,' states Khorshed.

Gerson da Cunha asks, 'Were the audiences in Bombay ready to greet that kind of theatre and that kind of painting and that kind of literature? Some were, because one mustn't forget that at that time a major part of the audience for everything was an expatriate audience. The Germans, the Swiss and so on who had fled from Nazi Germany, and others, Italians too. These days when you say Mumbai is cosmopolitan, what you mean is that there are Biharis and Tamilians and Kashmiris, not that it is the kind of world city that it was then. Then it really was cosmopolitan. And in any case the audience for anything, painting or theatre or whatever, was by today's standard very small, and a major proportion of it was expatriate and they were very appreciative. They understood, they were challenged, they were provoked.'

But Bobby was not creating in some sort of vacuum. There was already a vibrant theatre tradition. In 1943, when Marathi theatre celebrated its centenary, thousands thronged to watch the lead Marathi actress of the day, Vandana Mishra, perform on an improvised stage set up on Chowpatty beach.

A recently published autobiography of this actress of the 1930s, who could act in Marathi, Gujarati and Marwari, fills an important gap in the early history of theatre in Mumbai.

Vandana's initial training and debut performance was with Mama Warerkar, one of the pioneers of a Stanislavski approach to acting in Marathi. This approach, now known as 'method acting', equips the actor with the tools to create a deeply researched, emotionally true performance. Several days of script-reading and discussion, and the staging of largely realistic plays based on the Ibsen model was how she began her career.

But financial compulsions subsequently pushed Vandana towards the commercial Gujarati stage with its stylized performances against painted backdrops. I recall seeing a play in the late 1960s in the last days of the Bhangwadi Theatre in Kalbadevi, where Vandana had become a heartthrob twenty-five years earlier. The plays performed here belonged to the 'Parsi' style. The British tradition of the Victorian 'melodrama' usually mounted on a proscenium stage against a painted backdrop and wings, had taken effective root in Indian soil. In different pockets around India, this 'Parsi' theatre (as it came to be known in the country) created a vibrant tradition linking the local folk form with something more urban, more sophisticated. Myths and legends from history were played in an over-exaggerated style, with rhetorical, bombastic speeches, fainting heroines, rousing music and spectacular special effects. Many of these companies toured all over India, and influenced regional language theatre. Some even travelled as far as Indonesia and East Africa.

It was on this stage that Vandana played the romantic lead in the Marwari play, *Ramu Chanana,* which ran for two and a half years. This play had been a hit in Calcutta, and packing up the sets and costumes, the writer-director moved to Mumbai to restage it. While his brother played the hero, he looked for a lead actress. After hectic rehearsals over three weeks, mastering dialogue in Rajasthani, a new language to her, Vandana put on an elaborate eighty-panel ghagra and lots of gold jewellery to play the heroine.

Her nightly fee of Rs 350 was a princely sum at the time, and it had to be placed on her make-up table, before she started dressing for the show. The play was a melodramatic rendering of a love story between a poor goldsmith boy and a rich Thakur girl. It ended with her committing suicide when she sees the body of her lover. The suicide was often delayed as the audience insisted on her singing her last song over and over again before killing herself!

Thousands saw the play as it had tremendous 'repeat value' due to its catchy music. Many Marwari women would request Vandana to wear their real jewellery on stage for a show. She was one of the first female 'stars' of the Mumbai theatre and her autobiography gives us a fascinating peep into how Mumbai drama developed just before and after Independence.

But it was evident that change was in the air. New content was required for a new audience with new sensibilities. This decade, the 1940s, proved to be a watershed in the development of contemporary Indian theatre and saw the beginnings of three major movements.

The establishment of IPTA (Indian People's Theatre Association) was the first of these. Set up simultaneously in Calcutta and Bombay with the express purpose of producing plays strongly supportive of the national movement, IPTA helped mould many leading lights of contemporary theatre. Their trailblazing production of *Nabanna* that explored the different facets of the manmade famine of 1942, brought the downtrodden onto the Calcutta stage for the first time. IPTA's Bombay wing drew on working class and folk traditions.

Prithviraj Kapoor's travelling theatre company, Prithvi Theatres, that toured the length and breadth of India from 1944, was the second major movement. For over fourteen years, this group performed a repertoire of eight plays in 112 different cities of the subcontinent. Among their plays were *Gaddar*, *Deewar* and *Pathan* on social themes such as the need for communal harmony or the brotherhood of man. Other than Prithviraj's own family, the star attractions were the sisters, Zohra and Uzra Sehgal. Each performance ended with Prithviraj himself standing at the auditorium door, eyes closed, chadar in hand, asking people to donate generously for the victims of Partition.

Also in 1943, the Unity Theatre headed by Utpal Dutt in Calcutta came into being. Utpal Dutt moved from performing Shakespeare in English, to dealing with the plight of coal miners in a flooded mine in the elaborate staging of *Angaare*, to pathanatika (streetcorner plays) to writing and performing in jatras on themes as varied as the 1857 war of independence, the American war in Vietnam or the nuclear war. He went on to become a major Leftist, writing and performing plays across Bengal till the 1980s.

Bobby had been hugely influenced by the 'Group Theatre' movement. This movement that originated in New York shook up the theatre scene with its emphasis on idealism and artistic fanaticism. In the turbulent 1930s, group theatre had brought truth and realism to the stage with its exploration of the political and human dramas of its time. It wanted to give a voice to the playwrights and actors who were shut out of the commercial theatre. Bobby wanted to bring a piece of this to Bombay.

But in Bombay where the Theatre Group was just beginning to cultivate its audience, actually getting people into the auditorium was an uphill battle.

'We had to go from office to office, and plead with people to buy tickets. In those days the highest was five rupees or ten rupees at the most. And only the big-shot officers would buy those tickets. Some of them wouldn't come, they would just buy the tickets to please us. So we played to half empty houses over and over again. And then, Bobby came up with this idea of "no admission while the scene is in progress", and because of that many people used to feel very offended: we've paid good money and they won't even allow us in,' says Khorshed Ezekiel of those days.

'Alkazi and others eventually decided that we'd let people sit in the last two rows if they were late but they would not be allowed to move about and find their seats. That was one of the things that was very firmly established. Bobby probably started it but Alkazi made very sure that people actually complied.'

My mother recalls: 'It became a very large group and somehow it became the central focus of a lot of the intellectuals in Bombay. Bobby was able to create some sort of an aura around him... it became something people wanted to be part of. Once we began doing plays regularly, the house became such a lively place, with rehearsals going on all the time. Then Bobby said, "Let's have Saturdays as the day when all of us meet but just to enjoy ourselves, not for a rehearsal", and that's how the Hunt started.'

The parties were known as 'The Hunt', as this was where young men came to hunt for young women, or so my uncle Deryck thought. Deryck Jefferies, an Anglo-Indian, was pursuing the third Padamsee daughter, Shiraz. Hamid Sayani, soon to be a radio celebrity, was wooing the second daughter, Zarina, and of course Ebrahim was on the tracks of Roshen!

'We started having Saturday parties where we'd roll up the carpet and dance and play games and then the boys used to come over on several evenings in the week and we'd play mahjong

and carrom, and we also used to do séances and call spirits,' my
mother reminisces with a faraway look.

'It was great fun, very lively, and Mummy used to prepare
such nice things for us to eat. She would call us all in from the
terrace and we'd sit around the horseshoe table laughing and
talking and eating all those lovely snacks. Talking about our
rehearsals and all that had happened.'

Those heady years of teenage crushes and romantic interludes
in the midst of backstage banter, onstage applause and frenzied
partying would be echoed years later by my generation.

Four

Bobby's Death and After

'One steaming hot day in the city of Bombay with its mixed modern architecture and its trees centuries old and Sultan Padamsee just twenty-three, a voice and a flame that put itself out, a life that swallowed itself as a serpent might circle around and devour himself, and turned inside out, vanish quite from view—so it seems, he wished his own death and in an act invisible and yet felt like a scar across our lives, he chose to be dead.'

It was in this way, years later, that one of Bobby's closest friends, Jean Bhownagary, referred to his death. The shock and palpable sense of loss of all those who knew him closely is reflected in these words.

Bobby lived in a room by himself located on the terrace, away from the rest of his seven siblings. Zarina found him dead there with froth coming out of his mouth. She immediately phoned her mother to return from the Shiraz Furniture Store. My grandmother and mother rushed him to hospital but it was already too late. It was the 9th of January 1946. He had committed suicide by taking an overdose of sleeping pills. He chose to end his life at the age of twenty-three, having lived fully and feverishly all the experiences others space out over innumerable years.

In Alyque's words: 'On Bobby's death my mother became a ghost living in Kulsum Terrace. She sat in her room, on her rocking chair, didn't speak to anyone for a year, never had a bath for a year, never changed her clothes for a year.'

My grandmother felt it was not correct to weep in public and tried to hide her grief away from her children, bottling it up within herself. She was in complete trauma.

She had been extremely close to her eldest son. He was her golden boy, an over-achiever, a symbol of all she wanted her children to accomplish. As my mother put it, 'There was a very affectionate relationship between them and whatever Bobby did, Mummy would back. If he wanted to do a show, it was fine with her. If he wanted to have a party, that was good with her. If he wanted to wear her jewellery, fine, it looks good on you, that sort of thing. There was never any sort of disciplining, no "no you can't do that."'

In the same way, my mother was also very attached to her brother. Barely eighteen months younger than him, she was his muse. He lovingly referred to her as the 'Lady Roshenara'. She was extremely feminine—adhering to many of the 'womanly' virtues of the time, well-versed in household skills, in the kitchen and also in the bringing up of children (she brought up her youngest sibling Candy). She was an avid reader and a marvellous dancer. Her skills in cutting and tailoring were legendary. And she was happy to play second fiddle, for some years, to her brother Sultan and later to his protégé, her husband Ebrahim. Revolt only surfaced much later in her life, as she began to assert her identity as an independent modern woman.

In the brief years that had lapsed since his return from Oxford, Bobby had become a legend in his lifetime. He stood out from the crowd, often wearing a floor-length cloak over his clothes. Close family friend and producer of most of his plays, Khorshed Ezekiel recalls, 'He had twenty-five pairs of mojaris that he used to wear. Bobby used to get his kurtas dyed, and so Alkazi also got his kurtas dyed. Bobby would wear rather flashy kind of clothes and when he went out in the evening, he would wear his bandgala coat with his mother's necklace on top of it. Now everybody does this and nobody looks surprised. In those days most people, especially men, thought it was very odd.'

A flamboyant gay man was unusual in Bombay in the 1940s. Bobby's paintings are bold even when we view them today. Looking over his canvases and artworks, his interest and preoccupation with the male nude is palpable. One particular work that I remember vividly from my youth, as it hung next to the dining table in the Jefferies' home, was of two young nude men sitting on the ground, one with his arm around the other, their genitals clearly visible. Painted in vivid tones of rust and yellow, these virile bodies seem to almost burst beyond the confines of the frame.

Similarly this excerpt from one of his poems, clearly indicates that this love was not cerebral, but that he had certainly entered into intense, physical homosexual relationships. It is obviously an ode to a gay partner.

> Lips pressed softly on the thigh
> The shivering of slight golden limbs,
> Your figure a tautened bow
> And I the arrow at your loins
>
> Ah God! the sigh
> Of loving much.
> Our fingers joined within my hair
> And your hot breath upon my brow,
> Looking up then to see your eyes,
> Desire choked my soul away
> To meet your lips in hesitant embrace.

I kissed your hair
I kissed your throat
And like an anger in the blood
I kissed the skin stretched o'er your hips,
Your lips were lonely, mine too full
I paid my homage to your flesh.

As your wild beauty caught my heart,
I lit a candle at your head
I lit a candle betwixt your thighs;
Your beauty in their light was laid.

With fingers curved I touched your feet,
And with my hands I felt your form,
Up from your feet across your limbs
And shudderingly across your loins
And thrillingly across your skin
Reaching their last about your waist.
I fell like death upon you whole,
Your mouth was twisted in a smile
While penial terror lit your frame.
Ah, God the sigh
Of loving much
Ah, God! the sin of fruitless grain.

Pain
Closed in contact,
Sensuously ecstatic,
And limbs twined and twined again
In posture erratic.
Eyes in nearness sear their way,
Great pools of loneliness
The electric feel of skin stretched smooth
Here and there the creased flesh

Melts in union
With earth, thus earth
Moulded a little
Then—the lost ashes of desire.

Chill vapours thrive across the fields,
Harnessed clouds disperse,
Lust with a smirk hurries away,
Tripping with furtive eagerness,
Still wrapt in phallic warmth
And go prostrate myself, unwashed
Before the rising day.

The family shrouded his suicide in silence. Years later many newspapers would talk of his tragic death in a car accident! For to be openly gay in Bombay at the time was just not possible. Kulsumbai understood the situation well. Her eldest and youngest brothers were both gay. The family tried to 'cure' the youngest one by marrying him off and creating the Shiraz furniture business for him to run. He deserted his wife and never even stepped into the furniture store, leaving my grandmother to take over the running of Shiraz. Who would marry her three daughters, who were 'of age', if it was known that their elder brother was homosexual? And more importantly who would he marry? How would he survive in a reasonably conservative Khoja milieu?

But Bobby was not one given to cloaking any behaviour of his with ambiguity. His last will and testament clearly mentions that he is taking his life due to the unreciprocated love he had for a sailor, in port at the time. But life must go on, and so it did, even though Kulsumbai remained wrapped in grief for a year. Bobby's death was a deep scar that stayed with her for life. The scar never healed.

This large yet closely knit family found it impossible to react to Bobby's suicide in one voice. My grandmother withdrew into silence, alarming everyone. My mother was probably completely shellshocked as were her two sisters Zarina and Shiraz. Whether this was because they had come to know he was gay or the fact that he had committed suicide, we never knew. My father had been up chatting with Bobby till two a.m. the previous night and perhaps felt the death of his mentor most deeply. The younger Padamsee sibilings, Alyque, Chhotu, Aziz and Candy, were still teenagers, if not children. His suicide became a topic never to be spoken of. Questions remained suspended, unasked and unanswered. The uneasy silence that surrounded his death stayed unbroken for decades. If ever asked, my mother would reply, 'Those whom the gods love, die young.'

Thirty years later, Jean Bhownagary and my mother made a selection of Bobby's poetry and had it published by the Writers Workshop, Kolkata. A quiet tribute to the man they both loved and missed.

Alyque had this to say: 'After Bobby died there was a kind of pause because he was such a huge figure. Bobby and the memory of Bobby remained long after he passed away and people ten years later would say, "Padamsee? Are you related to Bobby Padamsee?" "Yes, I am his brother." "Really? Oh, I knew him so well, he was such a wonderful person, what stories he used to tell us!" Ten years after he passed away he was still a celebrity. Mind you, at that time in Bombay, there was a paucity of celebrities. Today there are too many.'

My grandfather was acutely aware of the whiff of scandal that had surrounded Bobby's death and he strove to protect his family from any further damage. His wife had retreated into herself, forcing him to take charge of all seven children. So he came down heavily on the freedom of his daughters and their suitors.

Khorshed recalls, 'After Bobby died, the girls were restricted to the house. If they wanted to buy some nail polish, I had to go to the shops and put a different colour on each of my fingers and each one would say which one they wanted, and I would have to buy it for them.

'Their clothes they would manage on their own but I went shopping for them for perfumes, make-up and lipsticks. I remember once Deryck gave Shiraz a swimsuit and she didn't have the nerve to tell her mother that he had given it to her as a gift, so she said, "You pretend you are selling it to me." So I pretended it was a swimsuit someone was selling, and then Mummy Padamsee allowed her to buy it. I think then Deryck took pictures of her in the swimsuit which was not quite the done thing, but it was all clean, open fun.'

Within less than a year of Sultan's suicide, the three eldest sisters of the family married. My parents married in a simple ceremony held on the terrace of Kulsum Terrace, while Zarina married Hamid Sayani who became a legend on the radio and in the world of advertising; and Shiraz married Deryck Jefferies, the lighting whiz of the Theatre Group.

All the spouses of my parents' generation had met through the theatre. Ebrahim, Hamid and Deryck had been nurtured and mentored through their college years by Bobby. The three were good friends, studying together at St Xaviers, and had been core and active members of the Theatre Group from its inception. Hamid had played Iago to Bobby's Othello, as later he was to play Claudius to my father's Hamlet. Deryck moved into the technical aspects of stage design and lighting, creating equipment in his own workshop at home. Occasionally he tried his hand at direction.

Three extremely young couples. My father with his curly hair, sturdy frame and eloquent gesticulation, able to recount any anecdote with humour and drama, and my mother, pretty and delicate, always immaculately dressed and ready to air her opinions. Zarina, the second Padamsee sister, was a real beauty who with her flawless milk-white complexion, expressive eyes and coiffured hair, looked like a filmstar of the 1940s. Her husband was the big-built Hamid of the baritone voice, with a cigarette case clasped in his hand. His mesmerizing eyes framed in heavy black-rimmed glasses and pencil-thin moustache added much to his allure on stage as an amateur magician.

The youngest couple, Shiraz and Deryck, were a study in contrasts. Shiraz was tiny and petite while her husband of British stock was a large man with a great interest in all things technical and a vibrant intellectual probing mind with an encyclopaedic knowledge of Western music from Mozart to Jazz.

All these marriages took place soon after a death that had cast a long shadow. Without meaning to, Sultan's suicide had propelled his sisters to marry almost immediately. Did they marry so soon to get away from the pall of gloom that still surrounded Kulsumbai? Or because of a fear that now their paths may diverge without the magnet that was Sultan holding them all tightly together?

Three marriages in a single year: my Khoja mother marrying into a relatively conservative Saudi Arab business family, Zarina marrying into a Shia family where her mother-in-law was an ardent Congress worker, and Shiraz marrying into a Catholic Anglo-Indian family with a background in railways, with her husband Deryck employed by the bus company BEST.

The courtship of the three sisters included some amusing incidents. One that my mother related to me was this: 'When the boys were courting us, my youngest sister Dilshad, Candy, would sit on the potty and when she'd finish she would start screaming, "Khalaas, khalaas". We would be terribly embarrassed. I don't know why we get so shy about certain things at a certain age. So we'd pretend that we hadn't heard and then Daddy would call out—"Roshen, Candy khalaas bol rahi hai, sun nahi rahe hain?" I would run there quickly, wash her, put on her panties and run back as if nothing had happened.'

If they were not allowed into the flat that particular day, the three suitors would hang around the bus stop across the road staring up at the windows and balcony, waiting for the sisters to emerge. While my father would pretend to be reading a book, Hamid would rehearse his magic tricks, preparing to become a performing magician. And Deryck would busy himself thinking of the next electrical invention he would build, while they all waited for their 'women' to appear! It was a Romeo and Juliet balcony scene played out in south Bombay, on a busy road with big red double-decker buses roaring past, three Romeos simultaneously waiting for three Juliets to appear together on the fourth-floor balcony!

My grandfather, Jafferbhai, was not amused. As my mother recalls, 'The second time I saw my father put his foot down was when these three boys were courting us and at that time our engagements where not finalized. They would appear every evening and we would sit in three separate rooms with the three boys. Mummy would circulate through the house the whole time, keeping a watch on us. One day Daddy just exploded and said, in his pidgin English, "Get it out of here, and don't come back to my house, you are trying to spoil the name of my daughters."

'They realized that they had better speak to their families if they wanted us and so everything got more or less formalized, because Daddy was not going to allow them to go on visiting us. When they returned it was actually with the idea that the engagements were to be announced and marriage would follow soon after.'

Over the next decade the pattern each of the Padamsee sisters' lives would take became clear. My mother, having had her first child within a year of her marriage, travelled to England with my father to develop her lifelong career as a costume designer. She was to spend much of her life abroad, over a couple of months every year, and her personal wardrobe always included pants and shirts, Western suits, 'twin sets'; along with saris. Both her younger sisters, Zarina and Shiraz, spent their entire lives in Bombay living within a kilometre of Kulsum Terrace. Their wardrobes remained crisp, starched cotton saris, glass bangles and inexpensive two-bar chappals. All the sisters wore their hair cut short through most of their lives. While Zarina led a life of leisure, never taking a job, Shiraz cast herself as a 'mother' completely preoccupied with the upbringing of the three children she had in the first decade of her marriage.

My parents moved into a flat on the third floor of Kulsum Terrace immediately after marriage. My father regularly joined his brothers-in-law (all nine years younger than him) to play cricket on the terrace that had been surrounded by thin wire mesh. They often smashed the ball on the door that linked the terrace with the drawing room. But it was all acceptable and easily tolerated. He built a large dolls house for Candy, who was only six at the time, and decorated it in detail, much to her delight. He also greatly enjoyed riding around my grandmother's house on Candy's tricycle, making it a point to ride over everyone's toes. Over the next decade he would figuratively step on their toes as well in many different ways, but for now he had 'arrived' in the Padamsee family and endeared himself to all its members.

Five

My Father's Backstory

At the age of fifteen, my paternal grandfather was handed a gun and asked to shoot a member of a rival tribal group. Hamed Alkazi refused and decided to leave home and find his fortune elsewhere. He had been born in Najd, in what we now know as Saudi Arabia. Within two months of his birth his mother died. She had been the youngest wife of a prosperous man in the area, and all my grandfather's step-brothers and sisters were years older than him. And now he had had enough.

Bartering his share of the ancestral property for a camel, he joined a caravan going via Kuwait to Basra, in contemporary Iraq. The only thing he carried was a letter of introduction from his father to a prominent business family, the Al-Bassams. Basra, at the time, was a bustling port town linked for centuries with trade across the Arabian Sea to India. Hamed's first job was stacking bales of cotton, but he soon graduated to being a scribe as people got to know of his excellent penmanship. This was an essential skill to write business letters in an age that preceded the typewriter and email.

The Al-Bassams, like many other Arab businessmen of the time, had been doing business in tea with India through the port of Calcutta. Each of the brothers in turn would travel to India to set up home for three years to carry out this family trade. And that was where they offered my grandfather a job. Once he moved to India he became a hot favourite, writing business letters in a neat cursive script.

Within months of his arrival in Calcutta, he had found a more lucrative position in Bombay and he relocated. Here he started his own trading business. A marriage was arranged for him a few years later. My grandmother had been born and brought up in India and the family business was trading in horses, especially Iraqi horses for the Poona races. Her family originally belonged to Kuwait.

In the busy Muslim-dominated area of Mohammed Ali Road my grandfather set up both office and home. This area is also known as Bhendi Bazaar. The name comes from the British referring to it as 'behind the bazaar' meaning behind Crawford Market, which warped into 'Bhendi Bazaar'! During the Raj, the area had been developed as a labour camp for workers who had come to build the city. Later, when the construction was over, the buildings were sold to individual owners. Mohammed Ali was a mass leader in the Non-Cooperation and Khilafat movements and also the Congress president for a brief spell.

Crawford Market just south of this road separated the city into the 'native' and 'English' parts of town. On one side lay the large Kalbadevi area that remains a busy, crowded market place with Hindu, Muslim, Parsi and Catholic shops next to each other and on the other the more Westernized parts of Bombay—St Xavier's College, Metro Cinema, the Bombay Gymkhana Club.

Next to my grandfather's one-room office, the newly married couple set up home in a single room on the same floor. As his wife was completely housebound, he wanted her to develop new friends. Among the first was a British lady, Audrey, who lived downstairs and regularly came up to spend time with my grandmother, to get away from her alcoholic husband. Over the years, and with the active encouragement of my grandfather, my grandmother developed the knack of befriending many women who lived in her vicinity in both Bombay and Poona, often becoming friends for life. As the family began to grow, my grandfather moved the family to Poona, a few hours away by train.

'This was because Poona was a military town known for its quiet environment, and salubrious climate, a good place to raise children,' my father remembers. 'I grew up in a family of nine children. Our house was just at the edge of the cantonment area, so we enjoyed the quiet of the military area but were not that far from Poona city.'

Hamed Alkazi continued to live in Bombay himself, travelling to Poona every Friday evening to spend the weekend before returning to Bombay. This was by the Deccan Queen, the train that had been recently established (in 1930), and that was crowded by daily commuters doing the up/down from Bombay to Poona.

'Beyond my immediate family, there were three other families living in the compound, each in their own villa. There was a Parsi family, where an èmigrè German-Jewish music teacher would come to give piano lessons every day. Then there was an English family in the next villa, and an èmigrè Persian family in the last. This created a very cosmopolitan environment. There was a tremendous feeling of good neighbourliness and a great tradition of visiting each other, very informally. On top of which every family—the Parsis, Christians and us—would celebrate their own festivals and invite everyone from the compound. This was a taste of the "communal" in the very best sense of the term.

'In the neighbouring compound, there was a long bungalow divided between a Goan Christian family and a Parsi one. The

Parsi women were very skilled at playing Western classical music, while the Goan Christian family loved jazz, so different types of music were constantly in the background as I grew up. Beyond the compounds were the green fields of a Maharashtrian farmer, from whom we bought our vegetables. He was one of my father's closest friends, although they really had no common language to communicate in. The farmer spoke only Marathi and my father had some knowledge of Hindustani but they were both drawn to each other.

'As I think back, all of this was also my education in theatre. Theatre is primarily about social observation and I saw a really rich slice of life, including a Parsi family that was like out of a Chekhov play. The sisters were all spinsters, and the one brother was a weak man, always drinking and borrowing money from the Pathan moneylenders,' my father recalls.

Being a self-taught man, my grandfather created libraries everywhere he went. These would include encyclopaedias, books in English, and he also subscribed to the latest journals from the Arab world, such as *Al Ahram* from Egypt. According to my father, 'We read Naguib Mahfouz when he was just starting out, long before he became famous or received the Nobel Prize.' Hamed firmly believed that their cultural roots lay in Saudi Arabia. Only Arabic was spoken at home, and they had a teacher of Arabic and Islamic studies who had come from Saudi Arabia and lived as part of the family. My father's eldest brother ran away from home early, and so my father took on the role of accompanying his mother to mushairas, as she had developed a great love for Urdu poetry.

Outside their immediate lives, great events were happening. Poona played an important role in the Independence movement, then at its height. Gandhi and other Congress leaders would be imprisoned in the Aga Khan Palace. At night the Alkazi family could hear Congress leaders working up the crowds. At the same time, there would be regimental bands marching through the streets, emphasizing the presence of the British army. It was both exciting and scary.

'I remember that on Saturdays, which were half-days from school, I would carry my bicycle over the sandy patch in the compound so that my mother wouldn't hear me leaving the compound. Some instinct would alert her, and she'd call out, "Ebrahim, Ebrahim!" But I'd pretend not to hear and cycle quickly all the way to Poona city. There I'd go to the International Book Service, which used to get the finest of new English literature from Europe. The intellectual fraternity of Maharashtra would also gather there, and they'd be discussing all the important issues of the time with the shop owner, a Mr Dikshit.

'I never had a day's vacation from studying. My brothers and I would return from our Jesuit school—St Vincent's High School—to the study of the Quran and its interpretation at home. My sisters were taught at home. This gave us a solid foundation in Islam and Islamic studies. The second great influence on my early life was also a person in charge of a library—Father Riklin, who was also the principal of St Vincent's, and it was he who encouraged me to participate in the annual school play. I acted in those plays from age nine to fourteen.'

Then World War II broke out in 1939, and a great transformation took place. The Fathers at St Vincent's were Swiss and German; the Germans were taken to the internment camps. 'We watched it happen, feeling almost bereaved. My father, who had bought a plot of land in our compound, also began to feel increasingly like an unwelcome alien. He had to carry his passport every Friday evening when he returned from Bombay, and he had to report to the police.'

Ebrahim left for Bombay soon afterwards, in 1941, to study

at St Xavier's College and to work with his father in the office. Bombay was where he was pulled into theatre and the Padamsee family. The contrast between the two households was immense. My father lived with his father and the cook Gulab (with henna-dyed hair!) in Mohammed Ali Road, sharing two pairs of pants between the three of them, so that only two of the three could go out of the house at one time! Or so the story goes. On the other hand were the Westernized, affluent and emancipated Padamsees and the charismatic Sultan.

Living in the cosmopolitan city of Bombay and without the constraints of life in Poona, my father threw himself into exploring the metropolis. 'You could go from listening to Gandhi at Chowpatty, to Mohammed Ali Jinnah's house to see what he had to say. I won an elocution contest on behalf of the Communists, and I visited Calcutta.

'While still in college I took up a teaching job at the Ismail Beg Mohammed High School in one of the mohallas of Bombay. I taught there for two to three years and found teaching so satisfying that I almost gave up my college studies. It put me in touch with students from a social level which I had never experienced. I began experiencing a kind of rawness of life. Life which was raw, violent, elemental in a manner my sheltered life at home had not allowed me to experience.'

After 1947 my grandfather, who felt a greater bond with the larger Islamic world, moved to Karachi. My father and two of his married sisters opted to stay on in Bombay. All eleven of my cousins from my father's family and six cousins from my mother's family went to the same school in Bombay. This was the Cathedral and John Connon School and often we cousins were studying in the same class!

My grandfather was extremely disappointed with Pakistan. The army had its eye on the building he owned, and one day they arrived, threw out all his beautiful furniture, and took it over. After spending several years in England the family moved to Beirut where the liberal atmosphere reminded the family of their years spent in Bombay and Poona. They would stay there for most of their lives, although later some of my father's family would move to Kuwait.

But my father identified completely with India. Dressed in kurta pyjama ever since his college days, he immersed himself in both the emerging theatre scene and the young contemporary art movement. The artists M.F. Husain, F.N. Souza and Akbar Padamsee, my mother's cousin, were among his closest friends. Despite bringing up their nine children in quite a conservative manner, my paternal grandparents, whom we knew as Ummi and Ubba, showed a tremendous liberalism in allowing their children to choose their own, rather unusual careers. Not only did they support my father when he chose to pursue a professional training in theatre in England, but they also supported two of his siblings, Munira and Basil, to become visual artists.

Six

Educating Themselves in Post-war London

After a pause, the Theatre Group decided to mount a production in memory of Bobby. They chose J.B. Priestley's *Music at Night* and it was very successful. Gerson da Cunha recalls, 'All the theatre groups that existed at that time got together to do it. In this play a violinist and a pianist play a sonata, more or less off-stage. And, as the audience listens to it, the play picks out members of the audience one by one, and goes into their thinking. They become single performers who deliver a monologue. And then another person delivers one. Terrific play.'

The *Times of India* wrote of this production: 'It is fitting that this production, which Mr Padamsee was working on at the time of his death, should become a milestone in the history of the amateur theatre movement. It gives evidence of a growing maturity in its conception of stage values, in its competent acting, its able direction, and its inspired handling of lighting and stage effects.'

While theatre took a back seat for a few months, my parents involved themselves in the exciting new changes occurring in the Bombay art scene. They bought a tiny little house in the environs of Matheran in the Western Ghats, which they wanted to turn into a kind of adda for artists as it was only a short train ride from Bombay. My father named it 'The House of the Foolish Virgin', after one of the stories in the Bible.

The Progressive Artists Group had come into being in 1946 and my father was invited to inaugurate their very first exhibition. Pride of place in this exhibition was given to the nude self-portrait of the young rebellious Goan artist Francis Newton Souza that shocked many viewers. Krishen Khanna, the eminent painter, remembers the strong reaction the painting got and the ridiculous way it was dealt with: 'Of course females in the nude were an acknowledged and much desired subject matter; but males, in spite of the legacy of Michelangelo, had to keep their underpants on and their flies buttoned up. The police intervened and the "offending" portion of the anatomy in the self-portrait was suitably covered, thereby attracting still more attention.'

Souza was a close friend of my parents. He had been born in Portuguese Goa, and spent the initial years of his life there. His father died when he was very young and he grew up 'fascinated by the grandeur of the Church and by the stories of tortured saints my grandmothers used to tell me. As far as I can recollect, strange fancies always occupied my mind. I seldom had companions. It created the artist in me.'

Souza's mother disguised herself and fled to Bombay with him, where she started working as a tailor. Souza found that Bombay was a completely different experience from Goa. He now lived in the middle of a busy city, in the final stages of the Independence movement. He chose a completely radical career for himself, the 'artist' and all the rebellion it symbolized. So he adopted the mantle of 'nationalist' and 'Indian', violently discarding being Catholic.

Joining the J.J. School of Art in Bombay, he soon realized that instruction was still carried out in the fossilized academic tradition. Students were taught to copy from the classical works of Greece and the Renaissance, focusing on a mastering of the art of perspective and proportion, while outside the classroom there was a vast Indian reality crying out to be captured on canvas.

The question of the meaning of art, in an India increasingly aware of its own unique national identity, was under furious debate. Major tectonic shifts were occurring beyond our borders. The whole notion of 'Orientalism' and the view of the East as being a colony of the West was being demolished. The Russian Revolution of 1917 had shaken the very foundations of aesthetics whether in art, theatre, music or literature, and now Europe was going through a vigorous churning of culture between the two world wars.

In such a charged atmosphere, Francis, with many others, chose to rebel. Along with five other artists, all belonging to a similar working-class background—S.H. Raza, M.F. Husain, K.H. Ara, A. Gade and S.K. Bakre—the Progressive Artists Group was founded in 1946.

Their intention was to 'paint with absolute freedom for content and technique almost anarchic, save that we are governed by one or two sound elemental laws, of aesthetic order, plastic co-ordination and colour composition.' Souza claimed that, 'Our art has evolved over the years of its own volition; out of our own balls and brains.'

Husain, another close family friend, decided to fully devote himself to painting when he was only twenty-two. He lived in a cheap room in the slum area near Grant Road and did all kinds of odd jobs. He painted cinema posters, designed nursery furniture, embellished cots and rocking horses with colourful designs. When Souza saw Husain's painting, 'Potters', at the Bombay Art Society's exhibition, he decided to bring Husain into the fold of the Progressive Artists Group.

All earlier art had either celebrated the divine in temples or in mosques or dealt with the life of royalty at court. Husain completely reversed this in his trailblazing canvases focusing almost exclusively, for his entire career, on the life of Mahatama Gandhi's 'last man'. Living and interacting on the urban street or the rural countryside, rarely within the interior of a house, surrounded by stoic cattle or prancing horses, the common man and more often woman, was the subject of his works.

They were all artists from the 'other' side of Bombay, the original 'native quarters', who were now crossing over to confront and take on the 'south Bombay' crowd. My father, living at Mohammad Ali Road, and Souza, living near Crawford Market, stayed a stone's throw away from one another, not that they would have met each other at their homes. For the meeting ground for many artists was the vegetarian restaurant and bookshop, Chetna, opposite Jehangir Art Gallery.

Sudhakar Dikshit, who set up Chetna, was a journalist with the newspaper *Indian Nation* and was a great supporter of the arts. He encouraged poetry recitations, book readings and discussions on art. Established in 1946, Chetna only served thalis, snacks and beverages. And it still exists in the very same location with more or less the same menu as seventy-five years ago!

My father's friendship with Souza was to last through Souza's life. Once he left India in the late 1940s along with my father, Souza never returned, except for brief visits, as he gained fame and notoriety in England with his paintings and anarchic writings, constantly taking potshots at authority. After living for twenty years in England, Souza moved to New York, attracted by the ferment and protest that had marked America in the 1960s. My father championed Souza's cause through life, promoting his work and writing.

Having been unanimously chosen to lead the Theatre
Group after Bobby's death, my father directed Shakespeare's
Richard III, even as the Naval Mutiny raged outside and the
sky reverberated with the sound of explosions. Rehearsals had
to be held during the day as curfew had been imposed on the
city. My sister Amal was born during a dress rehearsal of his next
production, *Hamlet*, produced immediately after Independence
in August 1947. Later the same month my father left to study in
England. He was soon to be twenty-three.

It was a tiny advertisement in *Art News* that enthused my
father to travel to England. The Anglo-French Art Centre in
London was offering courses in art, with a faculty that included
the great Matisse and Leger, who had broken much new ground
in the Modern Art Movement. Here was an opportunity not to
be missed.

My father managed to convince his family to loan him the
money to finance his trip. He also persuaded a close friend,
Nissim Ezekiel, to accompany him. Nissim, who went on to
become another lifelong family friend, was Jewish and belonged
to the Bene-Israeli community of Bombay. This community was
originally from Konkan from where they migrated to Bombay,
Poona, Calcutta and Karachi. Many of them were very successful
in the film industry as actors, producers and directors.

Nissim gained fame much later as a poet writing about
common and mundane things, as in his poem 'Night of the
Scorpion'. He was similar in this way to M.F. Husain, who
could turn an everyday object, like a lantern or an umbrella, into
something fraught with symbolism.

Due to his close friendship with my father, Nissim decided
to accompany him and do his further studies in England. Both
of them shared a bed in London! And were soon joined by my
mother and Souza along with his wife Maria, a dressmaker.

After a three-and-a-half-year stay studying Philosophy at Birkback College, Nissim made his way back to India as a deck scrubber on a ship carrying arms to Indo-China.

For my father, travelling by ship to England in September 1947 must have been a unique experience. It was his first trip away not only from his own home, but also from his wife and newborn daughter, Amal. The journey would take twenty-one days, the other passengers, a cast of characters to him, and the long, lovely yet lonely stretches of the ocean would have given him time to reflect and contemplate on the choices he had made in life. He had broken away from his conservative Arab family, chosen a path radically different to that of his businessman father and married outside the community. He was now travelling alone, far from home to England to pursue a career in the arts. Before setting off on the journey, someone had given him a copy of Mordecai Gorelik's *New Theatres for Old*. Reading this book, now a theatre classic, opened his eyes to the new world he would soon explore in England.

For my mother, who joined him less than a year later, leaving baby Amal behind with Kulsumbai, England was a place where she had grown up. But hers was a different England that now seemed to belong to a more pristine, idyllic age, a land of country cottages and boarding school life. Ten years after she had left, she encountered an urban metropolis severely hit by the war. The comfort of the wealthy Padamsee home that she was used to had been replaced by the bohemian not-so-affluent lifestyle of the artist Alkazi. It would require a period of adjustment. As for her separation from her baby daughter, it probably caused her more distress than it did Amal, who quickly became the family pet, especially with her Uncle Alyque and Aunt Candy, with whom there was only a seven-year age gap.

London in the post-war years was not the bustling London

of today, a bit frayed at the edges, but still vital in its core. The
Blitz had taken a huge toll on the city, and the British were
exhausted by the war. The city was unpainted, the buildings
bombed out, stained, grey. The Clean Air Act had not come
into being—sudden dark fogs engulfed the cracked and dull
city frequently. People continued to dress in their 'austerity'
clothes, everyone would be indoors by ten, there were no good
restaurants. Rationing was still prevalent and the Dining Rooms,
subsidized during the war, were often the only places one could
eat in a whole stretch of streets.

As my father wrote, 'Souza, Nissim and I would debate long
over whether we should have tomato soup or pea soup (which
was a halfpenny cheaper) at the Lyons Corner House when
we ventured out to treat ourselves. At the butcher's we would
content ourselves, once a week, with leftover slivers of meat and
with broken biscuits at the baker's, because that was all we could
afford. Heating your room was done by putting shillings in the
meter, household refrigerators hardly existed, and television was
yet to arrive.

'Food was rationed, and I used to be followed by elderly
sweet-toothed women who were keen to get my chocolate
and cigarette tabs, for which I had no use. That was the only
following I ever had in my life.

'Every Saturday about noon we would drift towards the
market at Portobello Road, a working-class district in those days
and not the tourist attraction it has since become, and buy
the leftovers for our weekly rations: strings of meat, broken
biscuits, a loaf of stale bread, discarded vegetables—all at reduced
rates. We couldn't afford more. We would shove the whole lot
together into a vessel. Put it on the fire, add enough water to
drown it, stir it into an unholy mess, and cackle over it, like the
bearded witches in Macbeth! Being a poet, Nissim would distil

out of this malodorous mixture a culinary concoction, which he would delicately serve out to us in meagre portions, rather like a starving haiku!'

But certainly nothing of their living conditions dampened their sense of humour and fun. My father would often gather a crowd around him as he banged on a postbox saying that the postman had locked one of his young brothers into it! Or the three friends would mount soapboxes at Speakers Corner in Hyde Park, haranguing the crowd in a language they would invent on the spot!

But as luck would have it, after he was disappointed by the teaching at the Anglo-French Art Centre, rather than attending art school, my father's feet gravitated towards the Royal Academy of Dramatic Arts (RADA). Because of his talent and his experience on the Bombay stage he won a scholarship waiver. RADA at the time taught the classical arts of acting with a focus on the delivery of Shakespearean verse, sword fencing, stage falls... It was as though the 'modern' movement in theatre had not yet entered the curriculum. Even as he actively participated in the RADA productions, my father was looking to learn direction in greater depth, and the director of RADA, Sir Kenneth Barnes, the iconic theatre critic, got him into the Producers Course of the British Drama League.

My parents worked feverishly, using every minute of their time in London to research and study in libraries, or to witness performances by many of the great actors of their generation. They had the good fortune to see the brilliant couple Vivien Leigh and Laurence Olivier on stage, acting opposite one another in Shakespeare's *Macbeth* and Oliver Goldsmith's *The School for Scandal*. All they could afford was 'a seat in the Gods', the third balcony from where you looked vertiginously down to the stage, getting a bird's eye view as it were.

But they found British theatre, though outstanding in performance and presentation, was still very conventional. The classics from Shakespeare to Richard Sheridan to George Bernard Shaw remained the popular long-running productions. My parents were keen to look beyond, to understand the much more radical and breakthrough theatre work that had characterized the theatre movement in Russia after the revolution of 1917. Luckily for them it was well documented.

Pre- and post the Revolution had been the Golden Period of Russian Theatre, when three Russian directors flourished alongside each other, each with his own signature style. And all of them had a completely unique, individualized, well-thought out vision of the theatre, that they could develop with their repertory companies. They had also conceptualized and created a specific kind of training to realize this vision, with the unstinted assistance of the Soviet State.

My parents read about the great Russian director Stanislavski's staging of Anton Chekhov's classics in a theatre specially built by him in Moscow in 1898 to produce 'naturalistic' plays, as opposed to the prevailing performance style of melodrama. This had required creating a completely new method of training for the actor. Stanislavski's approach tries to blend the actor's own personal memories with those of the character he is playing and is well documented by him in his iconic books, *My Life in Art*, *An Actor Prepares*, and *Building a Character*. Stanislavski had several British followers, most notably Michael Chekhov, nephew of Anton Chekhov who taught the 'Stanislavski technique'. As a result all his works had been translated into English and several workshops were on hand to learn his technique.

Meyerhold, who followed Stanislavski as a theatre 'messiah', focused on the learning of gestures and movement to understand the character. So while the Stanislavski approach moves from the inside out, Meyerhold moved from the outside in. My father experienced, grasped and internalized a lot from this sort of training.

Meyerhold had broken new ground in the years immediately following the Russian Revolution of 1917. His *Mystery Bouffe* was a seminal work when it was first staged in 1918. This allegory of international socialism, written by the poet Mayakovsky, introduced Meyerhold's unique style of direction to the public. His work combined American jazz, tap dance and other popular traditions, with clowning and acrobatics and games played with the audience during the interval. Sirens, factory whistles, cannon blasts, searchlights all played as much of a role as the actor. Being put in charge of theatre in the Soviet state, he was now able to create a sustained yet novel approach to the theatre.

Vakhtangov, who married the styles of Stanislavski and Meyerhold to create his own theatre company in Moscow, was my parents' third Soviet hero. Vakhtangov's innovative production of *Turandot* had mesmerized audiences as the actors transformed themselves on stage moving from the formal behaviour necessitated by their conservative evening wear into a Far Eastern 'exotic' fairytale setting, before their very eyes. Emphasizing the 'make-belief' world that the theatre actually is, was his forte.

My parents' notebooks and sketchbooks from these years stayed with them, their constant companions through life. This was in an age before photostating or using your mobile phone to take pictures. Everything was therefore copied out by hand in notebooks that were numbered.

While my mother spent her days at the Victoria and Albert museum and its costume collection, copiously drawing and sketching the designs of famous designers like Motley or Tanya Moseiwitsch, my father was hard at work at the British Library and the University College of London Library seeking to understand the antecedents of the birth of the 'modern' movement in theatre elsewhere in Europe.

Years later, through her fifties, sixties and seventies, my mother retraced her steps to the Costume Institute where she had worked while in her early twenties. Every summer when she was in London, for a month or two, she would spend four or five hours everyday in the V&A library, researching for the volumes she was writing on ancient and medieval Indian costumes. She was loath to take a taxi there, as she knew the 164 bus route well! Old habits die hard.

My father's research into iconic directors led him to the work of Max Reinhardt of Germany. He had brought together music, stage design, choreography and text to completely revolutionize German theatre over a thirty-year career in Germany. Here he managed eleven different companies, even as he presented his work regularly in London and New York, moving finally to directing films. Reinhardt viewed the director as a creative artist who 'orchestrated' the entire production. He worked in a range of theatre sizes, choosing them so that they would be suitable for the style of the script. While he used tiny intimate spaces to stage Oscar Wilde's *Salome* and Maxim Gorki's *The Lower Depths*, he presented Aeschylus' *Oresteia* in a 3000-seat theatre. For *The Miracle* in New York, he converted a commercial theatre into a Gothic cathedral, and his production of Shakespeare's *A Midsummer Night's Dream* was staged in a forest in Oxford. Like several of his contemporaries who moved from Germany to America following the rise of Hitler, Reinhardt influenced American theatre and its aesthetic considerably.

Great stage designers, Adolphe Appia and Gordon Craig, were also studied in detail. Appia was an outstanding Swiss lighting designer who used colour to great effect. He believed lighting could convey both the inner and outer worlds of the character. He wrote: 'Light, just like the actor, must become active; it can create shadows, make them living, and spread the harmony of their vibrations in space just as music does.' To create and enhance the three-dimensionality of the actor in the performance space, he created the concepts of 'active' and 'diffused' lighting.

Meyerhold, Appia and Craig were all part of the Symbolist Movement that emphasized the need to look beyond surface reality and discover the more poetic aspects of life. It was like the coming together of Impression and Expression in art.

The illegitimate son of well-known actress Ellen Terry and architect Edward Gordon, Craig saw the actor as a 'marionette'. His emphasis on creating an 'atmosphere' on stage attracted directors like Stanislavski in Moscow who invited him to collaborate on a production of *Hamlet*, and he was also a part of many assignments across Europe. Neutral, mobile and non-representational screens were used by him to create unique stage pictures. Craig's lifestyle was extremely bohemian too. After leaving his wife, he fathered several children with his three lovers, including the modern dancer Isadora Duncan.

No less fascinating was contemporary French theatre: the Comedie Français Company in Paris, the first Avignon Festival established by Jean Vilar and the work of Jacques Copeaus and Michael St Denis. My parents were exposed to the vibrant theatre movement of their generation, with its star director designers, who had crossed national boundaries and become legends in their lifetimes.

Dartington Hall, which my father visited in 1950, was the third major takeaway from his three-and-a-half-year stint in England, other than his formal theatre training and long hours of self-study in libraries.

Lord Elmhirst, who had set up the Dartington Hall Trust along with his wife, had served as Rabindranath Tagore's secretary in 1921. He had helped Rabindranath establish an Institute of Rural Reconstruction in Sriniketan, close to Shantiniketan. In the subsequent three years he travelled the globe twice, mobilizing the money required to run Sriniketan. Rabindranath encouraged Elmhirst to start a similar initiative in England. The focus was to be on the arts, social justice and sustainability. The couple returned to England to set up Dartington Hall hoping to impact rural reconstruction in the very poor agricultural economy of Devon.

At Dartington Hall, my father interacted with several stellar personalities from theatre and the other arts: Michael Chekhov, an ardent follower of the Stanislavski method; American theatre critic Harold Clurman; Rudolf Laban, who had created a system of movement training for the actor; Arthur Waley, the distinguished scholar and translator of Chinese poetry and Beril de Zoete, whose books, *The Other Mind* on Bharatanatyam, and *Dance and Drama in Ceylon,* are recognized as classics.

My father's exposure to these seminal minds from across Europe had a lasting impact on his theatre practice. He understood that any space could be a performance venue and formal auditoriums were no longer necessary. Whether he performed later in the lawns of the Bhulabhai Desai Institute or on the terrace of our flat in Bombay, in the tiny eighty-seat studio theatre in the National School of Drama (NSD), or created the open-air Meghdoot theatre around a vast peepul tree in the NSD or carved out a magnificent performance space in the ruins of Purana Qila in Delhi, one can see the seed of this idea had been planted in a cold library in London!

Looking beyond Stanislavski and his 'method' acting, he could sense the possibilities of training actors in our own vibrant folk and classical traditions whether Yakshagana, Tamasha or Bhavai or even looking further afield for inspiration to the Kabuki and Noh theatre traditions of Japan. Light, sound and overall visual design were crucial to his productions and he built on many ideas of Appia and Craig, and developed them further.

No idea is sacrosanct, no tradition inviolate was certainly what my parents experienced in their years of early adulthood in London.

'Nissim Ezekiel, Souza, Maria, and my wife Roshen and I, along with Krishna Paigankar, a superb film and literary critic who was settled in England, constituted an intense and earnest little group of expatriates, amidst the dismal ruins and choking smog of post-war London, which still wore the stale, drab, dreary and exhausted appearance of the city as described by Dickens in the nineteenth century,' my father wrote, recalling those seminal years.

But theatre was only part of the story, even though it was taking up a majority of my parents' time. Exhibitions by Picasso, Degas, Mattisse, Cezanne, Van Gogh and others, all in the original were to be seen and savoured by the five friends, as were poetry readings and other events at the Institute of Contemporary Art (ICA).

As with many of that generation, and even now, this charmed group of Indian intelligentsia who read and thought and talked only in English, even among themselves, were to become leaders in their own respective spheres when they returned to India after their years abroad. Nissim, Souza and my father reached the top of their vocations in a few years, my mother was the unparalleled costumier and gallerist of her generation and Souza's wife Maria's clothes soon graced the cover of *Vogue* magazine. Krishna Paigankar, filmmakers Jean and Freny Bhownagary, artist Akbar Padamsee, were friends with whom they spent time in London and Paris. Ideas were being tossed about, regarding what shape the new Indian arts scene would take, and how they would contribute.

It was time to return home.

Seven

The Theatre Group Splits

Five years after winning our freedom, the euphoria lingered. Along with an idealistic government headed by Prime Minister Jawaharlal Nehru, and taking their cue from the crucial role that artists had played in the aftermath of the Russian revolution, artists drawn from various disciplines were working at creating a new Indian 'nationalist' identity. This was particularly evident in the field of art, theatre and cinema. My parents were in the midst of all of this in Bombay, which was certainly the fulcrum.

As M.F. Husain put it, 'We had our own parallel national movement to evolve a language that is rooted in our own culture. It was important because any great change in a nation's civilization begins in the field of culture. Culture is always ahead of other political and social movements.'

Music and dance were revisiting older classical traditions and there was a huge interest in the elite (many of them for the first time) in Hindustani and Carnatic classical music and in the dance forms of Bharatanatyam, Kathakali, Odissi and Kathak.

Patronage for the arts at this time didn't come from the government but from enlightened individuals, wealthy entrepreneurs and industrialists of Bombay and elsewhere.

Lawyers like Bhulabhai Desai, business houses like the Sarabhais and the Tatas among others, now played the role of patron, replacing the maharajas who had supported so many artists and art forms in the past.

And the Indian art scene had also received the attention of several émigrés. To escape persecution by the Nazis in Germany and Austria, three Jews had moved lock, stock and barrel to set up home in Bombay, then seen as a thriving cosmopolitan port of India where it would be possible to live, as most people (of a certain class) spoke fluent English! Walter Langhammer, Rudy von Leyden and Schleisinger quickly gathered around them Indian artists who were all still in their early twenties. Every Sunday at his Napean Sea Road residence, Walter Langhammer, himself a practicing artist, organized soirees.

These three men coming from Europe and conversant with the vibrant modern art traditions being created there, proved to be among the catalysts of the art movement in Bombay. They had no connect with the academic tradition that was still being taught in the J.J. School of Art, they were men of the present, and proved to be enthusiastic and vocal supporters of a movement still in its nascent stage.

While Walter Langhammer became the art director of *The Times of India* in Bombay from 1938 onwards, Rudy von Leyden became its art critic. He was known to cycle down to the press after the opening of a show so that he could write the review on the day itself. 'Uptil that time a staff reporter used to be sent to cover art shows and he would make a routine report saying so and so painted a cow in a garden or whatever. I think the review and the talk about art, the writing about art, the war effort, the one-man shows all came together and stimulated a new atmosphere,' he wrote.

In Bombay, with the active support of Kekoo Gandhy who

framed many of the first paintings of the Progressive Artists Group, Walter Langhammer created an 'open house' and often provided free studio space to Indian artists. Bombay in the 1940s and 50s was in the throes of a cultural revolution.

Gerson da Cunha recalls, 'I don't think anyone realized that life at that time was going to be as good as it gets. No one realized what a great city this was, and what a privilege it was to be a citizen of it. The infrastructure, the water and the sanitation and the Central and Western Railways, and the electricity, all of that was more or less suited to the needs of that population.

'Travelling by tram and bus at the time was not downgrading yourself at all. It was just logical and we all did it, because what else would you do? Take a taxi, but why pay immense amounts of money?

'Secondly, the hotels and the restaurants were really very lively. In the late 1950s, as I recall, you had eight important jazz swing groups in the restaurants, The Volga, The Other Room, The Little Heart, Berrys. So it was a city where the city matched the needs of its population. You even had a great university, the Bombay University.

'In other words, Bombay was a knowledge centre that could not but have its effect and impact on all of us. The quality of discussion at a party at that time was amazing. By contrast, today you are suddenly aware that you are talking more about the inanities of domestic life, the fact that you don't have a cook and where do you get your next driver from? At that time this was not the case.

'There were seminars that were run by people like Deryck, people like Alkazi and by people they invited. Rudy von Leyden would talk about modern art. There was that kind of interactive chemistry that ended up in benefit to both sides.

'Then there were these spaces that become the focuses of

stimulation, the newly established Jehangir Art Gallery and soon after, the Bhulabhai Desai Institute. The Progressive Artists Group in Rampart Row was where modern art, modern painting was going on. We had in this city two symphony orchestras: the Bombay Symphony Orchestra and the Bombay Philharmonic. So, there were these focuses of enlightenment, if you like.'

When my father returned to India, coincidentally on the exact same ship that had taken him there three and a half years earlier, he was bursting with new ideas that he wanted to execute immediately. Beyond theatre, was his first love: art. That was what he had wanted to study when he went abroad, as he was already an artist himself. His fine black-and-white drawings, often pen-and-ink renderings of the delicate yet sensual relationship of man and woman or his charcoal sketches exploring themes related to the life of Christ, had won him an exhibition in London at the prestigious Leicester Gallery.

In one of her earliest poems, my mother wrote of my father's paintings:

The brutal strength of nudes
Completes and yet denies
The suffering Christ
His wasted flesh
Embalmed, immersed, and crucified
Another way of life
All conflict is resolved
In landscapes that conceal
Reveal
A shimmering maze
Of past and present caught
In muted notes of grey
And black and clear translucent whites

Mysterious play, yet not unmixed
With shades of not far distant day
Freed from the weight of time
They live
In pauses deeply felt
Between the words of life.

He still had many friends among the Progressive Artists Group, even though Souza had left. Nissim, my father and mother had made it a point to visit museums and galleries and seen the best of English, American and European art in their years in England. It was time to make a concerted effort to expose the Bombay intelligentsia to what was happening in the art scene abroad.

'This is Modern Art' was a series of exhibitions mounted by the Theatre Group in 1954. All the five exhibitions were held at the Jehangir Art Gallery which had only been built two years earlier. Although originals were not available, recourse was had to large-size reproductions of the Impressionists, Cubists, and the Surrealists. Several art books were undone, their pages perfectly removed and tastefully framed.

In a delightful series of black-and-white photographs of people attending Nissim's first talk on Modern Art, that accompanied the exhibition, one can make out the young artist Krishen Khanna, and of course the whole of the Padamsee clan, with Pearl Weiz, later to be Alyque's wife, sitting in the row just in front of them. In the background can be seen my father's Arab brothers-in-law in lounge suits. There is a palpable sense of the excitement and joy of an art movement then in its nascent days.

Raza, another major artist of the time, recalls, 'We were particularly torn between Western academic ideas and traditional Indian art springing from the Renaissance in Bengal which drew us by its attention to our own tradition. The works of the French Impressionists and the German Expressionists inspired us.'

Active involvement in the art scene resulted in my parents even courting arrest. This was to express solidarity with Akbar Padamsee whose nude painting had been taken to court on charges of obscenity. How could an artist depict a man with his hand gently cupping a nude woman's breast? Part of the argument put forward in the court included images similar to Akbar's, taken from the twelfth-century Khajuraho temple panels.

On the theatre front, my father galvanized the scattered members of the Theatre Group and created three training courses of different durations to impart much of what he had learnt abroad.

Although each course was independent, his idea was to carry students forward into the subsequent one, as the training was designed to become increasingly intense. The focus was on imparting practical training through yoga, movement and speech classes along with the actual production of plays staged before a live audience. Classes and rehearsals were supplemented by lectures, poetry readings, talks on art appreciation. Open classes were organized too, that could be attended by the lay public. The idea was to not only train students as professionals, but also to prepare the ground for the proper reception of good and meaningful theatre by an informed and appreciative audience.

One of the first productions he directed was Ibsen's *Ghosts*, staged in the tiny Institute of Foreign Languages Auditorium in 1952. With the audience seated on opposite sides of a small acting area, this was perhaps the first 'arena style' staging in India. Ibsen's powerful play had a stellar cast. Usha Amin played Mrs Alving to my father's Pastor Manders, while Alyque played Engstrand and Sylvie da Cunha, Gerson's brother, played the young Oswald. 'The sins of the father should not be visited on the children' is the bottom line in this play that explores inheritance, hypocrisy, incest and syphilis.

T.S. Eliot's verse drama, *Murder in the Cathedral*, and Jean Anouilh's *Antigone* were also performed to critical acclaim, as was Strindberg's *Miss Julie*. My father's training was already evident. Dissecting the play's text, reading between the lines— the subtext—exploring detailed characterization over a month of rehearsal along with using stage design, costume, choreographed movement, music and lighting to enhance the complete theatre experience were on show.

French playwright Jean Anouilh was acutely aware that it is from the Greek myths that we have constructed our notions of good and evil, what constitutes a man and who is a woman, justice and loyalty, allegiance to tribe and nation, the individual and his/her responsibility to society, borders and boundaries. By exploring these themes through the prism of the present, Anouilh attempted to give them a contemporary resonance.

His retelling of Sophocles *Antigone*, positioning it in World War II France under the Nazi occupation, was a masterstroke. Creon, the weary and cynical dictatorial uncle of Antigone as well as the ruler of Thebes, refuses to give her permission to bury her dead brother Polynices. She rises in revolt against him and is sentenced to death. The power of the state, the resistance of the individual, the tragedy of youthful idealism crushed forever, are its themes. Hamid Sayani played Creon to Pheroza Cooper as Antigone. Gerson recalls, 'It was an instructive technical and emotional experience for us all. Pheroza was a composed young woman. We watched as Alkazi provoked her with examples and parallels to heights of fury and violence at a great distance from the serene person we knew.'

The Times of India reviewed this production, saying, 'The

production amply demonstrates how fearlessly the Group tackles productions that even professionals might think twice of attempting. Every emotion of this headstrong, stubborn young girl was played to perfection by this actress (Pheroza Cooper). Creon played by Hamid Sayani was another excellent performance and the long scene in which Creon and Antigone matched their wits and laid bare their innermost thoughts, was a real joy and real theatre.'

By bringing European drama, in translation, to the Bombay stage, eminent Indian playwright Girish Karnad believes an entire earlier tradition of the Shaw play set in a drawing room was thrown out once and for all, and Indian theatre took a refreshing new turn.

In a wonderful detailed video interview by Shanta Gokhale and Sunil Shanbagh, Karnad says, 'Alkazi's productions of Anouilh opened my mind to the idea of reinterpreting our own myths. In our Puranic tradition there can be no tragedy. We know that whatever the travails of Raja Harishchandra, his bhakti will finally bring salvation to him. When I saw Anouilh's *Antigone* and *Eurydice* directed by Ebrahim Alkazi in Bombay in the late 50s and early 60s, it opened my eyes to this new possibility. I turned to the *Mahabharat* for inspiration. My first script was an interpretation of Yayati and was an immediate outcome of seeing these productions.'

Luigi Pirandello's *Six Characters in Search of an Author* and Jean Paul Sartre's *Crime Passionel* and *No Exit* were among the Theatre Group's first forays into European theatre in translation. The contemporary churn of Samuel Beckett and Eugene Ionesco, Edward Albee and Harold Pinter were only to come in the late 1950s and early 60s; and dealing with Indian themes, characters and situations almost a decade later. Hamid directed two of J.B. Priestley's plays, Sylvie da Cunha directed *Six Characters*,

Kersy Katrak directed *Tiger at the Gates*, Alyque directed numerous productions as did my father.

Alyque's early years (1950s) were spent in exploring and recreating the classics: Sophocles' *Antigone*, Congreve's *The Way of the World*, Shakespeare's *The Taming of the Shrew*, Marlowe's *Dr Faustus*, Goldsmith's *She Stoops to Conquer*, Wilde's *An Ideal Husband* and Bernard Shaw's *Candide*. Perhaps this was reflective of his own training in and exposure to theatre in England. Yet he was acutely aware of the limitation of an English-speaking audience. And so he decided to adapt Western plays into Hindustani.

Shaukat Azmi, Shabana's mother, acted in two of Alyque's Hindi productions in the 1950s, the first being *Sheeshe ke Khilone*, an adaptation of Tennessee William's *The Glass Menagerie*, with Shaukat playing the overbearing mother, who is extremely protective of her shy and socially challenged daughter. The other was *Sara Sansar Apna Parivar*, an adaptation of Arthur Miller's *All My Sons*, in which Shaukat played the mother again. Both productions were very successful.

Kaifi Azmi himself came to some of the 'soirees' organized at my grandmother's house to recite his beautiful poetry. In small, tiny, almost hesitant ways the Theatre Group was beginning to 'let Hindi in'.

In many other spheres, such as stage design and lighting, Uncle Deryck regularly interacted with the Indian National Theatre, a leading group of the Gujarati stage. Since the Theatre Group kept up with many of the latest techniques of the West, it served as a conduit for the rest of the theatre community. There was a healthy interest and co-existence among the Marathi, Gujarati, Hindi and English language groups in Bombay.

But trouble was brewing within the Theatre Group. A range of different directors doing a range of different plays was not something that my father appreciated or was even willing to accept. Khorshed recalls, 'I don't think the Padamsee family was ready to accept somebody taking over Bobby's mantle, which was what Alkazi was doing. He was putting down the rules and saying that we should do this and not do that. Eventually some people felt that just "art for art's sake" and "theatre for theatre's sake" was not the thing they wanted. Alkazi's plays were never money-making, they had a certain strata of people who came to see those plays and appreciated them, and who would stay and talk about them. So there was a big gap among members of the group about what theatre should be.

'Alkazi's was more of a thinking man's theatre than entertainment, and eventually after Alkazi broke away, the Theatre Group balanced it. They would have two or three plays making money, and one or two which they wanted to do as "good theatre".'

Alyque clearly remembers that fateful day, when the Theatre Group split and compares it to the Potsdam Conference at the end of World War II! 'Eventually, the split came because Elk, one evening, called all of us together in the Theatre Group, and said, "Look, I want to announce a policy, I am the president and from now, there is going to be only one director, because too many directors are misleading actors about what acting is all about."

'I was very pissed off, so was Sylvie. I said, "But Elk, this is not democracy." He said, "There is no democracy... theatre is life, theatre is religion". And then Mehlli Gobhai, one of the members, said something that has gone down in the annals of the Theatre Group. He said, "Elk, I don't understand what is all this façade about a religion." Elk stood up and shouted, "FAÇADE! You're calling my work a façade? You miserable little shrimp!" And he just went on. Mehlli got a shock. I think shortly after that he quietly snuck away from the meeting. But that was a very memorable evening.

'The next thing we heard was that Elk had decided to form his own group, and those members of the Theatre Group who wanted to join were welcome, but they could never again act for the Theatre Group. Or anyone else. They could only act for the Theatre Unit. For me, it sounded constricting. But several people did it. Kersy (Katrak) said, "Yeah, I am joining. Because he is a very good teacher." I said, "I agree with the teacher, but he only teaches one way, and I don't think that's a good thing. You should have a variety of experiences. Now what would happen if you had had only one teacher throughout your career in school?"

'It was a sad day, but Deryck was very strong. He said, "Alyque, you're right. Why should we give up Bobby's Theatre Group, just because Elk says he wants to be the only director? I also want to direct." And he did direct. He, together with Adi Marzban made a very good directing-producing pair. He did one of the biggest hits the Theatre Group has ever seen, called *The Little Hut*.'

On one side was her husband, on the other the rest of her natal family. It would have been a tough decision for my mother to make. But she knew within herself that my father had established very close ties with all the Padamsees, Kulsumbai downwards, and was well loved. He had shown himself to be the true torchbearer of Sultan's ideals—and so things would get sorted out over time. Already eight years had passed since Sultan's death.

Eight

Early Years at Vithal Court

On the day I was born in 1955 my father was blinding himself. On stage, of course, as Oedipus, the king. This brilliant Greek tragedy tells of a man who finds out he has killed his father and married his mother. My father played the lead.

Our family had recently moved out of the third floor flat at Kulsum Terrace, and we were now at Warden Road. We had bought this flat while it was still under construction and my father had chosen to do away with all the interior walls (except thankfully those of the kitchen and bathroom!) and create an amorphous large freeflowing space that could be divided, by curtains, into living and sleeping areas. More often than not it served as a rehearsal space. One wall of the room was clad in stone. Another large rock served as a bench. Floor to ceiling bookshelves, African masks, a mobile by Alexander Calder, an elegant Bodisattva sculpture, contemporary art and furniture built for plays were all aesthetically placed in the artistic interior. Outside the front door a beautiful stone sculpture framed the nameplate.

The flat was bright and airy, being on the fifth floor of Vithal Court. The sound of many voices raised in prayer, or singing together, often wafted in from the church next door. Or the strong rhythm of drums in the night accompanying a raucous Marathi folk song from a wedding being celebrated in the large colony of servants who lived in a slum behind our building. From our windows we could see the wide expanse of the Arabian Sea stretching till the horizon. And at low tide, you could smell the sea too! The view from our balcony allowed us to look directly across the road to 'Allah Beli', the Irani restaurant, which served scrumptious keema pao. Down the road at Breach Candy, a five-minute walk away, the Bhulabhai Desai Institute had come into being, an interdisciplinary arts hub. This was where my father held his rehearsals and sometimes performed.

Amal recalls, 'I remember my father getting up in the morning, and putting on music and he would come and gently wake us up. Feisal and I would be sleeping on one side of the room and my parents would be sleeping on the other side. From early in the morning till late in the evening there would be people visiting the house. The first visitor would be a carpenter whom my father was very fond of. My father liked to add new things to the house or build new sets for the theatre. The poet Nissim Ezekiel and the art critic and enthusiast D.G. Nadkarni would come and have breakfast with us after their morning walks. By the time I came back from school in the evening, the house would be full of actors and rehearsals would begin. This kind of life seemed very natural to me.'

But Nissim and Nadkarni were not the only guests. My parents regularly hosted many of the greats in contemporary theatre, dance and music from around the world. Outstanding modern dance choreographer Merce Cunningham came to dinner as did John Cage, the great musician. I remember my mother recounting to me that John Cage refused to spit out the vegetable drumsticks that she had served him, and diligently chewed them till he could swallow them all!

'Our home doubled up as my father's workspace, and so all his activities, be they discussions, rehearsals, the recording of music for his plays, the preparation of posters, the mounting of slides required as illustrations for his many talks, all these were done in full view of the family, and he actively involved us in all of them. Thus we imbibed and developed a love for art, architecture, dance, music, theatre, literature, poetry in a natural way as he awakened our sensibilities to space, light, form, colour, movement, rhythm and texture,' recalls my sister.

My father's first few productions for the newly established Theatre Unit explored poetic speech and stylized movement, both of which were to mark much of his theatre career. To this he added a dimension that he had not explored before, working with visual artists of exceptional calibre like M.F. Husain, or the sculptor Adi Davierwala, to create visuals of striking originality, that added their own dimension to the productions.

Murder in the Cathedral, T.S. Eliot's poetic rendition of Thomas Becket's last days, is a compelling verse drama. It tells of the individual's opposition to the king and was written by the eminent modern poet as a reaction to the rising tide of fascism in Europe in the 1930s. The play captures some of the spirit of the medieval morality plays in a contemporary fashion.

Becket, the bishop, struggles with his own conscience and a chorus of poor women serve as a counterpoint to him. When the play opens they await Becket who has just returned from a seven-year exile, and are worried by his volatile relationship with the king, Henry II. The Tempters arrive to lure him over to the king's side, and their arguments parallel the temptations of Christ in the Bible. The first offers physical safety, the second offers power and riches if he will serve the king, the third suggests that Becket should join the barons and resist the king. And then the Fourth Tempter speaks, suggesting martyrdom; Becket losing his life. Becket refutes all these arguments.

After a dramatic second act when they confront and finally kill him, the Tempters turn to the audience and defend their actions. Becket's murder was for the best reasons, in the right spirit, sober and justified, ensuring that the power of the Church would not undermine the power of the State.

My father directed this play twice over in quick succession in Bombay. For the first production for the Theatre Group (1953), M.F. Husain created the painted crucifix for the set and the half masks worn by the chorus members. Sculptor Adi Davierwala created the crucifix that was the main element of the stage design when he once again mounted it as the first production under the Theatre Unit banner in 1956, staged at the Bhulabhai Desai Institute.

It was only natural that from here he would move to explore the world of classical Greek drama. Over 2,000 years ago, the three great Greek tragedians, Sophocles, Aeschylus and Euripides, monopolized Greek Theatre (fifth century BC). Their hour-long plays were performed during the day in the open air, playing to an audience of thousands. They explored their own rich mythic tradition in play after play. Sophocles' *Oedipus,* considered one of the greatest tragedies of all time, is a fast-moving, almost detective-like drama. Choral speech, the stylized dance-like movement of individual actors against the mass of chorus, draped royal robes in deep rich tones, sonorous voices raised in rhythm became my father's signature style in presenting the Greeks to modern audiences.

He actively involved himself in all aspects of theatre, except costume, which was my mother's domain. I remember him laying out metres of hessian on the terrace and himself putting a brush into Plaster of Paris to paint the curtain that was an integral part of the *Eurydice* sets, or painstakingly rehearsing and re-rehearsing music cues of a play to get it just right. Girish

Karnad recalls seeing *Miss Julie* and how, when she comes to the end of her climatic speech, 'Kill me, kill me too, if you can kill an innocent bird', that was accompanied by 'sentimental music', my father, playing Jean, struck a match and on cue the lights brightened and the music was killed! Such precision and sophistication of presentation was new to Bombay theatre and Girish says it opened up new dimensions of the theatre experience to him.

My mother was the backbone of the Theatre Unit. Always doing the costumes on a minimal budget, often acting, sometimes even dancing. Administratively she ran the group—looking into advertising, ticketing, filling the auditorium, even seating the audience. Without her unqualified support, my father would never have made it as a director.

The single-storeyed Bhulabhai Desai Institute faced the Arabian Sea, with waves that furiously lashed the rocks across the road. It was here against a simple set of Greek pillars and a red drape, that my father brought alive this Greek tragedy. Elsewhere in this building there were artist's studios, including that of Gaitonde, one of India's first abstract painters, next door was Ravi Shankar's Kinnara Institute of Music and upstairs, on the roof and occasionally in the large semi-circular garden, my father performed his plays.

Madhuriben Desai, who created this first multi-arts centre in India, was an archaeologist, art critic and daughter-in-law of Bhulabhai Desai, the eminent lawyer. The rental for the art studio was only a rupee a day! Gaitonde recalls, 'Artists need to be in touch with other professions: music, theatre, books, you cannot stop thinking. A writer must know what music is, a dancer must know what theatre is.' This close-knit community of artists revitalized and nurtured one another till the late 1960s when the building came down and the locus (for theatre at least) moved to the ground floor of Walchand Terrace.

My mother often told me how Waheeda Rehman used to wait patiently to practice her Bharatanatyam in the same room my mother was dancing in, or how actors would drop in to watch Gaitonde or Husain at work during a break in the rehearsals. Panikar's yoga class went on in one of the rooms, and Sakina Mehta, wife of the eminent artist Tyeb Mehta, ran the bookshop. Years later another artist, Bal Chhavda, would open Gallery '59 on the premises.

Because its reputation spread quickly among artists, musicians, dancers and theatre workers in Bombay and elsewhere, and also because the events organized there reached out to a discerning public, the popularity of the Bhulabhai Desai Institute grew. Alyque referred to it later as 'a disorganized, free space to creatively explore the arts. A pleasant "gadbad!"' Artists of different styles, artists working in different languages came together to celebrate the interdisciplinary nature of the arts. Ideas flowed freely, minds were ignited.

It was an informal space where the audience and performer were not segregated by a raised stage, and a darkened hall. In fact, Ratna Pathak Shah says in an interview, the 'distance was minuscule'. As compared to the Marathi and Gujarati stage of the time, it was run by people not interested in making profit or the 'commercial viability' of a play. At most a production ran for six to eight performances, and then work began on a new one, totally different in style, in staging and execution. And theatre was only one among the many arts practiced here.

My father's landmark production of *Oedipus* was to travel to Delhi the same year to be staged at the first ever Festival of Indian Theatre. It was to capture the attention of the prime minister of India, Jawaharlal Nehru, who subsequently invited my father to lead the National School of Drama. But my father felt he was not yet up to the task, and needed a few years to prepare for the post.

So he established a School of Dramatic Arts and his very first student was Vijaya Mehta, who later became a legend in Marathi theatre in her own right. Among those who had their initial theatre training here were film director Vijay Anand (Goldie), actor Amrish Puri, actresses Kusum Bahl and Alaknanda Samarth, both of whom continue to be involved in theatre, and the maverick Satyadev Dubey, to whom my father left the Theatre Unit when he moved to Delhi.

International experts gave talks on theatre music, the masked theatre of Bali, stage design in the West, voice modulation and movement, amongst hundreds of lectures that were organized at the Bhulabhai Desai Institute. My father also regularly ran short-term courses sponsored by the Ministry of Education at different locations in Bombay and Poona. He even travelled across India conducting workshops in Shimla, Ranikhet, Darjeeling, Baroda and Matheran. He was preparing himself to head the National School of Drama.

Years later, after my father had completed fourteen years at NSD, my parents found a work space similar to the Bhulabhai Desai Institute in Triveni Kala Sangam in Delhi. Surrounded by the beauty of Joseph Stein's architecture and the sounds of ghungroos and tablas from a dance class, or the mellifluous Manipuri singing that accompanied Guru Singhajit Singh's productions being rehearsed on an outdoor stage, or even the chatter of students from the art studio, they must have recalled their initial years at the Bhulabhai Desai Institute. A coming together of all the arts and artists, so essential for the creation of a vibrant culture.

Coming from such disparate backgrounds and completely different experiences of childhood, parenting posed its own problem. While my mother had grown up in a liberated Anglicized world, my father's initial years meant speaking Arabic at home, praying five times a day, being protective to women even as his schooling at a Jesuit institution paralleled my mother's education. With my elder sister they tried to strike a balance between the two. Amal was pulled out of Cathedral School when she became an adolescent and put into the Urdu medium Anjuman Islam School for Girls, but only briefly. When she returned to Cathedral, she wore a salwar under the regulation uniform of a skirt and a blouse, the only girl to be dressed in this way in the entire school! Similarly it was thought she should learn the namaaz, but when maulvi sahib suggested covering all the artworks in our flat with little white curtains, my father swiftly got rid of him. By the time I was born, 'experimentation' time was over and I had the best possible Montessori education.

Childhood was a time of fierce friendships. Just opposite us, in Dr Maniar's flat, were two young boys of my age who along with me performed the escape of Shivaji from Agra in a fruit basket, in Marathi, when we were around seven! Diagonally across, a young friend of mine was later to give up his middle-class background and join the Naxalite movement. Or so his father told me years later, when he saw my stage adaptation of Mahasweta Devi's iconic novel *Hazaar Chaurasi ki Ma*, on a similar theme. Razia, who acted with me, belonged to a Bohri family on the fourth floor and Amal and I loved eating a meal with her family, everyone's hands dipping into the large communal thali, on which Bohri food is traditionally served and eaten.

On the first floor lived the 'stingy Manjis' who had no ceiling fans in their flat that spanned the entire floor! An oblique salute to how well ventilated our flats were at the time. And on the ground floor there was a large Parsi joint family, with many of the youngsters being part of the Vithal Court gang. On either side of our 'tall' five-storeyed building (or so we thought in those days!)

in two tiny, single-storeyed houses lived Mihika and Sreela, two Gujarati girls my age, and in the garden of the other small house, a large wooden swing was the location of many antics, much laughter and occasional accidents.

Several children in the building joined my mother's creative drama classes on the terrace and we once all came together to act in Sai Paranjpye's *Land of Cards* in Hindi. The children of many other family friends also made up the cast, M.F. Husain's children, Raissa, Akila and Mustafa, played key roles as did my cousin Munira Padamsee and I.

Every year at Janamashtami a huge human pyramid of lithe young men climbed over and on top of one another to reach the Dahi ki Handi that often hung as high as our fifth-floor balcony; Christmas meant large paper 'stars' displayed on many balconies; Diwali, a plethora of diyas and a communal celebration on the terrace, where families gathered to light rockets, enjoy fountains and dance with phuljhadis (sparklers) in their hands.

But that was only part of my childhood universe. Because there were also all the cousins from my mother's side who were in school with us! Closest in age to me was Rhea, Deryck and Shiraz's daughter, and we were inseparable friends through childhood, adolescence and into adulthood. We regularly performed plays in the Jefferies' drawing room to an indulgent family audience, where Rhea played Rapunzel to me as Prince Charming, and we battled her elder brother Renan as the Wicked Witch. All this against a black and white checkered floor and a castle made out of brown paper wrapped around their dining table. Another play I recall is *Bluebeard*, and then along with my cousin Ranjit Choudhary (Pearl's son), a Japanese play, *The Half Lie,* presented by Al-Jeff-Dhry. This was a comic made-up name for our 'performance company' combining Alkazi, Jefferies and Choudhary!

All of these plays were under the expert direction of Aunty Shiraz. She went on to become the drama teacher at Cathedral School, and so did my other aunt, Pearl Padamsee, who taught at Campion School, Fort Convent and J.B. Petit. Several of those who trained with them went into full time careers on the stage or screen later.

My mother was my constant companion in my growing-up years. I remember lying in bed with her as she read me a story before my afternoon siesta, or her patiently feeding me as I was a reluctant eater, or teaching me how to wash my hands with mud taken from pots on the terrace when we accidentally locked ourselves out of the house one day. I was into a lot of creative play and had an entire cupboard of toys, into which I could crawl, and where I spent many hours.

Theatre was often an evening activity with me and recently, viewing an exhibition of my father's work, I realized I had been on stage at the ages of four, five, six and seven! As the washerwoman's son in *Yerma*, as Medea's son in *Medea*, as Flipot the servant boy in *Tartuffe*. Later in Delhi, as a teenager, I featured in many of my father's productions.

Sound, smell, touch, flavour. Open windows that allowed the world in, and that allowed me to peep into the world from my tiny height. Not the isolated ivory tower of the Padamsee childhood but a vibrant, open, engaged view of the world.

Kulsumbai of Kulsum Terrace. Photo: Pablo Bartholomew

Jafferbhai and his young wife Kulsum

The Padamsee clan—Jafferbhai and Kulsum with Sultan (standing, right),
Roshan (standing, left), Shiraz (seated, centre), Zarina (seated, right)

English sojourn, 1938—Kulsum Padamsee with Roshen (left), Bobby (right), Aziz (seated on stool), Zarine (seated on carpet) in Owistree England

All in the family—The Padamsees with the three sons-in-law, Deryck, Ebrahim, Hamid, and Alyque Padamsee (standing, from left to right)

The Alkazi clan: Hamid Alkazi, father of Ebrahim Alkazi (top left), his mother Mar (top right), and, (below) Ebrahim aged 11, (second row, right) with his siblings in Poona

Tragic genius—Bobby Padamsee at home in Bombay with his trophies, 1944

Companions for life—Ebrahim and Roshen on their wedding day, October 1946 (ab

London days—Rosh
with Nissim Ezekiel
(left) in London, 194

A mother, grandmother, gallerist and costume designer—Roshen Alkazi with Feisal, aged 2, (above) and (below) with granddaughter Zuleikha

Growing up—Feisal, aged 7, with Amal in Matheran (top left); with his 21st birthday (top, right) and (below) with friends at the Cellar, Delhi

Photos: (Top, right), Pablo Bartholomew; (above), Ram Rahman

Finally, a family man—Feisal and Radhika on their wedding day with
(from left to right) Ram Rahman, Pablo Bartholomew and Ayesha Sayani and,
below, sons Zaen (left), and Armaan with Radhika (right)

Married to theatre—Alyque Padamsee
in *Death of a Salesman* (top left),
Pearl Padamsee (top right) and
(below) Amal and Nissar Allana
Photo: (Top right) Pablo
Bartholomew

Theatre in their veins—Roshen Alkazi
(top left), Amal Allana (top right) and,
(below) Ebrahim Alkazi
Photos: Pablo Bartholomew

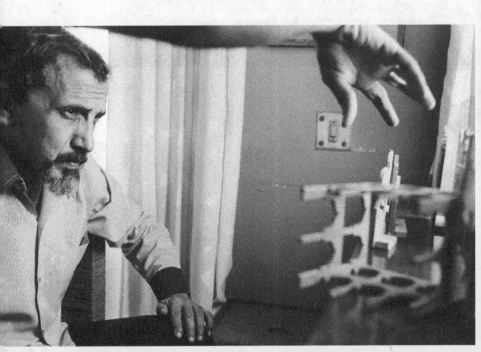

Where it all began—the horseshoe-shaped dining table in Kulsum Terrace, as it is to

Nine

Six Women Who Revolt

The terrace above our flat was large as it stretched over four flats, and one day my father rented it at the princely sum of Rs 150 per month! Here he built a small eighty-seater open-air theatre he named Meghdoot. The distant roar of the sea and the vast open sky with the twinkling stars above formed a perfect backdrop to the six productions he staged here.

Molière's *Tartuffe* was one of my father's favourite parts on stage. He played the lecherous godman in two back to back productions in Bombay (1960) opposite Usha Amin and Yasmin Mody (later to marry Farley Richmond, the American scholar of Indian theatre); and in Delhi (1964) for Yatrik opposite Joy Michael and Indira Kohli (later to emigrate to England and be a part of the crazy TV series, *The Kumars at No 42*).

Molière's sharp and biting satirical comedies remained part of my father's repertoire for forty years. From the more farcical, physical, knock about humour of *The Physician in Spite of Himself* and *Scapin*, to the wonderful, warm and witty portraits of despicable characters in *The Miser* and *Tartuffe*, to the social exposè of *The School for Wives*. *The Physician in Spite of Himself* ran for eight performances across Bombay in 1956, *Scapin* was presented both in English as well as in Hindi as *Bicchu*. The

Hindustani version got a new production in the National School of Drama with half masks and stylized costumes. *The Miser* he first staged with Bomi Kapadia in the lead role in Bombay, and then in a marvellous Urdu adaptation, *Kanjoos*, with Om and Sudha Shivpuri in the lead roles at the National School of Drama. This production ran for years.

The School for Wives, rechristened *Bivion ka Madrassa*, had the multitalented Rajesh Vivek in the lead role and was a perennial favourite of the National School of Drama Repertory Company. The use of a walking stick or umbrella handle to beat up or trip people, over-exaggerated simpering women in ghararas, lascivious old men lusting after young girls, avarice and greed, loneliness and redemption, love and betrayal found easy echoes in the Muslim milieu into which three of the plays were adapted. I recall my father sending Om Shivpuri, Sudha Shivpuri, Ramgopal Bajaj and Kamlakar Sontakke to Chandni Chowk, Jama Masjid and Old Delhi Railway Station to observe people in their own setting and use it to colour their characterization.

Sudha Shivpuri recalls, 'I went to Jama Masjid—at that time India and Pakistan were again at loggerheads—and stole into a house. A chik hung in the doorway. I stood behind it as I watched how Muslim women of a certain class behave, how they apply black powder to their teeth, how they slice supari, how they eat paan, and how they spit out the juice. I observed this carefully.'

Looking back at my father's choice of plays in his last phase of directing for the Theatre Unit in Bombay, I see a discernible pattern in his decisions. Six of the plays deal with the theme of a powerful female central character, and are also named after them. Henrik Ibsen's steely *Hedda Gabler*, August Strindberg's assertive *Miss Julie*. Jean Anouilh's young protestors, *Antigone* and *Eurydice*, Lorca's passionate peasant *Yerma*, and of course the quintessential wronged (and wronging) woman in Euripides' *Medea*. It is as though through exploring the inner and outer worlds of these titular heroines, he is trying better to comprehend his own equation with women. These are all modern women, strong and resilient, asserting themselves, questioning the prevailing social and institutional structures.

Girish Karnad, who saw some of these productions, also speaks of how finally a central woman character had replaced the male. Every script in theatre history till this time focused exclusively on the travails of the rather lonely and troubled tragic hero.

Hedda Gabler is Ibsen's most enigmatic heroine. Ibsen wrote at the time he was working on this play, 'The great tragedy of life is that so many people have nothing to do but yearn for happiness without ever being able to find it.'

Over the 130 years since it was first performed, this character has been interpreted as a closeted lesbian, a pregnant mother, a jilted lover and yet her 'truth' escapes us. She seems to have a need for freedom, and to wield the power to shape another's destiny. Her aim seems to have a warped personal logic, but despite getting what she wants, what she wants is not what any 'normal' person would. Oscar Wilde when he first saw a production of this play, said, 'I felt pity and terror, as though the play had been Greek.'

Medea is yet another example of a symbolic act of feminine revolt. Medea, a foreigner in Greece, has helped her husband Jason, who is Greek, kill her father and recover the golden fleece. Years later, angered by her banishment by the king, and deserted by her husband, Medea rebels by killing their two sons.

The psychologically complex character that Euripides creates is both attractive and repulsive. She is a foreigner in Greece and is therefore perceived as being the 'other', she is a woman in a male-dominated Greek society and above all, she is intelligent and vocal in her dissent.

Yerma is about a woman who cannot conceive. Her name in Spanish means 'barren'. Her yearning for a child, the pressure of a society of shepherds and washerwomen who surround and deride her, and the desperation that engulfs her leads her to kill her husband, beating him to death. Lorca creates his own style, blending the cadence and rhythm of Spanish (that even translates well into English) of a peasant culture, with images of a life lived in close communion with nature. The bleating lamb, the call of the shepherd's flute, the rhythm of clothes being washed on stones in a gurgling river, the belief in magical spells and potions to help a woman conceive and the annual religious pilgrimage, are all strong motifs in this play.

Vijay Tendulkar, enfant terrible of Marathi theatre, was struck by my father's production of this peasant tragedy and urged others from the emerging New Wave Marathi theatre community to see it.

The 'image' my father creates in each one of these plays speaks volumes. Dressed in a long black, velvet gown, Hima Devi with her deep throaty voice and impassive mask-like face, holds a long cigarette in her hand and looks broodingly out. She is the perfect Hedda Gabler. Alakananda Samarth as the young, alluring vivacious daughter of the Count, Miss Julie, is the ideal foil to my father's sexual predator Jean, the valet in Strindberg's masterful interplay of sexual tension across the class divide. Usha Amin's powerfully beating her husband to death in *Yerma* as he unfairly accuses her of adultery, or the same actress killing both her children as her husband announces his marriage to another, in *Medea* are iconic, elemental characters.

Each one of these women exemplify, elucidate and expand on the spectators' understanding of self, society and the 'other'.

It is, in a way, my father's exploration of trying to understand the woman of today, examine his own marriage that is failing and his involvement elsewhere.

One of these women kills her husband (Yerma), one kills her children (Medea), one kills herself (Hedda Gabler), one chooses to be condemned to death (Antigone). Each one of these women, along with Eurydice and Miss Julie, find that their path to self assertion and a search for their own identity, distinct from the world of men, ends in tragedy. To conform is to be unhappy, but to rebel is to die.

Seeing my father's production of *Miss Julie*, Girish Karnad wrote: 'When I walked out of the theatre that evening, I felt as though I had been put through an emotionally or even a physically painful rite of passage. I had read some Western playwrights in college, but nothing had prepared me for the power and violence I experienced that day. By the norms I had been brought up on, the very notion of laying bare the inner recesses of human psyche like this for public consumption seemed obscence. What impressed me as much as the psychological cannibalism of the play was the way lights faded in and out on stage.

'Most of my contemporaries went through some similar experience at some point in their lives. We stepped out of mythological plays lit by torches or petromax lamps straight into Strindberg and dimmers. The new technology could not be divorced from the new psychology. The two together defined a stage that was like nothing we had known or suspected. I have often wondered whether it wasn't that evening that, without being actually aware of it, I decided I wanted to be a playwright.'

My father's directorial process was detailed and always started with a close study of the period of the playwright, why he had chosen to write this particular play and how it was related to his other writings and the times he lived in. So for him a familiarity with the writer's entire ouvre was a necessary precursor to the production of this particular script. The ideas and art of the time of the playwright also coloured his perceptions.

The colour, fabric and drape of costumes of a particular historic period was an essential part of my mother's approach to costume design. After all, the way a Greek unstitched garment falls and is draped is completely different to the silhouette, cut and drape of a Renaissance garment or the complete camouflaging of a Victorian woman's figure, covered from head to toe, in an Ibsen play. Each epoch also creates its own style of movement: the courtly bows and exaggerated curtsies of an Elizabethan era, the coarse clowning of a French peasant, the teasing fan and fluttering eyelashes of a Restoration comedy. This combination of text and movement, costume and gesture creates a style that evokes an entire era on the stage.

Documentation of every production that he directed was another strong point of my father's. In Bombay he worked closely with Mitter Bedi, who was till then largely an industrial photographer, and drew him into shooting for the stage. A separate photoshoot session would be planned and the production shot in elaborate detail.

But not every production got a positive response from the press. Often they were strongly critical and my father responded in kind, either writing directly to the newspaper in question or publishing a riparte in the Theatre Unit Bulletin he brought out for years.

Anthony and Frieda Toyne, Derek Bond and Patsy Dance, among other expatriates, acted in the Theatre Unit plays. Anthony and Frieda played the cuckolded husband and aggressive mother-in-law, whom Tartuffe tries to fool in *Tartuffe*. Derek Bond of the British Council played Hedda's weak husband, Tesman, in *Hedda Gabler* and also a key role in *Eurydice*. Patsy Dance acted in both *Volpone* and *Eurydice*. These were only some of the foreigners living in India at the time, as were the three Jewish émigrés who had helped the Indian art movement mature and grow.

But it was the young men and women starting out in theatre who would develop into actors of stature under my father's direction. Kusum Bahl (now Haider) was only sixteen when she ran away from home in Delhi to pursue an acting course at the Theatre Unit. She stayed with us initially, sleeping on a chattai in a corner as I am told, as I was only two years old at the time! Alakananda Samarth of Shobhana Samarth's family and film star Nutan's niece, doubled up with Kusum in *Eurydice* and also played Miss Julie to my father's Jean. Kusum was both Eurydice and Antigone, and years later she was to play Yerma and Blanche Dubois (in *A Streetcar Named Desire*) in Delhi under my father's direction. Her theatre work took her places, but of that, more later.

These actors were, and continue to be, 'family' to us. Alakananda played Bernarda Alba years later in Amal's adaptation, *Birjees Qadar ka Kumba*, and Kusum did several plays with Amal, most prominently Gabriel García Marquez's *Erindera*, Mahesh Elkunchwar's *Sonata* and a new reworking of Ibsen, *Metropolis*. She has also worked extensively with me in Marsha Norman's *Night Mother*, Peter Nichol's *Passion Play* and Shelagh Stevenson's *The Memory of Water* in the 1990s.

Usha Amin was in a class of her own. With her striking, even piercing eyes, deep sonorous voice and strong stage presence, she played Yerma in *Yerma*, Medea in *Medea* and acted opposite my father in Tennessee William's *Suddenly Last Summer*, and in *Tartuffe*. Her husband Kersy Katrak played her husband in both *Yerma* and *Medea*, and then in an all-male cast (rare for my father!) Kersy played Estragon in Samuel Beckett's *Waiting for Godot*.

In *Medea*, my neighbour from downstairs, Razia, and I played the two children that Medea gives birth to, and then kills. I remember crouching backstage with a torch, chewing my nails, reading a comic version of H.G. Well's *The Invisible Man* with Razia, even as Usha stormed across the stage, screaming vengeance to the skies.

In our own immediate family, all four of us, my father, mother, sister and me appeared together in two productions of the Theatre Unit: Lorca's poetic tragedy, *Yerma*, and Euripedes' *Medea*. My sister and mother appeared in several other plays and often my father both acted and directed. *Volpone, Miss Julie, Suddenly Last Summer, Medea, Tartuffe* and *Waiting for Godot* were some of the productions of the Theatre Unit he acted in.

It was in these years that Husain came home to Vithal Court to get all four of us to pose for a family portrait. He also made great friends with Kusum Bahl, my father's actress, and she served as his muse for several years, appearing in many of his paintings.

And then one morning when everyone was recovering from the performance of *Medea* the previous night, M.F. arrived with a sketchbook tucked under his arm. He had quietly snuck into the show after it had started, perched himself in the very last row and his gaze moved from stage to sketchbook to imagination and back again. Before the show ended, Husain had already left.

A series of striking drawings rendered in black charcoal captured moments of high tension, passion and drama from the play. In his characteristic way Husain had not tried to realistically 'capture' the action of the play, but used the performance as a springboard for his own creativity.

Amal describes the Meghdoot Theatre days: 'I was barely thirteen or fourteen years old at the time, and besides helping my mother with getting the costumes ironed, setting up props, or laying out the cushions of the wooden bleachers/risers that were the seats, I was sometimes required to act in some of the productions as well. My most important job, however, was to serve steaming cups of coffee to members of the audience, punctually at the exact time the intermission bell sounded. The coffee was on the house, our way of thanking the audience for their strenuous effort of climbing up to see a performance. I remember it was quite a feat for me to organize the making of eighty cups of coffee in our minuscule kitchen.'

My father recalls: 'In those early days, Feisal and Amal imbibed the atmosphere of the theatre and because of the early exposure developed a very serious commitment to theatre. The atmosphere inflamed their minds with a tremendous passion for theatre. What they have learnt from me was discipline and the idea of social commitment. The idea that theatre is an important instrument of social transformation and not just entertainment. This is particularly evident in Feisal's work.'

A long line of people winding down six storeys would wait patiently to be let into the Meghdoot Theatre. Among them you could find the doyenne of Indian handicrafts, Kamala Chattopadhyay, or Pupul Jaykar, or even the young Girish Karnad with his friend Meghnad Desai. There was no lift and the other residents must have been very patient with the heavy footfall every weekend in 1960 and 1961. At night of course, like in all other Bombay buildings, the very same staircase would see the domestic help from various households roll out their meagre beddings and curl up to sleep.

Ten

Last Year in Bombay

The violent disintegration and collapse of a family that gets torn apart, beyond repair, links the themes of *Medea* and *Suddenly Last Summer*. And even as my father directed these two plays one after the other and staged them in a space—the Meghdoot Theatre—open and vulnerable to the elements, our own family was disintegrating in its own way.

A possessive and grasping matriarch whose gay son Sebastian is driven to suicide constitutes the plot of Tennessee Williams' *Suddenly Last Summer*, and the script has some echoes of the story of my grandmother and Bobby. Set in a fecund overgrown garden with maneating plants like the Venus Fly Trap, Mrs Venable (Usha Amin) must conceal the truth behind her son's death in any way possible. Standing in opposition to her is Catherine, the young man's cousin and a witness to his death. A charming silent onlooker is a doctor, played by my father.

Mrs Venable wants to bribe the doctor to perform a lobotomy on Catherine. Instead he injects her with a truth serum. She talks of how her cousin used her to procure young men he was sexually interested in, and how a group of cannibalistic young boys killed and ate him. It is an interesting script as Sebastian, the protagonist is absent. 'We all use each other, that's what we think of as love,' is Catherine's take on it.

The setting of my father's production, with a large Sri Lankan devil mask and numerous plants gave a sense of something primeval, and was symbolic, linking Sebastian to a barbaric past that an ostensibly 'civilized' present seeks to 'contain'.

As Tennessee William's writes, 'Man devours man in a metaphorical sense. He feeds upon his fellow creatures but people use each other, devour one another without conscience.'

This was the first, and one of the few American plays my father ever directed. Almost forty-five years later he directed Tennessee William's *A Streetcar Named Desire*, Arthur Miller's *Death of A Salesman* and Eugene O'Neill's *Desire under the Elms*, the first two in Hindi and the third in Punjabi.

Medea and *Suddenly Last Summer* were staged alternately with two very different plays: Ben Johnson's *Volpone*, a merciless satire of greed and lust written in 1606, and Samuel Beckett's exploration of the Theatre of the Absurd in *Waiting for Godot*, written in 1956, 350 years later. These four plays talk of greed and avarice, lust and lost love, the 'civilized' and the 'forgotten', the 'acceptable' and the 'unacceptable', they explore the lives of those who choose to go beyond the boundaries of society's restrictions.

Volpone was originally produced in collaboration with the Nalanda Arts Centre in Bandra where my father had conducted a month-long workshop every year for several years. Since it did well, he included some of the students from the original cast in his remounting of it for the Theatre Unit.

Ben Johnson's script is considered the best of the Jacobean comedies and is periodically revived around the world. The story revolves around a man pretending to be on his deathbed, to avoid repaying loans. All the characters are named after animals: the Vulture, the Raven, the Carrion Crow. There are even hermaphrodites and eunuchs as part of the cast. Dennis Fernandes played Volpone, the fox to my father's Mosca, the fly.

Waiting for Godot, the ultimate pathbreaking Theatre of the Absurd script by Samuel Beckett, was his last production in Bombay for the Theatre Unit. After its first Indian production on our terrace it has been a perennial favourite of Indian directors. The tramps Estragon and Vladimir wait patiently through the changing seasons for the arrival of Godot. The play works as metaphor, raising several questions related to human existence, the meaning of life and the universal need for hope.

Kersy Katrak and Manohar Pitale played the tramps, Gerson da Cunha with his booming voice and popping eyes played the exploitative Pozzo while my father played the woebegone Lucky at the end of a long rope, literally. It is interesting that in all these four final productions in Bombay, my father cast himself in varied roles, displaying as it were, the entire range of his dramatic skills. It would be the last of his appearances as an actor on stage, the sole exception being his new production of *Tartuffe* in Delhi for Yatrik with him reprising the titular role.

It was a busy year full of performances on the floor above. My sister recalls, 'Our flat on the floor below became the backstage area where costumes were ironed, tea was made, and actors came to relax between scenes. They roamed in and out of the house, exchanging a few words with me, a little girl who found herself entirely at home in this world of make-believe. Actors transforming into Jason, Medea, Yerma or Estragon, uttering very grand dialogues—full of pain. My father would often play the lead in his own plays, and was in the habit of keeping us waiting outside the only bathroom we had, while he rehearsed his lines in privacy... or so he thought!'

Four diverse productions of a Greek tragedy, a Jacobean comedy and two contemporary 'classics', all with topnotch actors who had honed their skills over several years with my father, all productions performed open-air in the Meghdoot Theatre.

Waiting for Godot alone played for twenty-three performances. Not having to pay hall rental allowed the Theatre Unit to do long runs of its productions with an almost repertory type company in place. 1961 was a year of crowning glory for my father.

A very different production that my father directed before leaving Bombay for Delhi was *The Prince of Peace* for an institution of Jesuit fathers in Chembur, then a distant suburb. It was Gerson da Cunha who had seen a rehearsal of it and was upset by its level of amateurishness. He invited my father to take over the direction. The production was on the life of Christ and my father completely removed all the dialogue, substituting it with excerpts from the Bible, read by Gerson and himself, accompanied by a haunting score of classical music. My mother's perfect Biblical costumes and his choreographic compositions lifted this religious tale to an artistic level.

It was his first attempt to do a production on a lavish scale, working with a large cast. Years later in Delhi with *Andha Yug* at Ferozshah Kotla and three productions mounted at Purana Qila, he had mastered this style.

Visiting us at Vithal Court at that time, the artist Krishen Khanna recalls, 'Within the first week of my being in Bombay, I somehow graduated to see the Alkazi household... in fact, it was an induction into a whole world of total culture, by that I mean, high culture. Literature, painting and of course drama, and no distinctions were made between them... they were just a part of living, a part of life... it leads me to think that real culture is a day to day affair, and not a little injection that one is given to become cultured. So, it's the whole time, it's life which goes into it, and it widens people, it softens people.'

A healthy respect for, and interaction with varied aspects of Indian culture marked my parents' last years in Mumbai. My mother had had a fascination for dance, not only ballroom, waltz, foxtrot, rumba and samba but also the more exotic Dance of the Seven Veils she had choreographed and performed in Bobby's version of *Salome* when she was only nineteen. She felt increasingly drawn to Bharatanatyam and decided, at the age of thirty, to learn the form. On the suggestion of Indian scholar Dr Narayana Menon, she travelled to Madras to convince the greatest of all Bharatanatyam dancers, Balasaraswati, to be her guru.

Bala was already a dance legend internationally. She belonged to a family of traditional devadasis who devoted themselves to dancing in the temple. Her family included percussionists, violinists, vocalists and flautists. And yet she made space to accommodate my troubled Westernized mother who was seeking to understand something of her Indian roots at the age of thirty. It was a warm, loving and healing relationship for my mother.

They began on a journey that they undertook together as guru and shishya, which developed into a close family relationship that lasted long beyond Bala's death. For two years my mother along with my sister, then nine, and me, only two, lived at the YMCA in Madras and we spent every day in Bala's house. As Amal recalls, 'She studied the Natyashastras, she learnt, through Bala, the history and tradition of Bharatanatyam, the life of the devadasis, while side by side she was tutored in vocal Carnatic music. More enriching was the close intimate relationship that blossomed between her and Bala. Bala's mother, Veena Dhanama, Bala's brother, the great flautist Vishvanatham, and Ranganathan, the mridangam player, as well as Bala's daughter Laxmi, all welcomed her warmly into the charmed sanctum of their family life. Going in and out of their home, attending concerts, this entire experience for my mother was like entering an entirely new world, a world that was very grounded, a world steeped in tradition. For her this was what she had always been searching for... an "Indian world", which she had, till then, known only as a distant observer. Now she was enveloped by it, experiencing it first hand. It was during this time that it became clear to her what form and shape the trajectory of her life must follow. From this point on, hers was to quest and delve deep to discover the roots of our very ancient civilization and find out for herself, what it meant to be an Indian.'

As far as I can recall, Bala's house was in Adyar, a leafy suburb of Madras. While my mother practiced with Bala, I would play in the red mud outside, building different types of structures. The melodious Carnatic flute, the sound of ghungroos, the Bharatanatyam 'bol' and the stamp of feet, along with the smell of rasam, the sweetness of coconut water, the scent of the veni that Bala wore every day in her hair, became part of my consciousness. It was a different kind of 'rehearsal', that I was witnessing here, an opening of my mind to a different worldview and culture. Now, sixty years later, I still feel strangely at home whenever I visit Madras (now Chennai) for work.

The two years we spent together in Madras brought my sister, my mother and myself very close. A photograph of my mother and myself as a young child shows her beaming, while I look out at the photographer with curiosity and contentment in my lively eyes below a curly mop of hair.

My father had always had a fascination for Kathakali, ever since Bobby had urged him to learn some of its techniques for the production of *Chitra* by Rabindranath Tagore that Bobby had begun directing, just before he committed suicide in 1946. He now learnt more about it, even as he began to read and write Hindi. My mother also directed two plays in Hindi, *Neki ka Rasta*, a puppet play which she worked on with a traditional kathputli artist, and *Patte Nagri*, a play for and by children.

Mine was an unusual childhood, some would even say a

disrupted one full of travel, varied living spaces and constantly being in the midst of performances of both drama and dance, and yet some things in my life did remain the same providing me with emotional stability. There were still the mandatory Sunday lunches at my grandmother's place. Except for Deryck, none of the other sons-in-laws (my father and Hamid) attended. These lunches typically began around two p.m. when the five Jefferies would arrive at my grandmother's flat, often directly after attending mass in church. The other five of us, my aunt Zarina and her daughter Ayesha, and the three of us Alkazis, would be waiting patiently yet hungrily, for the spread my grandmother always provided. My grandfather would join us at the horseshoe table restricting himself to bajre ki roti and a chutney of smashed garlic and ground red chilies, typical farmer's fare in Saurashtra.

After a long, leisurely lunch which usually ended with plates of cut up mangoes in the mango months, the adults would all retire for their siesta, while the six cousins played table tennis or dumb charades till it was tea time. Then we all headed out to see a movie together! Everyone except my grandfather. These were always the latest English films: *The Snows of Kilimanjaro*, *Lady of the Camelias*, even a Hitchcock film. We usually saw them at the New Empire or the Excelsior cinema which also meant gorging on bhelpuri from Vithals next door.

I don't recall eating a single Anglo-Indian dish at my grandparent's home, except for caramel custard. But when all the Padamsee sisters set up their own homes, menus and palates changed forever. Cutlets, macaroni, bakes, roast chicken, bread pudding and jelly regularly appeared at meal times, along with several Goan dishes because much of the domestic help and all of the cooks came from there. Spices were roasted instead of being fried, prawn and sea fish, vindaloo and cafreal became an intrinsic part of our diets. Tomato ketchup and Maggi noodles were still a generation away. Food habits so completely reflect a family's culture and its gradual transformation.

A great fun experience of my childhood was being a part of the short film *The Case of the Missing Corpse*, written and directed by Alyque and Deryck, and starring all of my cousins. It was a 'cinema noir' thriller with several identical-looking dead bodies (all played with elan by Alyque!), a couple of crooks (one of whom came out of a fridge!), me as a weeping policeman (aged four) and lots of laughter!

I also 'starred' in one of Uncle Hamid's advertising films dressed for different roles: a painter with a beret and palette, a businessman, a cricketer. What the product was that I was promoting I have long forgotten.

My strong connection with my grandmother and both my aunts, Zarina and Shiraz, that had nurtured me though the Sunday lunches, overnight stays and these collaborative projects, helped to sustain our family through the darkest days that were just around the corner. My aunt Zarina held court every afternoon with always a few guests for lunch, whether it was a family member or someone from the film fraternity. It would be served on a trolley in her bedroom. My other aunt Shiraz had cast herself completely as a fulltime mother, even getting up every night to slow the regulator of the fan in the room where her three children slept.

And as I 'grew up' from being a five-year-old to the age of eight, I was allowed to cross the road for a haircut at the Variety Hair Cutting Saloon, or go to buy flowers at the shop at the corner, 'Flamour Florists'. This was run by the kindly Mrs Allana, soon to be my sister's mother-in-law. Amal and Nissar, her boyfriend, met over dissecting a frog. While this process was still on, the frog freed itself, jumping out of the window. My sister was distressed, Nissar was amused. And in this way they bonded for life!

Looking back on those early years, the range of stimuli I got is mind-boggling. Chanted verses from the Greek choruses of *Medea* mingle with the voices raised in song from the church next door and the mellifluous singing in Carnatic style that accompanies Bala's dance performances. Smells mingle too: the acrid tempering of rasam with spluttering mustard seeds and hing that is added in the last stages, as Bala herself demonstrates to my mother how to make the 'perfect' rasam, co-exists with the heady smell of fried onions that are liberally sprinkled over my grandmother's food or the warm familiar baked smell of a macaroni pie made by my mother. The absurd dialogue of *Waiting for Godot* is challenged by the screams of frightened birds on the soundtrack of *Suddenly Last Summer*, and is tempered by the Christian prayer 'Our Father who art in Heaven' that we recited every morning in my initial years attending Cathedral School in Bombay.

M.F. Husain's 'Blue Nude' hangs tranquilly on the wall at Vithal Court, light years away from the Victorian aesthetic of my grandmother's drawing room, or the austere interiors of Bala's house where a single lit agarbatti suffuses the house with the heady scent of jasmine flowers.

All of this and more is 'home' for me.

Eleven

Delhi—An Altered Reality

AND THEN suddenly one day in October 1963 my parents
decided to separate. Suddenly for me. Maybe Amal had
known for some time or suspected something. She was fifteen, I
was only eight, soon to be nine.

Amal and I had come up to visit my father in Delhi where
he now headed the National School of Drama. It was the long
Diwali break that Bombay schools give. Living with him in his
flat in Nizamuddin was a woman unknown to me, Uma Anand.
Gracious with a deep commanding voice, sophisticated. Her
parents were also staying there. As a naive eight-year-old I was
comfortable with being pampered by both my dad and Uma.
I remember I spent hours in the barsati playing with the glove
puppets I had bought from Cottage Industries. Or watching the
fluttering pigeons my father kept in a huge wire mesh cage on the
terrace. The Diwali holidays came to an end and yet my father
insisted that Amal and I stay on in Delhi.

On a dark October evening while we were at dinner, my
father's cook answered a doorbell downstairs and came up to
tell my father that there was a woman at the door asking to meet
him. It was my mother, looking sad and desolate with a small
suitcase clutched in her hand.

My parents and Uma disappeared together into one of the bedrooms for over three hours. Amal and I sat in the cold night, wide awake below the bare tree trunk with which my father had decorated his living room. We were the two loneliest children in the world that night. We knew our fate was being decided in the next room and we had no part to play in shaping it. We knew life would never be the same again.

Soon after, my mother pulled us out of school in Bombay and we moved to Delhi, taking up a flat in Defence Colony. My father continued to stay on in Nizamuddin.

Delhi was a completely new experience for us. Living in a single-storeyed bungalow instead of a five-storeyed cooperative housing complex took some getting used to. Having a large garden in front of our house instead of playing in the empty spaces between parked cars. Sleeping on the roof in the summer on a 'charpai', after wetting the terrace floor, and keeping water cool in a 'surahi', waking up at dawn to the sound of roosters. We were now certainly living in 'India'!

We seemed to be perennially short of money in our early years in Delhi. I remember my mother anxiously watching the meter of the auto-rickshaw we would be travelling in and then calling out to the driver, 'Yahin utaar do, ghar pahunch gaye' (Drop us off here, we have reached home). We would jump out and walk another ten minutes, heads held high, before we actually reached home! My woollen school socks were often torn and occasionally even wet when I wore them, as we couldn't afford a third winter uniform.

And the interiors of our house had floor-level seating as we couldn't afford furniture. Mattresses covered in vibrant patterned bedspreads with colourful mirrorwork cushions were the seating in the drawing room backed by a large, rather grim Tyeb Mehta painting of a woman disrobing in shades of grey and brown. The dining table was a Japanese-style bench around which we sat on floor cushions. We could afford meat once a week.

The contours of my world had entirely changed. Far from the colonial port city of Bombay, I now attended Modern School in the heart of Lutyens Delhi. For prayers we would sit cross-legged on durries instead of standing and singing the Lords Prayer as we did in Cathedral in Bombay. Instead of Miss Le Monjan (yes, that really was her name!) I had Sharmas, Vermas, Chatterjees and Banerjees as my teachers. While Bombay meant acting as an elf in *The Shoemaker and the Elves*, emerging from a plywood toadstool cottage, Delhi meant participating in a play on the National Struggle for freedom. In the art room at school we made batiks rather than Christmas tree decorations.

My mother ensured that I built close friendships in the neighbourhood by starting drama classes for children at our house. Very soon I had a wide circle of friends, similar to my gang at Vithal Court and virtually the whole of C-Block Defence Colony was known to me. I would be out everyday till eight p.m. playing seven stones or maran pitti in the park or chess or monopoly indoors.

She herself was often preoccupied with herself and her own situation and was obviously in depression. She continued doing the costumes for my father's plays even though they lived separately, so every day she encountered him at the NSD. Often she would be sitting in the costume department quietly eating the sandwiches she had brought from home, as he swept past in his car, taking Uma out for lunch.

A poem she wrote at the time expresses her dark feelings.

The Weight of Loneliness

The weight of loneliness is like a stone
Which slowly sinks into the dark

tarns of the soul
There trembling eddies form
Rippling vainly towards a distant shore
Where no one waits
Its form is round and smooth
Its sinking slow and sure
And as it sinks the grey becomes
A black oppressive thing
Against whose deepening power
There's no escape

An aspect of Delhi that fascinated and endeared itself to me right from my first visit to the city were the many ruins of the past that dotted the landscape. Layers of the seven cities of Delhi would be suddenly seen through a doorway: a dome, a minaret, glimpsed through the trees. They were 'lonely' monuments, alone, by themselves, appearing to have outlived the hustle of people who once inhabited them. It was as if a large section of India's past, long before the colonial powers arrived, was revealing itself to me in small bits and pieces. I fell in love with history. My father was completely enamoured by the ruins of Delhi and on Sundays he would often drive my mother, Amal and me in his small grey Standard Herald car to picnic in one of the areas around the Qutab Minar.

My mother kept alive the tradition of Sunday lunches, whether enjoyed outdoors as a picnic or at home. It was the only time in the week we spent together as a family. Though my mother occasionally did make these lunches awkward and formal by insisting that Amal and I be well turned out, every hair in place and a smile plastered on our faces when my father arrived. He often brought along a particularly bright or difficult student from the NSD, seeking to 'soften' them by a shared lunch with his family. I remember the lively Srilata Swaminathan and Neelam Mansingh, the well-known director of today, joining us. On other occasions a theatre person visiting Delhi would accompany him. I recall that Badal Sarkar, the playwright and rebel of the Bengali theatre, was a guest at one Sunday lunch.

But to return to the monuments of Delhi. Early in his theatre career in Delhi my father had used Ferozshah Kotla and the ruins in Talkatora Gardens effectively to mount his legendary production of *Andha Yug*. Fourteen years later he would restage it in Purana Quila too. The huge stained stone walls, aged by time and witness to history provided an eloquent background to this story of the aftermath of the Mahabharat.

Three productions directed by him in his initial years at NSD stand out in my memory. His very first play *Ashad ka Ek Din* by Mohan Rakesh, narrates a story that almost ran parallel to his own life. A young girl, Mallika, is Kalidasa, the poet's, muse, but everything changes for her when he moves to the capital, deserting her, marrying the princess and becoming the court poet.

NSD was then situated in a small bungalow, A-6 in Kailash Colony, that was a distant suburb of Delhi at the time, hardly built up. To reach there you passed by fields of mustard, a railway crossing, and sometimes you could even hear the call of a jackal. My father constructed an open-air setting and seating for the spectators in the back courtyard of the building. It was reminiscent of an eastern UP village with a mud hut, mud flooring and a chabutra near a tree. An intimate audience of under a hundred witnessed the poetic beauty of Rakesh's writing in an evocative setting. The acting by first-timers, Om and Sudha Shivpuri, Ram Gopal Bajaj, Mohan Mehrishi, Sai Paranjpye, among others was outstanding. Hindi theatre had come into its own.

He followed up this pioneering production with another open-air experience, Dharamvir Bharati's *Andha Yug* in Ferozshah Kotla, a powerful indictment of the horrors of war. Though it is set in the days after the carnage of the Mahabharat war, it brings to mind the aftermath of the bombing of Hiroshima and Nagasaki. A gigantic wall adorned with a broken Ashoka chakra dwarfs the actors. On top of the wall are wire sculptures of vultures waiting, a telling image of annihilation and destruction. The costumes are all in black, white and brown.

Pandit Nehru came to see this production and his security personnel actually ran onto the stage, disrupting the performance, when one of the actors called out his line, 'Maar diya. Usko maar diya' (We've killed him). The security personnel thought that this was an attempt on the life of the prime minister, not realizing it was a line from the play! A wonderful 'head off' between bureaucracy and culture!

Kalidasa's Sanskrit play *Abhigyan Shakuntala* was directed by my father for an international Sanskrit convention. I remember helping to glue sheets of gold paper ('there must be no wrinkles') on the plywood cutouts of trees, their design derived from miniature paintings, that made up the stage setting.

In the summer of 1964 the entire family travelled together, first to Beirut to spend a month with my paternal grandparents and other members of my father's large family who lived there, and then on to Italy and Greece for another month. My first image of my grandparents was of my quiet and reticent grandfather, Ubba, sitting in a chair on the balcony and enjoying the sight of the azure blue Mediterranean Sea, while my plump grandmother, Ummi, was constantly talking with us in Hindustani. The family had spent the major part of its life in India and my father's five sisters were always around chattering with each other over cups of black Turkish coffee. Their language was a wonderful blend of

Hindustani, Arabic and English. They would excitedly reminisce about their early years in Poona.

It was the first time I was travelling with my father who turned out to be an anxious traveller, always getting us to the airport hours in advance of the flight. He must have been tense meeting with his family after a gap of many years and keeping up the pretence that we all lived together in Delhi. It is interesting that in the fifty years of his life that he lived with Uma, he never introduced her to his own family, though I think most of his siblings and his parents were aware of the situation. They went out of their way for my mother, accepting her completely, as they had eighteen years earlier when my parents were newlyweds. She would be cooking with my grandmother in the large kitchen, shopping with my father's sisters, being congratulated on having such well-spoken and confident children and was generally much feted, celebrated and often consulted on family matters.

This was to remain the pattern for all of her life as almost every alternate year we travelled as a family, most often to London, where lots of Dad's relatives lived permanently or temporarily. She never lacked respect in either her own family or with her in-laws.

My grandparents lived in a beautiful flat with one of my aunts, Lulu, looking after them. It overlooked the changing colours of the Mediterranean Sea, right on Beirut's iconic water front. While waves lapped at the Pigeon Rocks, seagulls flew over the harbour full of luxury yatchs. At the time Beirut was the 'Paris' of the East, and all my aunts and cousins wore the latest high fashion and had chic haircuts. Right next door lived Dad's sister, Noorie, her husband Abdullah and their five children. We could literally call out to them from my grandparents' kitchen window. Three young cousins of mine, all female, all in college, had their own flat with screeching parakeets in the drawing room. Down the road were Fatima and Rimmy and their six children. Round the corner lived my youngest aunt, Faiza, and uncle Mohammad, and Dad's other two siblings, Munira and Basil, both artists came and went regularly from Beirut. And even though three of Dad's siblings never married, they were never short of 'family' as nieces stepped in to play the role of caring children.

The interiors of my grandparents' flat on the third floor were flooded with light. The walls were adorned with large photographic blow-ups of cave paintings from Lascaux in France. Other walls had my aunt Munira's delicate abstracts on display, or some of Faiza's collages.

On the weekends we would drive up into the hills of Lebanon and stop at a roadside eatery with wooden tables, where we would eat wonderful 'mezze', mouth-watering kababs and grilled fish. Often enough these restaurants had a mountain stream gurgling through them.

This was my first interaction with many of my cousins while the rest I hadn't met for a few years since they relocated from Bombay. My cousin Tariq and I were the only two boys surrounded by thirteen Arabian teenage beauties. And was I spoilt!

On our last evening in Beirut, my aunts indulged me, taking me first to my first-ever Bond film, *Goldfinger*, and then they whisked me off to see the fabulous Las Vegas type show at Casino du Liban. Here a drop of gold paint fell on me from one of the topless women dancing on a moving chandelier that glided above our table! I was only eleven, and that drop anointed me and prepared me to step into the gawky world of my adolescence.

Next we visited Italy and Greece and it was a feast for the senses. Paintings and sculptures by Leonardo da Vinci and Michelangelo, Tintoretto and Titian, Giotto and Botticelli accompanied by my parents' vast encyclopaedic knowledge of art and artists, enthused my sister and me. In Greece we got tickets to watch Zeffirelli's production of the opera *Othello* in a Roman amphitheatre, Herodicus Atticus, located on the hill just below the Acropolis; in Florence we went to a football match played by torchlight in medieval costumes and in Greece, after doing the four-day classical tour, we crossed the bay from Athens and trekked to the vast 3,000-seat theatre at Epidaurus to see a production of *The Trojan Women* in the original Greek. A feast for the senses! My mother captured much of these trips in one of her many poems.

Greece

Its song streams down the hills
The vales are full
Of lights that swung to rest
Two thousand years ago
The dreams Penelope wove
Haunt shepherds' looms
In huts of stone
When winter signs
And all the past awakes
To blast the fragile webs
That hang around to smear
The freshly moulded stones

So let another land
Another age
Fall on my brow
And smooth its creases

Twelve

The Changing Fortunes of
Theatre in India

Moving to Delhi in 1962 meant moving away from a city with a vibrant theatre tradition in several languages, some of which had existed for over a hundred years. By comparison Delhi was a cultural desert, without a single auditorium to perform in. There had been a rich tradition of urban theatre in other parts of India and it had grown and developed from its beginnings in 1795, but not in Delhi. As a teenager I remember seeing a production by the Gujarati Natak Samaj that worked out of Bhangwadi in Bombay with my mother and grandfather. This was one of the most successful and long-lasting companies. The name Bhangwadi indicates what happened in that area: the opium and bhang trade. In the midst of this business district was a large theatre that staged plays that ran for hundreds of performances. Many of these productions were in the Gujarati Rangbhoomi tradition with an emphasis on songs and musical accompaniment. Song books were placed on each seat and when it was time for a song the auditorium lights brightened so that the audience could sing along. Someone who worked there remembers upto fifty victorias (horse-drawn carriages) pulling out of the theatre entrance at two a.m.!

The play that I saw was *Ra Mandlik,* a historical set in the eighteenth century. A key turning point in the play was the curse of a Charan woman on the king who broke out in smallpox. To lighten the mood of this rather grim play, at regular intervals a drop curtain would come down, and a comic subplot involving a woman with her two lovers and a lot of live singing, would be enacted in front of it. Meanwhile behind the drop curtain a huge new painted setting was being swiftly erected.

In the heyday of Bhangwadi, money would be thrown on the stage in appreciation of a particularly poignant scene or the performance of a popular song. Not regular coins, for they could injure the actors, but silver coins in velvet pouches. So many were thrown at each performance that a special scrim curtain was lowered for the songs, so that the pouches wouldn't spread across the entire stage! The idea of an encore was so linked with Bhangwadi, that the word for 'encore' in Bombay theatre circles became 'Bhangwadi'. The popularity of their songs often drew courtesans of the area keen to hear, hum, sing along and in this way learn the song that they would perform in turn for their patrons, while their musicians feverishly put down the musical notations during the encore. This was in an age before any recording devices. There could be upto ten encores of each song, each one only made possible by additional money being thrown on the stage!

Fashions for women were set here: the latest hairstyle, the drape of a sari, the style of jewellery, similar to the contemporary Hindi film that dictates popular fashion.

And then the movies came into being, snatching audiences away from live theatre forever.

Interestingly, it was a Russian who directed the first regional language play in a regular proscenium theatre in India. Imagine yourself in a tiny little theatre in Calcutta over two centuries ago. There are boxes all around you, full of excited Bengali gentry, while backstage a young man of Slav descent, Lebedev, paces up and down waiting for the curtain to go up. Lebedev has managed the near impossible, a cast of men and women acting together, and throwing open the auditorium to an Indian audience. The year was 1795, the date was the 25th of November, the play *Love Is the Best Doctor*. And when the curtain rose on this performance, modern theatre in India began.

Who was Lebedev? A talented musician with a burning passion to see the world. Lebedev's travels took him from Russia to Vienna, Paris to London, and in India from Madras to Calcutta. But though his show was an unqualified success, the British authorities did not take kindly to the activities of the Russian traveller and expelled him.

But Bengali theatre never looked back. It went on, moving from strength to strength. In 1813, the prestigious Chowringhee Theatre of Calcutta that had been until then only reserved for the British opened its door to Indians. The result was that about a thousand people were turned away and we had our first recorded 'box office hit'. By 1835, scenes from *Julius Caesar* and *The Merchant of Venice* were regularly performed in Bengali, but it was not till Michael Madhusudan Dutt had written *Sharmishta* that original Indian plays were performed.

But beyond Bengali, Calcutta also nurtured the theatre movement in both Hindi and English. While in Bombay theatre flourished in as many as six languages: Marathi, Gujarati, Urdu, Konkani, Marwari and English.

In 1776 in Bombay the first theatre was built, called the Theatre on the Green, followed fifty years later by six new theatres at Grant Road, turning this area, now quite a rundown part of the city, into a 'theatre district'. Because of their location on the border of both worlds, the Westernized Fort and the native quarters, these theatres became popular. In 1879, two new grand theatres were established in the vicinity of Victoria Terminus, the Gaiety in 1879 and the Novelty in 1887. They both had a large stage, an auditorium that could seat 1400 people and a front curtain painted by a famous German artist.

One of many Gaiety Theatres built across the world simultaneously, the Bombay Gaiety no longer exists, but the tiny Gaiety Theatre in Shimla is still in use 132 years after it was established. Here my theatre group, among many others, still performs on a regular basis. It has perfect acoustics, a delightful yet tiny twenty-feet wide stage, and ample backstage area, while for the seating there are gilt boxes in blue and gold that surround the stalls. In its heyday with its pride of place on the Mall in Shimla, it must have been worth visiting. Phaetons would draw up at the colonnaded entrance and British women in evening gowns and men in tailcoats would enter the theatre for an evening of fun and entertainment. The wonderful theatre exhibition on the first floor of the theatre displays photos of all the Amateur Dramatic Club productions since their first play, *Time Will Tell*, was mounted in the newly built theatre on 30 May 1887.

But beyond the large capacity proscenium theatres, money was to be earned on the road by travelling theatre companies. Parsi theatre companies used the newly established railway system to travel with their plays, usually performed in Urdu, from Lahore to Benares, from Dharwar to Calcutta. This resulted in the birth of local theatre companies based on the same tradition though performing in the vernacular. Scripts began to get published, advertisements appeared in the local newspapers, theatre songs became immensely popular and theatre flourished.

The cosmopolitan population of Bombay, in particular the Khoja and Bohra communities, became major patrons, flocking to fill the auditorium of the Parsi Natak companies. In addition, packed trains from Surat and Baroda would ply to Bombay. They were colloquially known as 'so-and-so play's train' carrying audiences hungry for theatre to Bombay. And as time wore on, religious themes brought a new audience in search of 'darshan', and soon nationalist themes pulled in even more people, eager to watch ideas of political resistance disguised as history or myth.

Building on the same tradition a group of actors led by a British couple, Geoffrey and Laura Kendal, created 'Shakespeareana', touring the whole of India in the 1930s, 40s and 50s performing Shakespeare, among other playwrights, in theatres, schools, colleges and occasionally at the royal court of a local raja. Several members of Prithviraj Kapoor's family worked with them and finally Shashi Kapoor married Jennifer Kendal.

But it was the Marathi stage that has had the longest continuous tradition of making and watching theatre. Its beginnings are credited to Vishnudas Amrit Bhave who dramatized stories from the Ramayana and presented them at the Sangli Court as early as 1843. Moving to Bombay later, his plays are considered to be the first ticketed shows in Marathi in that city.

Marathi theatre simultaneously traversed two routes: the first of scripted plays without music on quasi nationalist and social themes, and the much more popular form of the 'sangeet natak'. The Kirloskar Natak Mandali, with Kirloskar himself and often the female impersonator Bal Gandharva acting, was very successful from 1875 right upto 1935. They drew on the vast prevalent music traditions of the time, from Carnatic music, to religious keertans, folk songs to popular women's songs.

The Indian National Theatre sponsored new productions in both Marathi and Gujarati in the 1950s and this, along with the highly competitive one-act play collegiate festivals gave the

Marathi stage a new lease of life. Vijaya Mehta and Satyadev Dubey changed the face of the Marathi stage forever with their experimental productions for Rangayan in the early 1960s.

The commercial stage flourished alongside. I got a close look at the professional or should I say commercial English language stage in Bombay, and how it functioned in the 1970s when I was backstage for a production directed by Adi Marzban. It was a long running 'sex' comedy then in its fortieth show. It was already 6.28 p.m. and the lead actress, Ruby Patel (Shernaz Patel's mother), was yet to arrive, even though the first two bells announcing the performance had been given. At exactly six-thirty a taxi pulled up, Ruby emerged dressed for her part, and in one smooth movement, crossed directly from the backstage entrance onto the stage and made her first appearance! Barely a minute had passed between her entering the building and the performance beginning!

Watching a performance with an audience sealed in the dark, all eyes focused on a brightly lit 'proscenium' stage that framed the action was a colonial legacy, and was seen as being the norm for a long time. By contrast our own vibrant folk traditions were played arena style and in the open, often in daytime hours. It would take years for the Modern Indian Theatre movement to break away from the proscenium format. My father, among others, took the first step towards this by staging *Ghosts* arena style in 1952 or in his use of an angan to stage *Ashad ka Ek Din* in Delhi in 1962 and in several other productions that used open areas or ruins to fashion a new 'performance space'. Indian theatre moved in this direction over the next decades, finally resulting in site-specific performances in garages and factories, in the middle of a forest or on the beach.

But the real lack across India was of scripts in Indian languages capturing the 'here' and 'now' of the challenging

1960s and the emerging dilemmas and disparities that India was facing. As Girish Karnad sharply commented years later, 'To have any value at all, drama must at some level engage honestly with the contradictions that lie at the heart of the society it talks to and about. The Parsi theatre society refused to acknowledge the existence of any problem. As a result, although it ruled supreme for almost seventy-five years, the theatre—and its many reincarnations in the regional languages—produced no drama of any consequence.'

With much prodding and probing my father unearthed two gems of Indian writing, both by authors well known as novelists and essayists. Even though several years had passed since the writing of *Ashad ka Ek Din* no one had produced Mohan Rakesh's play on stage. Dharamvir Bharati's *Andha Yug* had faced the same problem: no takers. Overall the lack of a good script or of a company willing to produce it reflected the very limited theatre movement in Hindi. Parsi theatre companies had certainly come and regularly performed in the capital, as had Prithviraj Kapoor, often staging his plays on the makeshift stage of the Regal Cinema in Connaught Place—a cinema hall being used for theatre performances!

Almost immediately after joining the National School of Drama, my father actively encouraged the translation and production of plays from regional languages into Hindi. Adya Rangacharya's *Suno Janme Jai* and Girish Karnad's *Tughlaq* appeared in translation from the original Kannada, Badal Sarkar's *Evam Indrajit* was translated from Bengali. Mohan Rakesh's entire oeuvre of plays got their first production by the team of Om Shivpuri and my father. *Lehron ke Raj Hans* and *Aadhe Adhure* both directed by Shivpuri appeared a few years after *Ashad* was first staged. I recall accompanying my father to visit Mohan Rakesh and Anita, his partner, on the morning of the dress rehearsal of *Aadhe Adhure* in its first-ever production in 1969 directed by Shivpuri.

Rakesh and Anita lived in a somewhat rundown multistoreyed housing complex in East of Kailash. He tended to be on the plump side with dark-rimmed spectacles and with a smile, at least for my father, Anita was wiry and much younger. I remember my father's roving eyes running across the interior of that flat, soaking in the atmosphere and he mimicked something of the same movement in the lighting he designed for Shivpuri later that morning.

The set of a shabby middle-class home with quite a lot of furniture and props were lit section by section as the play opened on the first speech by Kale Suit Wala Aadmi. The audience's eyes were led by the lighting to 'discover' the space. This script in Rakesh's newly evolved style of writing dialogue as incomplete sentences, went on to make theatre history and has had regular re-interpretations and revivals over the years.

In the early years of this century I spent five days with Rakesh's son, Shaleen, a prominent gay activist, at a workhop in Shimla that I and a colleague were leading on 'Gender and HIV' for the Ford Foundation. As we travelled together through the pine forests of Mashobra and over a high tea hosted by the Oberoi group at the newly refurbished Wildflower Hall, I gave Shaleen a glimpse into his father's link with the same landscape. Mohan Rakesh had stayed in a small Himachal Pradesh tourism guesthouse in Kufri, a nearby ski resort, many moons earlier. He was trying hard to complete the third act of *Lehron ke Raj Hans*. Also at the Institute of Advanced Studies in Summerhill near Shimla, he had presented his 'beej nataks', seed plays, bold attempts to break away from the writing tradition of the time.

The preface to *Lehron* and the wonderful theatre magazine *Enact* (that lasted for eighteen years) had done a marvellous job of recording theatre history as it happened. Shaleen was completely unaware of his father's legacy and listened eagerly to my recounting.

Mohan Rakesh is certainly the most important Hindi playwright we have had so far. Of course, Girish Karnad has written many more plays over the years in both Kannada and English, but Rakesh's reputation rests on just three scripts, all perfect examples of the 'well made' play.

Ashad ka Ek Din, written for radio in 1954 and presented on stage for the first time in 1963, introduces us to Rakesh's signature style that develops and gets greater refined over time through *Lehron* to *Aadhe Adhure* in 1969. He creates his characters in pairs, either two people who complement each other, or two who are diametrically opposed to one another. Usually those who complement have rhyming names like Rangini and Sangini, Anuswar and Anunasik or Datul and Matul of *Ashad*, Shwetang and Shyamang in *Lehron* and the sisters Binni and Kinni in *Aadhe Adhure*. For most characters there is almost always a 'shadow' self, the negative, the opposite. If in *Ashad* it is most obviously Vilom (that means the opposite in Hindi) to Kalidasa, there is also the princess Priyangumanjari as opposed to Mallika, the heroine.

In *Aadhe Adhure*, instead of two 'opposites' there are four polar men: Mahendranath, Singhania, Jog and Juneja, all to be played by the same actor .

The plot lines are simple, the situations of the play easy to relate to even if they are set in the past. The dilemmas are always contemporary and the yearning woman is his leitmotif: a woman searching for the 'perfect' complete man, whom she can never find. *Aadhe Adhure*'s Savitri is a distant cousin of Ibsen's *Hedda Gabler*.

Another iconic script was *Andha Yug*, by Dharamvir Bharti,

who served as the editor of the weekly newsmagazine *Dharmayug* for over a quarter of a century. In bleak rhyming verse he creates the post Mahabharat world, full of wounded survivors who seem to be emerging from a nuclear winter. Till today, fifty years later, every year a director from some part of India attempts his own unique interpretation of this text.

By the end of the 1960s, the disenchantment of the populace with the Indian state had begun and the opening scene of Girish Karnad's *Tughlaq* echoes this, though he cleverly sets it in fourteenth-century Delhi with the people reacting to the medieval monarch Mohammad bin Tughlaq, in place of Jawaharlal Nehru.

In just thirty years, the concerns of theatre had completely shifted from poor copies of Shakespeare to a re-exploration of our own history, whether through the personal stories of Kalidas or Tughlaq, or the reinterpretation of India's mythic past in *Andha Yug*. A 'National' Indian theatre was beginning to emerge.

But beyond subject matter, the real issue was of finding a voice and the right theatre language. At the time my father wrote: 'Each night, when I return from rehearsals of plays written in a language which is a travesty of the spoken word, my constant relief is the speech of my mali, a UP peasant who speaks the gentle Poorbi. I am repeatedly thrilled by his originality of expression, by his spontaneous imagery and the curious dream-like cadences of his speech-rhythms. There is nothing forced or studied in his words. The poetic images arise naturally and without any self-consciousness. This is characteristic of our rural people. Language is the communication of a direct human experience. It is vital, living. Images arise from life and nature around them, which are a part of their being. References to gods or heroes are as of intimate and well-loved friends—known, adored, and feared. The cadences of speech have the grace and limpidity of a mountain stream; a crisp, fresh crystalline quality. The texture of words, often with an earthy roughness, reveals the nuances of human relationships.

'The peasant or worker responds with strength to the impulses. Sexual image and abuse spike his language with a piercing force. There is nothing abashed or shame-faced in this. It is unpuritanic and free from salacious obscenity.

'The Hindi playwright needs to explore the possibilities of language and to create the style that is best suited to his particular vision and creative purpose. We are fortunate in having rich sources of inspiration. The collision of classes, the influx of the rural worker to urban areas and his spontaneous vocal response to his changed milieu; the highly coloured and rich imagery of the many dialects, provide some. Above all, the growing awareness of our playwrights themselves that they must accept the challenge of language in the theatre is our surest hope for the future. A language can never be foisted on a people from the top. Hence the patent failure of A.I.R Hindi. Language rises from the varied experience of different sections of society. It mingles, influences, absorbs, changes, above all it lives. It is for our writers to add meaningful dimensions to this living language of the people in the theatre.'

Thirteen

Early Years in Delhi

Four young kids crouched in a plywood 'well' waiting to be rescued, little knowing that all of them would grow up to be well known artists or impressarios. Pablo Bartholomew was there playing a tiger, growing up to be a much celebrated, internationally recognized photographer. So was Kristine Michael as the snake, now an extremely gifted ceramic artist. Chandrika Grover played the mouse and is now chief curator of the Swiss Arts Council office in India. And then there was me as the 'ungrateful man'. I was ten years old at the time.

This was a Yatrik production of David Horsburgh's delightful dramatization of the Panchatantra tale, *The Ungrateful Man*. Directed by Mina Swaminathan, the play was among the first few Indian scripts for children. I had performed the lead role of the Joker, in Hindi, in Bombay a couple of years earlier, in yet another wonderful Indian children's theatre script, Sai Paranjpye's *Land of Cards*, directed by my mother. These were the rare few Indian plays for children, much needed in a world where our imaginations were still dominated by Western fairytales and Enid Blyton.

The very next year I appeared on TV as a Joker once again in *Joker Miyan Jo Hasne Bhule*, again directed by my mother, and produced by Sadhan Mullick, who was to become my father-in-law twenty-three years later! Acting opposite me in this first-ever children's programme on Doordarshan, was the six-year-old Sagari Chabbra, now an accomplished writer and filmmaker.

The core group that created the theatre group named Yatrik in 1964 in Delhi had come together after travelling with two productions directed by Tom Noonan of the USIS (United States Information Service), *Abe Lincoln in Illinois* and *All the King's Men*. Theatre enthusiast Joy Michael remained the cornerstone of this group all the way through till her death in 2018. Wonderfully talented actors Kusum Haidar (nèe Bahl), Sushma Seth, Roshen Seth, Salima Raza, Nigam Prakash, Rati Bartholomew and Marcus Murch were there from the start. My mother worked with Yatrik for several years designing costumes as did my mentor Barry John, directing adults and children alike and often delighting audiences with his own outstanding portrayals. The group worked out of Joy's house in Kaka Nagar for several decades. Here many rehearsals took place, parties were held and romances blossomed. Yatrik performed at the Defence Pavilion Theatre in Pragati Maidan trying valiantly, and occasionally successfully, in running a weekend theatre programme.

My father acted in and directed *Tartuffe* for this group soon after he moved to Delhi and Uncle Alyque came years later to direct *Medea* with Joy Michael in the lead role.

Yatrik became an easy, comfortable second home to me, as I had been so accustomed to spending my evenings at rehearsals in Bombay. Along with Joy's daughters, Meriel and Kristine, I would help usher audiences into their weekend performances. And Joy's home with Nana, her warm mother, always welcoming us with a slice of cake or a bowl of broth, and where Christmas pageants were performed in the back lawns, made the perfect Anglo-Indian bridge from Bombay to Delhi for me.

I became much more conscious of nature in Delhi than I had ever been in Bombay. Was it the age I was? Or the proximity in which one lives with it in Delhi with its changing seasons? In Bombay, my brief encounter with nature was limited to one with the tempestous sea that mercilessly beat down on the rocks at Breach Candy, or that breached the Marine Drive wall with huge waves every monsoon, drenching people in their cars. And of course in south Bombay one is always aware of the wonderful old trees with gnarled trunks and gigantic height that line many pavements.

In Delhi I became acutely aware of the drama of the changing seasons: the subtle changes in light, the variation in weather, the variety of tree, shrub, flower, bird as spring slipped into summer and then we would awake to the loud music of the thunderclaps of the monsoon months, till finally one day, winter was upon us, creeping up quickly, without any warning.

I could spend hours on the balcony of the Defence Colony flat where we lived for fourteen years, watching twilight falling on the gulmohar tree growing outside the gate. Squirrels gambolled on the branches of the tree, even as chameleons were snatched off the bark by violent crows. I would sit on a comfortable folding rattan chair with leather straps for arms that my mother had picked up in Madras.

Spring brought the fleshy petals of the pink and orange silk cotton that lasted only a brief while before littering the ground, followed soon by the pale lavender of the jacaranda and the happy drooping yellow blossoms of the laburnum, with green parrots shooting in and out of the trees. A peepul tree in our vicinity would be strangely naked one day and the very next full of tiny, glistening, oily, pointed leaves, each of which shook in the slightest breeze. Sparrows and crows perched on our balcony railing complaining loudly about the 'loo' winds of summer.

Bulbuls and the Seven Sisters joined this chorus of complaint even as the bright magenta and orange blossoms of bougainvillea burst into bloom. The hotter the temperature got in Delhi, the stronger and deeper the colours of the flowers in bloom became.

And even as the speckled flowers of the gulmohar were beginning to wilt in the heat, it was the rainy season. A distant rumble first, then a darkening of the sky, the hurried flight of birds trying to escape and then the sudden fragrance of the first fat drops hitting the hot earth. Delicious. Reminding me of the sky full of stylized clouds, flying swans and bolts of lightning in a Kangra miniature painting. My friend Malati and I had a deal that during the first monsoon shower, we would run up to the terraces of our respective houses and dance uninhibitedly, celebrating the rain!

Winter meant keeping the doors and windows tightly shut, gathering around the ineffective two-bar heaters in the long, dark, cold evenings, shivering as the hot water ran out during a bath and getting used to the smell of mothballs that lingered long in our sweaters, scarves and socks. Outside a million flowers bloomed on Delhi's many roundabouts, and the crisp sunlight that made up the brief hours of day encouraged us to just sit around, popping peanuts into our mouths and littering the earth with their shells.

And as I grew into my early teens, Amal and I would often accompany our father early on Sunday mornings, to the Chor Bazaar (Thieves Market) that was set up impromptu on the road leading to Jama Masjid in Old Delhi. Crowds thronged the road as the hawkers laid out chaadars on the pavement and covered them with their wares. Here, burrowing among the objects displayed, we would chance upon many 'gems'—publications from the British days, a stack of gramophone records, a forgotten eighteenth-century miniature, a small glass object. This sifting through abandoned or stolen items was the beginnings of my father's collection of nineteenth-century photographs in his later years, when he used the same technique, frequenting Sunday bazaars in London and smaller towns, building a rapport with the dealers and subsequently being offered hidden 'gems'.

My only other interaction with my father was when I would be roped in to play bit parts in some of his NSD productions or be allowed to watch rehearsals. My mother found every available opportunity to bring father and son together. She worried less about Amal, who was with him day in and day out from the ages of sixteen to nineteen, as she was a student at NSD.

Jean and Freny Bhownagary moved to Delhi in the early 1960s, along with their daughters, Janine and Ashoo. They lived close to us in Defence Colony and we often had a pot luck dinner together. Jean had been a central figure in the Theatre Group and a close friend of Bobby's. Along with Adi Marzban he wrote reviews, he also acted, painted, sculpted, made films and did magic shows, giving himself the whacky stage name, Foo Ling Yu.

With a Parsi father and a French mother and educated in France, Jean had moved to India at the beginning of World War II to do night shifts at Reuters, the news agency. He decided to stay on for most of his professional career. Later in life he headed the Films Division for several years and among his protégès were the outstanding filmmakers Sukhdev and Pramod Pati.

His daughter Janine remembers, 'His talent in discovering, choosing and trusting filmmakers became legendary. He encouraged a cross fertilization of talents, inviting musicians, painters, sculptors, dancers to direct short films for the Films Division.' M.F. Husain's pathbreaking *Through the Eyes of a Painter* was one and it went on to win him the Golden Bear at the Berlin Film Festival.

While Jean was in the Ministry of Information and Broadcasting as an UNESCO representative in the 1960s, his wife Freny directed an Ionesco play for Yatrik. Once again a coming together of theatre, art and cinema

Kusum Bahl, who had been one of Dad's major students in Bombay in his Theatre Unit days, now moved to our immediate neighbourhood with her dashing husband Salman Haidar who had pursued her across Europe till she finally agreed to marry him. This young couple took excellent care of me, Salman nurtured in me a love for books and I was often whizzing around town with them in their yellow Volkswagen beetle.

A big moment of my childhood was when the President of India, Dr Sarvepalli Radhakrishnan, invited Ashoo, my cousin Rhea and me to spend a day with him at the resplendent Rashtrapati Bhavan. This was quite usual for him, but a once-in-a lifetime experience for us, wandering through the halls usually populated by visiting royalty and politicians and chatting informally with the President as he lounged on his book-covered bed.

And there were also moments of national tragedy that stand out in my memory. I still remember the vast multitudes of people that filled the roads of Delhi on the day of Nehru's funeral cortege and cremation in 1964. My mother, sister and I were part of this weeping mass of humanity, aware that history was in the making. Milling crowds lined the streets, we all recognized that an era that still glowed from the idealistic embers of the freedom struggle was coming to a close. An unease had entered the public sphere: after Nehru, who?

Within a few years one of the songs we sang in school went :

Yeh bees saal baad bhi
Wahi hahakar kyun?
Doodh, ann, vastra ki goonjati pukar kyon?

Twenty years after Independence
Why the same demand
Why is there still a crying need
For milk, food, clothes?

I remember it was not much later that the story of President
Kennedy's assassination broke. The large format *Life* magazine
brought us pictures of the event in chilling detail: the rushing
car, the bloodstained body lying in the lap of a distraught Jackie
Kennedy. News had begun to force its way into our homes, and
distant heroes crumbled to dust before our very eyes. And in a few
years *Life* brought us the student protestors, helmeted riot police
cowering behind shields, exploding teargas, and the occupation
of the Sorbonne University in Paris all in stunning black-and-
white pictures, even as the napalm bombing of Vietnam awoke
the conscience of the world.

The world, as we knew it, had shrunk and national boundaries
no longer had the same meaning.

Delhi in the early 1960s was a 'young' capital city. It had
been a bare fifteen years since Independence, and in 1947
Lutyen's Delhi was sparklingly new with a bureaucratic, political
and commercial centre which had yet to evolve its own ethos
and culture. The divide—architecturally, geographically and
culturally between the traditional lifestyle of Shahjahanabad
(Old Delhi) with its sophisticated cuisine and tehzeeb, Urdu
language and literature, vital poetry tradition, bustling trade and
bazaars and the last remnants of a Mughal past was completely
in contrast to what the British sought to develop in 'New' Delhi.
But they never got a chance to do so, as independence came to
India just a few years after Lutyen's Delhi was built. There was
a formidable cultural challenge before the leaders, architects and
cultural tzarinas and tzars of the new nation.

My father was only one of the many who were seeking to

create a modern Indian voice in the realm of culture. Indrani Rahman with her statuesque body and expressive large eyes enthralled audiences as she revived the art of Odissi as did Yamini Krishnamurty with Kuchipudi while Birju Maharaj innovated in Kathak. Shombu Mitra and soon playwright Badal Sarkar were giving a contemporary turn to Bengali theatre, even as Vijay Tendulkar, Vijaya Mehta, Arvind and Sulabha Deshpande, and Amol Palekar among several other heavyweights experimented on the Marathi stage. Delhi was also witness to the exciting odyssey of Habib Tanvir who combined folk and urban actors in his many productions with Naya Theatre, and the strong support of Urdu and Punjabi poetry in the operas of Shiela Bhatia. And beyond the performing arts, the visual arts were spearheading a revolution as never before.

It became de rigeur to buy an outfit at Gurjari, read the first Indian English novels of Kamala Markandaya and to shop at the newly established Fabindia.

In other cities, other endeavours. The new contours of a planned city: Corbusier's Chandigarh. A new understanding of Indian design in Ahmedabad with the establishment of the National Institute of Design (NID) and in Pune, the establishment of the Film and Television Institute of India (FTII) that heralded a 'New Wave' in Indian cinema.

As Bombay in the heyday of the Empire in the 1880s had expressed itself architecturally in the extravagant overbearing buildings of the Raj, or how in the 1930s and 40s the city's architecture symbolized a new age, with its Art Deco-inspired residential buildings, so did institutional buildings epitomize Delhi in the 1960s.

Here the combined visions of architects Habib Rahman, Raj Rewal and Joseph Stein resulted in the building of several iconic structures that expressed the 'new' India, now free and standing tall. Habib drew extensively on an Indian lexicon using Mughal jaalis, covered corridors and arches from the Sultanate and blended them with an airy openness that marks his landmark buildings: Rabindra Bhawan and several of the multistoreyed housing complexes that dot the city. Stein, an American architect who made Delhi his home, with his signature sweep of landscape and low height structures created India International Centre and Triveni Kala Sangam, marvellous examples of the use of jaalis, lotus ponds, light and shade and dappled interiors rendered in a contemporary style. Raj Rewal's huge monolithic structures as at Pragati Maidan's Hall of Nations was yet another part of the evolving modern Indian vocabulary in Delhi's long building history.

To create a 'new' culture, state patronage of the arts in the form of three academies—Lalit Kala, Sahitya and Sangeet Natak Akademi—came into being. They were all housed together in the iconic Rabindra Bhavan designed by Habib Rahman. The building was one of a kind with its triangular staircase, three wings jutting out in different directions, with Mughal-inspired jaalis and heavy stone cladding linking it to Delh's architectural legacy.

Here, on different floors, literature and music, dance and art co-existed. The third floor housed the National School of Drama from 1966 to 1976. In the immediate vicinity over the years the Shri Ram Centre for Performing Arts, Triveni Kala Sangam, Kamani Auditorium and Sapru House concentrated culture in one part of the city.

Not far away in the midst of the colonial style colonnaded arcade of Connaught Place, the shopping centre, perched on an empty plot, was the rather untidy, makeshift temporary structure of India Coffee House where Hindi writers and several artists met on an almost daily basis. This was adda baazi, Delhi style.

The National School of Drama worked out of a really small space. Within this my father carved out an excellent studio theatre by removing a wall between two rooms to make an eighty-seat auditorium and a stage as large as the seating. Many 'huge' productions of classics, Sophocles' *Oedipus* and Shakespeare's *King Lear* were presented here in Urdu, while later Mohan Rakesh's *Lehron ke Raj Hans*, among others, got its first production.

In 1967, my father created an outdoor performance space behind Rabindra Bhavan, built by the students themselves. As noted director M.K. Raina recalls, 'NSD had a meagre budget those days. We worked three hours a day building this theatre and Mr Alkazi carried bricks along with us.' He named it the Meghdoot Theatre once again.

The huge peepul tree that formed the backdrop to the acting area lent a real gravitas to any production mounted before it. For different plays, different habitats were constructed. *Godan* by Premchand in a stage adaptation titled *Hori* saw a field of corn and a couple of village huts typical of eastern UP, for *Tughlaq* elegant arches framed the space while *Yerma* was played against the textured white walls of a Spanish village. Years later, long after my father had left the National School of Drama, I had an opportunity to direct *The Jungle Book* in this magnificent open-air setting with the tree as a central character.

Creating something out of nothing at all—a Mumbai terrace transformed into an open-air theatre, a peepul tree defining a stage, a curtain of hessian splattered with Plaster of Paris to create a setting, requires real imagination. My father excelled at this and also worked at next to no cost.

In his fifteen years spearheading NSD, he created a well-formulated teaching programme and a formidable reputation as an actor trainer. For the initial seven years as Director, NSD, along with his trail-blazing *Ashad ka Ek Din* and *Andha Yug*, my father did new productions of plays he had directed earlier: Sophocles' *Oedipus*, Strindberg's *The Father*, Ibsen's *Ghosts*, Beckett's *Waiting for Godot*, Anouilh's *Antigone*, Moliere's *The Miser* and *Scapin*, this time around in Hindi or Urdu. These are all theatre 'classics', staple fare in acting institutions across the world.

For the next seven years he vitalized the school's curriculum by inviting directors from elsewhere to interact and work with the students. From Germany came directors Carl Weber and Fritz Bennewitz to introduce the genius of Bertolt Brecht to Indian audiences, while from Japan Professor Shozo Sato directed an impressive Om Puri in the titular role of a Kabuki play in Hindi, *Ibaragi*. Along with these was a trail of plays by emerging Indian playwrights, many appearing on the stage immediately after being written.

NSD at the time mounted rivetting productions in the folk form of Gujarat, bhavai, in Shanta Gandhi's *Jasma Odan* and B.V. Karanth's Yakshagana rendering of *Veer Abhimanyu*. Vernacular theatre traditions from different corners of India were beginning to enter mainstream urban culture. Within a few years, NSD graduates returned to explore their own roots, whether in Manipur with Ratan Thiyam or in Karnataka with Prasanna among others. Sanskrit theatre traditions were explored in *Madhyam Vyayog*, *Shakuntala* and *The Little Clay Cart*.

When he left NSD in 1977, my father went out in a blaze of light, mounting three huge productions in the Purana Quila Theatre that he had designed. As the blue leached out of the Delhi summer sky, and a heavy purple twilight descended, the jewel-like tones of my mother's costumes appeared against the weathered stones of Purana Qila. Here, as the distant roar of lions from the nearby Delhi Zoo could be heard, the tragic tales of Razia Sultan and Muhammed Bin Tughlaq were played out. A long flight of steps led down from a huge archway that was sometimes filled by the ceremonial procession of a king, and at other times resounded to the clash of swords as Razia Sultan battled for her life and yet at other times was full of the rushing, rioting mobs hungry for food in Girish Karnad's *Tughlaq*. Delhi's history came alive at Purana Qila.

The third play to be mounted here was *Andha Yug*, now in a completely new production avatar, fourteen years after it was first seen at Feroz Shah Kotla in 1963. Inspired by the stylized movement of Yakshagana and Kabuki, the universal theme of the futility of war set after the Mahabharat battle was performed with the grace of a dance to a sung chorus composed by Vanraj Bhatia. To clothe the characters in this new interpretation, my mother drew on Japanese and Indian garments accompanied by Yakshagana-style headdresses and make-up.

From these large, sweeping, spectacular productions that still inhabit the imagination of Delhi audiences to the small, intimate, emotionally heavy world of Jimmy Porter and Alison in John Osbourne's *Look Back in Anger* played out in the studio theatre of the NSD, my father had demonstrated his prowess over several genres of drama.

His thorough grounding in aesthetics and theatre in England and Bombay had borne fruit and nurtured several generations of theatre workers, on and off stage, in rural and urban India, creating a national theatre movement. At its apex, at least in those years, stood the NSD. Very few other national institutions ever gained that stature.

Interestingly when he left, he selected B.V. Karanth as his successor, a person completely unlike himself in background, exposure, personality and outlook. Karanth, an ex-student of NSD, had worked in a commercial theatre company in Karnataka, learnt classical music in Varanasi, then used his NSD training to break new ground in theatre and cinema. He was to lead NSD in a very different direction. In a similar fashion my father had left Theatre Unit in the hands of Satyadev Dubey in 1962 when he moved to Delhi, again an immensely talented individual with a very different 'take' on the world.

As Neelam Mansingh, one of NSD's star alumni and an eminent director, was to write years later, 'Both Alkazi and Karanth not so much created a revolution as they put stakes in the ground, drew a boundary... created a new planet, where theatre artists could come and discover their own beings in a mixture of rational, creative, historical and traditional ways.'

Through the 1960s and 70s, my mother continued to design the costumes for each and every one of dad's fifty-odd productions, as she had done earlier, for their Bombay productions in the Theatre Group and Theatre Unit.

My sister recalls, 'Sitting on her bed, with hundreds of swatches of different weights, weaves, colours and textures laid out in front of her, Roshen looked like a painter with her palette, as she now began the task of colour-scheming. It was evident that it was during this activity, more than any other, that the creative juices were flowing most spontaneously. Holding each swatch between her fingers, she gently rubbed it, felt it, while her eyes wandered away to ruminate and imagine the colours she would co-ordinate and select in order to infuse a scene with power, or use the subtlest of nuanced colours to suggest, to underscore, or to create counterpoint, in another sequence.

'In Delhi, there was a new dimension added to her costume work as she increasingly had to design for Indian plays. For costuming productions like *Andha Yug* based on the Mahabharat, or *Ashad ka Ek Din* set in the Gupta period, or *Tughlaq* in medieval India, Roshen had been disheartened to find little or no costume reference material readily available for herself as a designer. For researching into the history of Western costumes, there was a wealth of material available. She resolved to somehow fill this lacunae in Indian costume history. With no background at all in Indian history or a college education to guide her into a methodology of approach, Roshen just simply picked up the gauntlet, as it were, and set to work! Knowing only too well what kind of reference material a costume designer might be looking for, she embarked on this huge historical enterprise and began an exciting journey towards understanding the country and its people, through clothes.' Her research resulted in her writing two outstanding volumes: *Ancient Indian Costume* and *Medieval Indian Costume*.

And was my mother innovative! For the costumes of *Hori*, she bought second-hand rags and saris from the pavements of Old Delhi to clothe the actors. For *King Lear* and *Oedipus* she created wooden designs based on motifs of the period that were handblock printed onto the garments. From hairstyle to footwear, she was able to create the right 'look' for any period of history.

Learning how to wear a costume and make it your own was another part of my mother's training of an actor. I recall sharing the lift with the young Om Puri and Naseerudin Shah at Rabindra Bhavan as they tried valiantly to cover their 'nakedness' as they sported my mother's tiny, Tarzan-like, nine-inch long leather loincloths for *Suryamukh*. Being comfortable on stage with a bare torso and bare legs is a real challenge.

Or Naseer and Ratan Thiyam strutting on the Kamani stage in *Dantons Death* set during the French Revolution, to get a feel of how to stand and gesture in a frockcoat and breeches. Or Manohar Singh trying to manage the flowing 'abads' that my mother dressed him in for *Tughlaq* at Purana Quila in the mid 70s.

And then my mother was offered a job by Kekoo Gandhy, an old friend of the family from Bombay and who had been a great supporter of the Progressive Artists Group. He was searching for a replacement for Richard Bartholomew to run the Kunika Chemould Art Gallery that he owned at Cottage Industries emporium on Janpath. My mother's active involvement in the art scene and the fact that the majority of artists were her close friends made her the ideal choice.

Not only did it bring in the much-needed extra money, it also allowed her to become her own person in carving out her own career, distinct from that of my father's, even as she continued to design costumes for all his plays at NSD.

The pattern of my life changed considerably. Since my sister would be rehearsing at NSD till all hours, I couldn't be home alone in an empty house. So after school got over at three p.m., I would walk down to my mother's office at Janpath and closing her office door, have a quick nap. Once I was up it was time for a snack at Bankura, the café downstairs, and often I would wander through the whole of Cottage Industries, keenly looking at the beautiful crafts on display there. This was where my keen interest and knowledge of Indian crafts developed. We would make our way home only at seven-thirty p.m.

My mother always encouraged artists to drop by for a cup of tea and an informal chat at the gallery. Because she was so graceful and gentle, artists were easily drawn to her. She was never in a rush, and lived an unhurried pace of life with always enough time to stop, look and listen. Her days were never packed with appointment after appointment. She had time for everyone, particularly struggling young artists. Touched by her individual concern, around her grew an increasing tribe of them. From old friends M.F. Husain, Tyeb Mehta, Krishen Khanna, Ram Kumar to the entire newly emerging Baroda 'gang': Jeram

Patel, Nasreen Mohamaddi, Gulam Mohammed Sheikh, Nilima
Sheikh, Bhupen Khakkar, Jyoti Bhatt and their guru K.G.
Subramanyam.

I recall travelling with my mother from Delhi to Baroda in
the deluxe chair car and arriving at this old-world, princely state
of a small town. I must have been around fourteen and in my
mind's eye I can still see the young, bearded and bespectacled
Gulam Mohammed Sheikh excitedly sharing with us the first few
issues of the publication *Vrishchik* with monochrome graphics
by Jyoti Bhatt, or K.G. dressed in his characteristic white lungi
and kurta showing us the toys he had created of wood and
leather, even as the long curtains draping his windows billowed
in the breeze.

Or eating Jeram Patel's masala khichdi as we watched him
working with a blowtorch on wood, or the first glimpse of
Bhupen's calendar art-inspired pop art 'naïve' paintings. K.G.
Subramanyam had created a wonderful blend of art and craft
at the Baroda School of Art, encouraging all around him to
experiment and innovate with traditional craft materials.
He himself was already creating terracotta plaques and glass
paintings.

Many of these artists had their first-ever shows at my mother's
gallery, including the crazy opening that heralded the arrival of
the one and only Bhupen Khakkar. An openly gay man who
gave up his career as a chartered accountant to become a full-time
artist, learning on the job and creating quaint, well-observed and
detailed images of life in small-town Baroda, Bhupen entered
the art scene in style in 1970. For this first opening he created
what Richard Bartholomew described as 'a kind of happening',
starting with the bright 'gulabi' wedding-style invitation cards
and moving on to a mock wedding procession assisted by art
critic Geeta Kapur and artist Nasreen Mohammadi. He never

looked back, going on to become an internationally recognized and much feted artist.

From Bombay emerging voices Gieve Patel, Sudhir Patwardhan and Nalini Malani had their first one-person shows here. Their works reflected the life of the citizens of that city, from Gieve and Sudhir's large imposing canvases capturing the grim lives of industrial workers to Nalini's glimpses into the drawing rooms of middle-class Bombay.

One particular painting lingers in my memory. In this canvas by Nalini Malani the square space is dominated by a large maternal figure rendered in stabs of colours and swathes of brown and grey. For years this painting cast its own magical spell in our home because it reminded us all of my grandmother, Kulsumbai.

In a similar fashion, many Delhi artists, among them Paramjit Singh, Arpita Singh, Meera Mukherjee, Vivan Sundaram, Saroj Pal Gogi, Rameshwar Broota, first exhibited at Kunika.

Several women artists of eminence today like Arpita Singh received a nudge towards making art a full-time career from my mother. Arpita often recounts to me that it was during one of her conversations with my mother at Kunika Chemould, that she bemoaned the fact of her life becoming confined to her house as her daughter was still a baby. My mother encouraged her to paint. Arpita asked, 'Paint what?' And my mother responded, 'The objects you see around you.' Arpita's first few canvases in her signature quirky style were just that, a collection of household objects, gaily coloured, suspended in space.

Paramjit's beautiful haunting landscapes, Vivan Sundaram's powerful voice against Indira Gandhi in the Emergency years, reflected in his startling portraits of her, and Broota's brooding ape men, all appeared for the first time on the Kunika Chemould walls.

Anyone who interacted with my mother still remembers her crisp, cool cotton saris perfectly starched in summer, the beautiful silks with matching shawls and coats in the winter, her numerous caftans. Art enthused her—performance, music, painting, sculpture, photography or installation. There was no jargon involved, no following of a fad or an 'ism'—she responded directly, emotionally. She was the ultimate 'rasik'.

It was a heady time for art and my mother was its empress. She had come into her own. It was in these years that she wrote this poem in the Japanese style of haiku:

The solitary bird
Sings.

Fourteen

Companions for Life

Eight close friends saw me through my teenage years in Delhi. Five male, Yusuf, Pablo, Koko, Ram and Rajeev, and three female, Malati, Meera and Tani. The quiet and reticent Yusuf Mehta with his nose always stuck in a book and the feisty troubled teenager Pablo Bartholomew, now an immensely creative and world renowned photo journalist, were among the earliest. Yusuf was the son of Tyeb Mehta, one of India's foremost painters, and Pablo was the son of the outstanding art critic Richard Bartholomew and his wife Rati, who was completely immersed in Delhi's theatre scene. Malati Khanna, the vivacious, intelligent and pretty daughter of Krishen Khanna, the artist, was often the Fourth Musketeer! Living in close proximity in Nizamuddin, Mathura Road, Jangpura and Defence Colony, we would occasionally walk, or rather amble across to each other's houses, to spend a leisurely afternoon and evening. These walks were on the railway tracks, sometimes even late at night, when we would loudly belt out the latest Beatles number or *Mera Naam Hai Shabnam* as we marched in rhythm, arms linked, down the tracks! Or we could spend hours together listening to the Doors or the Jimmy Hendrix Experience.

The tremendous vitality and ferment in the Western music

scene was very much a part of our growing up. From the Beatles to the Rolling Stones, from Janis Joplin to Joan Baez, from The Who to Santana, lyrics of protest set to unforgettable melodies and dense instrumental tracks were to be heard, absorbed and danced to.

And did we dance! Every Saturday night a bunch of my friends and I could be found 'grooving' for at least four hours at the newly opened The Cellar in CP (as Connaught Place was known) or Wheels at the Ambassador Hotel. The Cellar was the beginning of the discotheque culture in Delhi, and we were among its first patrons, adorning the ceiling with our names etched in smoke! Foreign hippies in their lungis and tee-shirts, high on ganja or whatever else, brought an edge of curious excitement to our Saturday nights. After all, we were the *Dum maro dum* generation! The Cellar was situated in the basement of Regal building and the excitement and apprehension of being in Connaught Place at night lent its own thrill to every visit.

Wheels near Khan Market drew a different, older, more sedate crowd, the yuppie professionals of south Delhi, whom we could elbow off the floor with our vigorous dance moves. *In a Gadda da Vida* and *Hotel California* were our favourite dance tracks. We did this from the ages of seventeen to twenty-three. Seven years on the dance floor every Saturday night! Talk of Saturday Night Fever? The phrase could have been coined for us.

All four of us were children of practicing artists and performers. Books lined the walls in all our homes, divans were draped with handloom bedspreads and the walls covered with contemporary art, arresting photographs, classical sculpture or an occasional African mask. Food was often a Burmese dish of noodles and soup called Mahmi, or a detectable Bohri mince pie or best of all, hot chicken patties from Wengers.

Our parents were friends, part of a large and growing circle of artists, who had chosen to gravitate to Delhi and to live in or around Nizamuddin. Gaitonde, Ram Kumar, M.F. Husain among others were part of this charmed circle.

The 'younger' lot of artists, somewhere in age between our parents and us, were Eruch Hakim and Nasreen Mohamedi. We would occasionally drop in at their barsati-cum-studio apartments, to watch them create their black-and-white drawings. Nasreen introduced us to green tea, Eruch was always ready to roll a joint.

There was an amazing camaraderie and willingness to help one another within the artist community. They were beyond friends, they were family. When the Mehtas relocated from London to Delhi, they stayed with us for the initial month. When Pablo's parents travelled to the US for a year, as Richard won the prestigious Rockefeller scholarship, Pablo stayed with us. Going out of your way to help a friend in a very tangible way was an integral part of my mother's personality.

Husain was already an icon in Indian art, an artist who stood apart with his characteristic white beard, long paintbrush and bare feet. Tyeb was more quiet, the 'intellectual' of the group who had recently returned from several years spent in London, Krishen had only just given up his regular job in a bank to become a 'full-time' artist.

Husain enjoyed gathering many of these families together, bundling us into his Fiat with his iconic horse painted on it, and dragging us off to see Helen dancing in *Inteqam* at Golcha Cinema in Old Delhi, followed by a meal at Flora in Jama Masjid. He knew exactly what time Helen's dance sequence was, so a large group of us would walk into the hall minutes before the dance, and exit immediately after it was over. A compliant management and Husain, the charming smooth-talker, made such a privilege possible.

It was my first encounter with Old Delhi at night with its

crowded lanes, women in burqas, the smell of frying kababs, the flavours of dum pukht biryani and the call of the azaan. I wondered if this was similar to Mohammed Ali Road in Bombay where my father grew up. It was an alien, exotic world aeons away from my Westernized, though bohemian, childhood in south Bombay. Little did I know at the time that I would soon spend ten years working in Old Delhi!

It was also my first encounter with the magical, fantasy world of Hindi cinema of the 1960s with its larger-than-life heroes, heroines and vamps. The kitschy sets, the pulsating, percussive, heavy O.P. Nayyar or R.D. Burman music, the heavy-bosomed heroines in tight kurtas and fitting churidars being pursued across the mountainscape of Shimla or Kashmir by heavy-hipped middle-aged heroes was like entering a new, bizarre, garish, yet captivating universe.

Binaca Geet Mala hosted by my uncle Ameen Sayani with his gravelly voice and his characteristic over-the-top style, and Vividh Bharati, with its requests for *Jhoomaritaliya*, had turned film music into a cult classic. Across the country, on their little transistor radios, people were listening to and singing *Roop Tera Mastana* or *Mere Sapnon ki Rani* or any other popular song from the latest Rajesh Khanna blockbuster. And he was the true superstar of our generation with his tilted head, closed eyes, a half smile on his always moist open lips, a picture of sensuality. It was a time when cinema hall marquees displayed gaudily hand-painted hoardings advertising the movie, often with heroines with bulbous lips and purple mascara, and with the hero dressed in 'bingle', a shirt and pant of the exact same colour!

Inteqam turned me into a Helen fan for life. My greatest teenage fantasy was to be one of the dancers who would appear behind her in a nightclub sequence in a B-grade Hindi movie!

Koko De and Meera Anand came into my life through my

participation in the Young Stagers Club that Barry John ran for Yatrik. Aloo tikkis, papadi chaat, borrowing books from the British Council library and never returning them, wearing eye make-up to parties, stealing brass nameplates from our neighbours' gates and throwing them into the Defence Colony nallah, creating largescale 'pop' art murals together, cooking exotic dishes and baking cakes were all integral to my friendship with Koko. Lots of food and fun, mischief and masti! He also lived in the same neighbourhood, Defence Colony. His mother, Ira De, wrote poetry as did my mother and his home was constantly full of a number of colourful and eccentric characters often with a wine or whisky glass in their hands.

Another eccentric, Amelita Stacy, lived down the road, and she would arrive at their house with a small dead chicken strapped to the back of her bicycle! She insisted on cooking it in 'just a brown paper bag, no spices' in Koko's mother's well-appointed kitchen. Surajit Sen, the AIR news reader, was a permanent fixture presiding over the weekly bridge table, all the four players conversing in anglicized Bengali. Sometimes Koko's brother would play a medley on the piano with a chorus of barking dogs. It was really like a household out of a Chekov play: mayhem, bonhomie, eccentricity, tolerance.

The city was our playground and I explored many parts of it for the first time with Koko. Shopping for Sanganer printed kurtas on Janpath, eating the delectable papadi chaat of Shah Jahan road with its imli and banana chutney, enjoying the inexpensive pastries of Defence Bakery. Sometimes we would get his father's office car, an off-white Ambassador, and its liveried chauffer whom we called Billi ki Aankhen, because of his green eyes! Most often we used buses, waiting patiently for the bus to come, as 'tantalizing tempters' (our name for auto-rickshaws) drove past us slowly, tempting us to take an auto that we really could not afford!

We would spend hours together seeing the latest movie at Priya in Vasant Vihar, then catching a bus to South Extension to buy a record at Rhythm House from our pocket money and then cooking a meal together for a sit-down dinner, invariably followed by a homemade scrumptious dessert. We believed that it was 'cool' for young men, beginning to sprout facial hair at fifteen, to be able to cook well.

Meera belonged to an army family and was the oldest of four sisters, all of whom acted in my plays. In our first play together for the Young Stagers Club, I had bullied Barry to let me play the villainess, much to Meera's chagrin. She played what Barry called 'the sexiest dragon in history', as another friend, Paro Anand, played my pet troll. They never forgave me for stealing the part of the evil Baroness Gudrun von Grubelstein from them. I played it with aplomb with newspapers stuffed into a 42B bra borrowed from Koko's mother to give me a cleavage, and a dress of red lamé first worn by Joy Michael in *Medea*. The things one does at fifteen!

Long rehearsal hours, shared interests and just generally 'hanging out' as teenagers, turned Koko and Meera into two of my closest lifelong friends. It was a sad day for me when they both moved to America.

And then there was school, Modern School where Tani Sandhu and I gravitated to one another as we were in the same class and were perennially late for school. We would disappear into the mist that enveloped the vast football field to slowly walk the two mandatory rounds as a punishment for late-coming. Tani's mother was the publisher of the well-known Hindi publishing house Rajkamal Prakashan that produced an arresting series of paperbacks in the 1970s, with works by famous artists on its covers. Tani was the brains behind the idea.

Tani and I were drawn together by a love for literature,

theatre and dance. Sitting cross-legged on the floor of her room as she sat behind her Gujarati accountant desk, we would while away an evening with delicious snacks appearing magically at regular intervals. In the final months before the school-leaving examination, we had a deal to talk on the phone at eleven every night. She had a close friendship with my mother who introduced her to the world of art. I remember one evening on her way out of our Defence Colony flat, she was drawn to a reproduction of three village women from the nineteenth century that hung on one of the walls of our staircase. Seeing her interest, my mother called out, 'Take it, Tani, it's yours.' Tani tucked it under her arm and whisked it away!

Tani and I hosted huge dance parties every New Year's Eve with a bunch of our friends, we wrote long descriptive letters to one another and we often fought and argued, always making up before the evening was over, often dissolving into peals of laughter. On leaving school we also entered into a suicide pact, deciding we could never 'grow up' and that life must be terminated at twenty-one. At twenty-one we renegotiated, swearing to end our lives together at thirty, and then finally when we turned thirty, life was so exciting and full of promise that we just decided to 'live on!' A friend for all seasons.

Ram Rahman, son of the accomplished dancer Indrani Rahman and India's foremost architect Habib Rahman, was a companion in crime for many years. Not only in Delhi but also in New York, Boston, Maine, Mexico, Bhutan, leave alone Bombay, Manali and Bangalore. With him later in life I explored Aztec ruins in Mexico, monasteries in Bhutan, MOMA (Museum of Modern Art) in New York and the temples of Belur and Halibiddu in Karnataka. Well-informed, with a vast range of interests, he was always ready for any sort of adventure. As Ram always sported a professional camera around his neck, many doors were opened for us in otherwise unreachable places. The latest salacious gossip about our friends, a strong sense of sarcastic humour, a shared delight in the world and a hunger to experience all it offered us, bound us together, almost like brothers.

Along with Ranesh Ray, who is now an eminent designer, and Himani Mehta, now a costume designer for films, Ram, Yusuf and I created a rather marvellous shadow puppet play, *Aranyakand*, based on the Ramayan, when we were all of fifteen. Wire hangers were twisted into outlines of faces, decorated with translucent beads, and along with shadows of our own hands, created the tension between Dashrath and Kaikeyi. Jatayu's body was cut out of an X-ray, lending it a tremendous vulnerability. Music and sound effects added much to this hour-long performance. Beyond staging it at home, we also did a performance of it during the Diwali Mela at school.

A lot of this shadow play was created in the Rahman's Shah Jahan Road flat. We could look out from the second floor, beyond the speckled orange blossoms of the gulmohar tree, beyond the long wafting curtains amplified by the breeze, to gaze at India Gate and other parts of Lutyens Delhi as night came to the city. It was the only house in Delhi from where I could look out at a height, something I was so used to doing in Bombay from my grandmother's fourth-floor flat or the Vithal Court fifth floor balcony. We rehearsed our shadow play in Indrani's dance room, with a Nataraja in the corner, far away from her bedroom where she would be having a siesta, muffling the sound of the telephone by covering it with a teacosy!

Ranesh, Ram and I also spent several hours creating 'batiks' in the wonderfully equipped art room of Modern School. Devyani and Kanwal Krishna, both outstanding artists, were our instructors and encouraged us to experiment with tie and dye, linocut prints and enamelling on leather. Imagine my delight on completing college to receive a call from Bishamber Khanna, my junior school art teacher, who had put together a portfolio of my work when I was nine, ten and eleven, and carefully saved it for me over the years.

In those days, Modern School, with its sprawling campus on Barakhamba Road, had an impressive array of artists manning its creative arts departments. Contemporary dancer Narendra Sharma, Uday Shankar's main pupil, taught us dance, eminent photographer O.P. Sharma trained us in the dark room even as Om and Sudha Shivpuri and Ved Vyas were our drama instructors. Under the creative and inspired leadership of M.N. Kapur, the school fostered the talent of several young minds of my generation. Theatre artists Maya Rao, Anamika Haksar and Anuradha Kapur, dancers Rasika Khanna and Madhavi Mudgal, musicians like Madhup Mudgal, art impresarios like Sanjeev Bhargava, and of course several of my contemporaries emerged from this institution. This stress on art and creativity as being completely on par with academic achievement can rarely be seen in any school today.

College saw me spending almost every day of three years whizzing around in the Fiat of the wonderful, warm and rather brilliant Rajeev Bhargava, a close friend and intellectual companion. From Sartre to Camus, Fellini to Fassbinder, Gandhi to Godse, ideas regarding life, art and cinema were our daily menu. We would spend hours late into the night, sitting in his car parked under the foliage of jamun trees somewhere around the arts district of Mandi House, furiously debating ideas emanating from what we had just read or seen.

Years later, when Rajeev had married Tani, the three of us went on a two-week driving trip around France 'sans Paree' (without visiting Paris). It was in our own quiet way a homage to visit the birthplace of Impressionism, Nihilism and Existentialism.

All of these friends came together, with the exception of Ram Rahman who was still in school, to help me mount my first 'ticketed' production, Mohan Rakesh's *Ashad ka Ek Din* in an English translation. Malati played the vivacious heroine Mallika, the 'muse' of Kalidasa the poet, graduating from a carefree adolescence to a mature, quieter older woman who still waits for Kalidasa's return. Rajeev with his deep, rich voice and magnetic stage presence played opposite her as Kalidasa, Yusuf Mehta played Vilom (the opposite) to Rajeev's Kalidasa, the dark mercurial man of the village who marries Mallika in Kalidasa's absence. Meera played Ambika, Mallika's tragic widowed mother always apprehensive about her daughter's future. Tani and Pablo played representatives from the royal court in Ujjain, Tani as a giggly young Rangini and Pablo, rose in hand, dressed in a pink and black dhoti as a courtier. Koko helped me to create the costumes, improvising from whatever was at hand. True teamwork and the absolute beginning of my career as a director for the stage.

Fifteen

Jafferbhai's Disappearance

M y grandfather spent the entire day rocking on his jhoola. Till one day when he was over seventy, he had had enough, packed his bags and left Kulsum Terrace forever—moving in with his mistress, never to return, except for his own funeral.

He was a large, corpulent man, always dressed in a meticulous long white shirt and loose pyjamas that he changed thrice a day. He was almost an invisible presence when we visited once a week on Sundays. Prompted by my mother we would rush into his room, give him a peck on the cheek, mumble 'Hullo nanibapa' and then run out again. He would join us at the lunch table, eating his customary bajre ki roti and lasun chutney. For the rest of the day, we would busy ourselves, paying no attention to the patriarch.

His jhoola was a large upholstered sofa suspended on chains that he would gently rock with his feet. Behind him on the wall arranged in a unique pyramidical design hung portraits, painted or photographic, of his own side of the family. The pictures are in black-and-white, the visages are grim. They have not been touched up, tinted, painted over in a photo studio like the ones in the drawing room. Facing him in a formal arrangement are sofas for his guests. Directly in front of him a large four-poster bed is where he naps in the day, sleeps at night, often it is draped in a mosquito net.

We occasionally glimpse a guest in his room sitting and chatting in Gujarati, or him getting a nice oil massage by the handsome young men from the barber shop on the ground floor. Never did we as kids realize that my grandparents had not exchanged a word with each other in our presence for over twenty years.

And then one day he is gone. No one asks where or why. We know it is yet another 'never to be spoken of' topic with my grandmother. Unused objects begin to pile up in his room. Family hangers-on sleep on his bed at night. It is as though he never existed,

Why did he leave? The big question, unasked and unanswered in the family. As I understand it today the marriage had broken down, many moons ago when suddenly the baby-making factory that was my grandmother put an end to co-habitation with her spouse and created her own bedroom and life. The years of living apart in Bombay and in England had allowed both to carve out their own lives in separate spaces. My grandmother was feverishly attempting to create an anglicized future for herself and her children, asserting herself as woman, wife and mother. My grandfather, after his return from England, retreated into the comfort of a traditional male existence, with, I am sure, enough contact with women and the outside world. Alyque suggests he had eight mistresses over the years, not at the same time, but sequentially!

From the outside, the relationship looked fine, independent roles and existences, no cracks visible on the surface. He stayed on till the last of his sons had married. Bubbles (Aziz) had chosen to ignore his mother's diktat and censure and marry his girlfriend of several years, Parveen, who was a Parsi. My grandmother in a grand diplomatic gesture decided to go to Pune on the weekend of the marriage so that the rest of the family could attend it. When my grandmother returned, it was to a vast, empty, silent house for my grandfather had used her absence to disappear himself. He no longer needed to keep the pretence of the marriage alive. He had fulfilled his last duty as father by being around when the last family member married.

He didn't move far, two kilometres down the road. Sitting back, looking relaxed, in a new jhoola! Attended to by a nurse who was his companion in many ways. With the exception of the Jefferies (who didn't even question where he had suddenly vanished), all of us visited him in his new flat. Certainly the space was smaller, but the interactions became less formal and more relaxed.

When he died a few years later, my grandmother insisted his body be brought to Kulsum Terrace before it went to the graveyard.

My grandmother herself disappeared a few years later, slipping into Alzheimers. Words began to escape her. My cousin Rhea, who lived across the hall, would often see my grandmother standing in front of the fridge, the door wide open, bemused by why she had opened it. The family took to labelling everything: 'milk, bread, butter...' but my grandmother became more and more silent and confused as she had in the year following Sultan's death till finally she passed away, five years later. Till the end, Rhea would lie on a chattai on the floor next to my grandmother's bed, holding her hand through the night. She had always called Rhea 'thingamebob' but in the end there was no recognition.

The woman of determination, grit, and tremendous courage, who had inspired her son Alyque to create the no-nonsense Lalitaji of the iconic Surf commercial, was no more.

And as for the jhoola? Years later, after my grandmother passed away, Alyque had it moved to his own flat in Breach Candy. His drawing room echoed his parents' flat, except for the large over-sized family portraits benignly glaring down at us. They had been replaced by contemporary art: M.F. Husain, Akbar Padamsee, Mickey Patel and interspersed with posters of Broadway shows. Alyque often took his own father's place on the jhoola, rocking gently, holding us enthralled with his mimicry and the fine art of storytelling. And when dinner was announced, my grandmother's signature dishes would appear on the table. I felt I was in a time warp!

And now when Alyque himself is no longer with us, what will become of the jhoola?

Sixteen

The Pearl Padamsee Story

The 1970s saw the gradual fracturing of the Padamsee family. Death and divorce came to stay. Many family members remained estranged for years, choosing to not even talk to one another. There were only three of us in the family who felt this was an issue to be addressed and that we must address it. My aunt Candy, my cousin Yohan and myself.

In August 1973, a sudden call from my cousin Renan to us in Delhi brought horrific news. My mother's younger brother Bubbles had died in a car crash on the Western Ghats, his two children were critically injured and in ICU. Only his wife Parveen, who had been driving the car, had escaped unscathed, physically. Mentally, the trauma of what was finally three deaths, her entire family, was to haunt her through her life.

My grandmother, even though she had never met Parveen since her marriage or even seen either of her grandchildren, was at the hospital day and night. Her only interaction with these two children were when they were dead and she paid the bill. But nothing changed or softened within her. Except there was an acceptance of Pearl and Raell as Alyque had already left to live with Dolly. The fragility of life and the vital importance of nurturing relationships came home to me in a big way. It was time to do something.

I began spending a large part of my summer vacation living with my aunt Pearl and my cousins Ranjit and Raell in Bombay. This was a part of the larger and extended family that my grandmother chose to ignore, and my aunt Shiraz had followed suit. It was interesting that, in those pre-mobile days, both my grandmother and aunt had to call on the landline to speak to me, so they automatically first spoke to Pearl as she often picked up the phone.

Pearl Padamsee was a most wonderful, vibrant personality. Tiny in height, but gigantic in talent. Theatre and music, acting and direction came naturally to her. With C.F. Andrews as her godfather, she had grown up in a Christan and Jewish household committed to the ideas of the freedom movement. Alyque and Pearl met in the St Xavier's Theatre Club which she attended in a khadi salwar kameez.

Alyque recalls their first interaction: 'When I went to St Xavier's College, I was dying to join the Drama Club which Bobby was responsible for starting many, many years ago. I went there, it was in the big courtyard, and there was a little girl with a big book, like a hisab book and she said, "Yes?" I said, "I want to join the Drama Club." "Oh, really, I see, well, have you had any acting experience?" I said, "A little." She asked me what that was. I told her it was the *Merchant of Venice*. She said, "What part did you play?" "Well," I said, "it was a silent part but my brother played the Prince of Morocco." She asked me who my brother was, and I replied, "Bobby Padamsee." "What? Bobby Padamsee is your brother?" "Yes," I said. "You know, theatre sort of runs in my family." She said—"It doesn't run, it gallops."

'And that person turned out to be Pearl Weiz. When my sister Zarina heard that I had met Pearl and I said that she was a very bubbly person and full of life, she said, "Alyque, I think that's a good girlfriend for you." And those words echoed in my mind and for thirteen years I pursued her, thirteen years!'

When Pearl's father, Altaf Weiz, became the first Indian high commissioner to Fiji, she moved from Bombay to Sydney to get a degree in archaeology. Alyque was away in England while she returned to India, got married and had two children, Rohini and Ranjit.

But her marriage didn't last long, and after doing some plays in Bombay with Alyque, Pearl went to the London Academy of Music and Dramatic Arts. Her great friend there was Janet Suzman, later to become a major actress in the West End and marry director Trevor Nunn, only to subsequently divorce him.

Divorce from her first husband and marriage to Alyque soon followed. The outcome of the marriage was that my grandmother banned the entry of Pearl to KT, though they had been great friends earlier. Alyque plunged into the world of advertising to earn a living and support his family. Pearl and he moved to Belha Terrace, not far from the Padamsee house. Every afternoon Alyque went to have lunch with his mother at KT.

And then tragedy struck. Pearl's firstborn, Rohini, died in September 1961, of nephritis. I remember the sombre atmosphere at the hospital after her death. It is one of my earliest memories. Alyque and Pearl's daughter Raell was born soon after.

Alyque and Pearl travelled to London and New York almost every year from the late 1960s to the mid 70s. This gave them an opportunity to regularly see, up close and personal, the exciting new experimental theatre work being done there. It was an age of Grotowski, Café La Mama, Richard Schechner's 'Living Theatre' and several other theatre collectives. The 67 Youth Revolution resulted in a major shaking up of the American and European theatre scene. New performance spaces—lofts, staircases, houses—were mounting shows created through improvisation with a lot of physicality. There was a palpable 'newness' in the air. The impact of these visits could be seen in the plays Alyque and Pearl chose to direct on their return to Bombay.

Alyque's production of Peter Weiss' *Marat/Sade* was staged in St Xavier's College, while Pearl directed her first play, Jean Claude Van Italie's *The Serpent,* in a church. Gerson played de Sade to Alyque's Marat in the bathtub, with Yasim Mody as Charlotte Corday who stabs Marat to death. The play is set in a lunatic asylum, where the inmates are staging their own version of the events of the early years of the French Revolution. Writhing masses of actors take the stage, sometimes come off it to attack the audience—this play is a visceral and disturbing experience. It pits the ideas of individualism and revolution against one another in a unique setting, an asylum. Weiss' own family history of having to flee Germany, because they were Jewish, resulted in his writing several powerful plays that drew on the dark satire of Kafka. Homelessness, isolation, repression and the State were his preoccupations. Alyque later remounted it in Hindi as *Pagal Khana* in a wonderful translation by Ismat Chughtai. In Delhi years later, Barry John was to direct it for Theatre Action Group (TAG).

Pearl covered the entire floor of the tiny St Thomas church with aluminum foil for her production of *The Serpent.* The actors formed the ever-changing stage pictures, bodies interwoven creatively, with words and phrases repeated over and over again to create a specific style of presentation. The play tells of man's first flouting of the word of God in the Garden of Eden. The author, Jean Claude van Italie, was an innovator in script and direction, work-shopping his way across the world.

But within ten years of getting married Alyque got involved with Dolly Thakore and chose to leave home and Pearl.

Life at the beautiful flat at Belha Terrace in which she continued to stay, was an invigorating affair, with constant guests from all over India and the world. The large drawing and dining room opened out completely to a large terrace at the same level. The water tanks (and in Bombay you can't avoid them!) had been painted by the young artist Mickey Patel with Aztec-type murals. On many evenings the entire space became a perfect rehearsal space with an audience seated on the terrace and performers in the drawing room. Late-night drinks and food under the stars, often with stunning mellifluous fine voices raised in song, followed. Exotic salads and Pearl's signature dishes. An avant garde lifestyle: heady nights!

Pearl Padamsee nurtured an entire generation of actors on this terrace and in her drama work in J.B. Petit School for Girls and Campion, an all-boys school. Shashi Tharoor (now a Congress MP) played Fagin to my cousin Ranjit's Artful Dodger in *Oliver*, Ronnie Screwvala (later to head UTV films) acted in several plays, comedian Cyrus Broacha was a regular while contemporary stage director Rehan Engineer was with Pearl the night she passed away. Ayesha Dharker, the international actress, and Faezah Jalali, now a director in her own right, made their first appearance, in school plays under Pearl's direction. From the Theatre Group, Homi Daruwala, Hosi Vasunia, Vijay Krishna, Ruby Patel, Roger Perera, Sabira Merchant, Soni Razdan (Aalia Bhatt's mother) were all close friends as well as actors. I first met Mahesh Elkunchwar, a young Marathi playwright, and Dadi Pudumjee, the puppeteer just returned from Europe, on this terrace. It was a constant open house at Belha Terrace.

Pearl herself was a fine actress, starting off as Kate in *Taming of the Shrew* with Gerson da Cunha as Petruchio opposite her. She played many leading roles in Theatre Group productions, the young teenage gossip who destroys a teacher's reputation in Lillian Hellman's *The Children's Hour*, the hysterical Abigail Williams in Arthur Miller's *The Crucible*, among others.

Looking at the list of plays she chose to direct, I am struck by the fact that she never chose one of the classics as Alyque often did. All the scripts she directed had been written in the 1960s, 70s and 80s. There is no Greek tragedy, no Shakespeare, not even a Moliere. The 'oldest' play she directed was Brecht's *Arturo Ui* written in the 1950s that follows the fortunes of the titular hero as he rises to power like Hitler. Another Brecht she attempted was *The Measures Taken*.

Many of her productions view Biblical tales through a contemporary lens, the musical *Joseph and His Amazing Technicolour Dreamcoat* by Andrew Lloyd Webber, Jean Claude van Italie's very contemporary take on the Old Testament, *The Serpent,* and the celebratory joyous circus-style romp on Christ's life and parables, *Godspell*, the musical which she directed twice over.

Another whole set of plays examines the male-female relationship up close and personal. *The Collector,* a dramatized version of the John Fowles novel, is a two-hander (Soni Razdan's first performance) of a young woman kidnapped and held captive by a young man. *Dangerous Liasons*, Christopher Hampton's contemporary retelling of an eighteenth-century Casanova and his 'conquests', starred Naseeruddin Shah, Sabira Merchant, Ratna Pathak Shah and Pearl herself. Neil Simons' *Last of the Red Hot Lovers* looks at an unlikely Casanova of today with three of his women friends, and was adapted by her to a Mumbai setting. The last play that she directed, Harold Pinter's *Betrayal*, explores the dynamics of an extra-marital affair. One doesn't need to be a genius to understand her preoccupation with affairs and adultery.

Other more commercial productions included Woody Allen's *Don't Drink the Water* and Michael Frayn's *Noises Off*. Another entire genre of plays was by first-time Indian playwrights: Cyrus Mistry's *Doongaji House*, Gieve Patel's *Princes*, Zarina Sayani and Freny Bhownagary's *Bedroom*. Sympathetic looks at the crumbling family in different corners of India. Supporting new playwrights, directors and actors were an intrinsic part of Pearl's personality.

And there was of course the vast range of plays written by Shirin Darasha, principal of J.B. Petit School for Girls, that Pearl directed every year, including the stories of Marie Curie and Helen Keller, and the more contemporary Mumbai stories of pavement dwellers or of a young Muslim girl from a conservative background who becomes a detective!

On the large screen, Pearl acted opposite Ashok Kumar in *Khatta Meetha* and with Amol Palekar and Tina Munim in *Baton Baton Mein*. For Granada TV she played a key role in *Staying On* with Saeed Jaffrey. For Govind Nihalani, she acted in *The Party* by Mahesh Elkunchwar and in Shyam Benegal's *Junoon* she played a cameo role. In her later years, Pearl acted in my serial based on Ruskin Bond's stories and in another serial of mine, *Khoj Khazana Khoj*, and also in the telefilm's *Roshini* and *Like That Only*.

A sharp sense of detailed characterization, a dramatic and mobile face, a melodious and expressive voice and superb comic timing marked every portrayal. I particularly remember working with Pearl on a scene in *Ek Tha Rusty*, a serial I was directing based on the stories of Ruskin Bond. She was playing Ruskin's grandmother and we decided to end one of the episodes with Pearl spontaneously singing and dancing a song of the 1940s. I had chosen the popular song 'Jealousy', and Pearl knew it well. So without any rehearsal at all, as the light was fading, I said, 'Roll camera' and 'Action'.

Pearl effortlessly glided around the small room in the Savoy Hotel in Mussoorie, moving her hands gracefully as she swayed to the rhythm of the song she sang. On her face nostalgia and remembrance of a now-dead partner played out. The entire crew was mesmerized and almost teary-eyed as it was the logical end to an episode of Pearl recounting to her grandson, the young Rusty (Zarul Ahuja) the story behind a particular photo in the family album.

'Cut,' I called out. Almost immediately I heard the sound of someone clapping behind me, and turned to see Ruskin Bond himself. I had completely forgotten I had invited him to the shoot. I was worried that he may object to this scene which features nowhere in his story. On the contrary, he just leaned across to me and whispered, 'How did you know "Jealousy" was my grandmother's favourite song?' And gave Pearl a thumbs up.

To me, Pearl was a larger-than-life character, straight out of the Old Testament. She had strong beliefs and an amazing sense of empathy and compassion for those who lived on the fringes or even beyond. Perhaps spurred by her own son Ranjit's battle with drugs over the decades, she reached out through the Seva Sadan Society, using her skills to nurture and to heal. Gay men and lesbian women were comfortable on her terrace and she always lent a supportive ear.

And even though Alyque's betrayal pained her deeply, she was always there for him, his constant friend and companion. My mother and Pearl bonded because of the similarity between their life histories and Pearl often stayed with us in Delhi. I remember her triumph when we hired a cook a few inches shorter than her, and the cook's triumph when later that evening he appeared with a chef's hat, a few inches taller than Pearl's height!

Regaling us with stories and songs, laughing with abandon, angry with purpose, despairing at the plight of the dispossessed. She wrote to all she cared for regularly. Just a yellow postcard or an inland letter jammed with news and opinions. I still have many of them in my bedside drawer. We were more than aunt and nephew, we were close friends.

In London she asked me to accompany her to the dress rehearsal of *Cats*, Trevor Nunn's first attempt at directing a musical. At the National Theatre we went together to see the young emerging actor, Anthony Hopkins, in a rivetting performance as Rupert Murdoch in *Pravda* and also the *Orestia*, the Greek tragedy trilogy. In her one-of-a-kind kaftans, embroidered and embellished, she personified a certain age of Bombay theatre.

In the last years of her life Pearl moved into her mother's flat at Churchgate in the building adjoining my cousin, Ayesha Sayani's. She redecorated it in her inimitable style with just a touch of whimsy. Next door, eager students of a piano teacher filled the atmosphere with music. Every evening she followed her mother's routine of a trip to the CCI club. Here she entertained her guests, read a little, gave interviews, met aspiring actors. Her end was a sudden heart attack. Luckily at the time the very young Rehan Engineer was with her. It was late at night, and early next morning I was there to be with her daughter, my cousin Raell. Alyque was away as was her son Ranjit, so it was just an overwhelmed Cyrus Broacha and I who accompanied her on her last journey to the crematorium. Till today, many years later, Raell celebrates Pearl's birthday with a group of friends who just can't forget her and the way she enriched the lives of each one of them.

Seventeen

The Heady Sixties and Seventies

'Trust yourself, dare yourself to be the person you have become and in so doing, resist the pressures that insist upon conformity.' A beautiful quotation written by I know not who, that has certainly been one of the guiding principles of my own life.

The need to develop the ability to trust oneself, keep oneself constantly open to experiencing the changing world and to be able to change is something I feel many people resist along their way to growing up. And certainly for myself 'resisting the pressures that insist upon conformity' holds great value. In my father's family, I am simply known as 'the rebel'.

A close friend of mine, Dina Kapur, who lived in the US and made occasional forays to India, sent me this quotation. I must have been around sixteen or seventeen. We were great friends, even greater correspondents as were many of our generation, and our letters were long, well composed, thoughtful and thought-provoking. Many of these from a handful of friends are still with me.

I was an unattractive young man. Thin and gangly with a head of unruly, unmanageable curly hair that could never be combed or controlled and a large pair of thick spectacles that were constantly slipping down my nose. By the time I went to college, my clothes and hairstyle loudly proclaimed my non-conformity. I had grown my hair into an Afro and often wore red pants with a red shirt or prints bought off a beach in Goa. My friends at the rather stuffy St Stephen's college that I attended called me 'Carnival of Eden'. I loved the title. For a phase in college, Yusuf Mehta and I wore checked kasai lungis, the ones normally worn by Muslim butchers, and kurtas, and I would be comfortable walking into the NSD dressed just like this. My parents, and I must hand it to them, never made an adverse comment about my appearance and I was comfortable in my skin, as much a non-conformist then as I am now.

I never really took to being at St Stephen's College and certainly the college didn't take to me. Perhaps I had travelled so far down the 'Indianization' process that Delhi in general and Modern School in particular had taken me far from my 'colonial' childhood in south Bombay. To me St Stephen's epitomized a way of life, a vanished time, a culture that I had consciously turned my back on. Certainly the teaching was largely outstanding and invigorating but the entire atmosphere and ethos—the P.G. Wodehouse Society, the Shakespeare Society, the donkey darby, the debate topics, the haw-haw speech—infuriated me. And the fact that the college principal went around carrying an umbrella when the weather report predicted that it might rain in Oxford that day!

Also, having started Ruchika Theatre Group while in my very first year of college, meant that I was always trying to escape classes to get into rehearsal. And that St Stephen's was all male at the time was even worse. I was extremely co-educational in everything. For me life without my women friends was no life at all. In retrospect, maybe I never gave my college a fair chance.

We were a generation ready to change the world, refashion it in our own image. Our icons were Gandhi and Che Guevara, our music, alternative, our literature R.D. Laing and Sylvia Plath, our lifestyle often just short of being 'hippies'. Drugs were a part of the scene, never of mine, but certainly of many of my closest friends like Pablo and Alok Nath. Fast bikes, fast girls (what a sexist phrase but popular in the 1960s), alcohol, cigarettes: all an essential part of growing up. And questioning.

We regularly rented out the barsati on our roof to augment the meagre family income. For many years a young woman who hung out exciting underwear to dry lived here, and later an idealistic young male scientist who opted for a vasectomy at the age of thirty. My understanding of the world was expanding.

A young British couple, Peter and Eva, came and stayed with us for a few months when I was fifteen. They were studying architecture under my uncle Chhotu in London. Eva often only wore a lungi tied under her armpits, and walked around barefoot. She went on to become a lifelong friend of my mother's and made a career as one of the main organizers of the World Music festival in London. Her alternative lifestyle was attractive, and I spent many hours at the dining table chatting with the couple.

In a similar way two of my cousins from Bombay came and stayed for lengths of time in our barsati. Renan had married the model Gulnar, Pooh (Ayesha Sayani) married Dhruv and for me, watching the vicissitudes of the 'modern' marriage of these two cousins was an education. Neither marriage lasted long.

Cross-community and cross-cultural marriages had always been the thing in the Padamsee family because all my mother's siblings had done so. Alyque married in turn a Christian Jew, Pearl Weiz, then lived with Dolly Thakore and finally divorced Pearl to marry the young singer, Sharon Prabhakar. His younger brother Chhotu married Margarite who was British, but had Jewish and Czech ancestry. Aziz (Bubbles) married a Parsi,

Parveen. Not to be left out, my aunt Candy married a Punjabi, Anand Bhatia! Our generation has gone the same way with Muslim, Hindu, Jewish, Catholic, Protestant, and Buddhist partners. We have had to be very inventive, constantly designing cross-cultural marriage ceremonies and have often had to rely heavily on texts like Khalil Gibran's *The Prophet*!

Many of my cousins have also followed the good example of my maternal grandfather of 'living in' rather than marriage! Today, of us fourteen cousins only six are married, a testament to the times. What's interesting in all of this, is that with very few exceptions, no one practices the faith they were born into. So I belong to a family that has literally lived 'out of the box'.

My sister continued dating the ever-dependable Nissar Allana, a doctor in the making, from the time she was fifteen. His constant trips to Delhi gave a stability to our family as he was the only 'male' member and my mother depended heavily on him. Not that he was a conformist at all. With the princely sum of thirty-five dollars in his pocket, which was all we were allowed to exchange in the late 1960s, he hitchhiked his way across Europe. He was on his way to meet Amal in East Berlin where she was studying theatre after completing her course at NSD and he often survived by selling his blood! The next year both of them made the trip together, hitchhiking from Kabul to Germany with many adventures along the way. Soon enough Nissar abandoned his original career plan of becoming a doctor and switched to designing for the stage.

A magazine that reflected the concerns of our generation completely was the *Junior Stateman* (*JS*) of Calcutta. With its bold, pop art graphics, fun content, including a much-awaited sardonic column by Jug Suraiya and a serialized novel on the Nazis(!) by a very young Shashi Tharoor, we read it avidly, devouring it from cover to cover. There was always substance there, beyond the style. An iconic publication of our generation.

Several of us from two batches of Modern School and some of my friends from the Young Stagers Club came together in July 1972 to form Ruchika Theatre Group. Drawn by a common love of and belief in theatre, we wanted to master all aspects of it ourselves, without any training or inputting by adults. We were between sixteen and seventeen, idealistic and determined. Forty-seven years later, many of us are still working together under the Ruchika banner.

How similar we were in age, energy and outlook to the Theatre Group! At Ruchika we chose to only do plays of social relevance whether in Hindi or English and the very first production I directed for the group was Mohan Rakesh's *One Day in Ashadh*. The very same script with which my father had begun his career in NSD.

In the initial years, Modern School gave us complete support, providing us with space for regular rehearsals. And once that came to an end, my extremely creative colleague Arun Kuckreja, rehearsed across Barakhamba Road, where Modern School was located, at the house of a classmate, Medha Gujral, while my plays got rehearsed in our home, C-442, Defence Colony.

Much of my mother's adolescence at Kulsum Terrace and adulthood at Vithal Court had seen the disruption of the living space to hold rehearsals, so when I began shifting the furniture and making numerous cups of tea for my young actor friends, she didn't even raise an eyebrow.

Ideas about how to shape and change our own futures and the world we live in were a constant in our conversations, whether we were in a university café or meeting at home for a Ruchika rehearsal. Hanging out in a friend's car at two a.m., drinking cold coffee at Devicos on Janpath, talking Nietzsche and Sartre, arguing over Gandhi's constant remaking of himself in our invigorating 'Thursdays at 5' sessions over a hot cup of tea and a plate of pakoras in the cold winter afternoons, making it a point to visit Max Mueller Bhavan or Alliance Français regularly to see and dissect the latest 'new wave' film from Europe, all helped mould us and colour our perceptions. But our reference points remained Western, not necessarily American but certainly European. Dealing with the Indian reality was yet to happen.

And it was this circle of friends and actors who grew together in an atmosphere of intellectual dissent and debate. Cameraman Anil Mehta, filmmaker Bina Paul, film professional Shernaz Italia, writers Susan Vishwanathan and Paro Anand, actors Neena Gupta, Sohaila Kapur, Pawan Malhotra, Harsh Chhaya, Alok Nath, Mona Chawla, who all went on to make a mark in their respective professional fields, began here their lifelong career in the arts. There were numerous others who contributed greatly and yet chose to earn their money elsewhere, never giving up their deep and genuine interest in the theatre.

Adjusting to the reality of making a career and earning your own money was complicated and difficult, as in this excerpt of a letter from Pablo to me: 'I have very strong demarcations of what is what. Where I'm whoring and where I'm doing things I enjoy. Working on film sets is a gross rape on the senses but it's good enough because then for the next fifteen days nobody is telling me to do this or that.

'The day I shoot I get my money in hand if not in advance. Very important. Not like advertising where you might not see your money at all. Or might see it after many many moons. Here you always remain fluid and the mobility of money lets you or gives you access, buys your personal time. Simple economics.

'Anyway, I will never be able to make that ultimate compromise of working thirty days a month under somebody else. I need my mobility. It's very important to my existence and work. Anywhere I am, I am always doing my own personal work on the side.

'And the film world is fascinating!

'People are afraid of going into anything because they feel that they'll get trapped. I'm too much of an outsider, too much of a nomad to be able to get stuck.'

Equally difficult was the process of adjustment to life at the top-notch universities abroad. Ram wrote, 'New Haven must be the pits of the universe or else I haven't seen it yet! I have been in the depths of depression ever since coming here. It's just a town with horribly negative and oppressive vibrations.

'Most of the students are the deadliest bores in the world. A number of them come from very well-off families and it's the first time I've come across art students who are very socially hung up. They dress in designer clothes, wash their arses with designer toilet paper and eat off designer dishes. Walk around with their noses up in the air. So good old me runs in off course, hangs my silk Indian flag in the studio and puts a number of Indian calendar paintings on the wall. I also behave very shockingly. And I am considered a total freak and of course I love it!' Ram however stayed through his course at Yale and when he graduated appeared in a complete American Indian outfit complete with a feather headdress. Of course this appeared on national television and Ram had made his point.

Theatre served as my entry point, my way of understanding a situation. And for the first five years as a director (1972–77), I explored the world of Absurd Drama in many of my productions.

The movement that came to be known as the Theatre of the Absurd had emerged in Europe during the 1950s and 60s as a reaction to a changing worldscape that no one could really comprehend. Where was man headed in an age of political discord, unruly mass movements and the constant ominous threat of a nuclear winter? Eugene Ionesco, Samuel Beckett and Jean Genet were the flagbearers of this new theatrical genre in

France, as was Harold Pinter in England. Even more interesting to me was the work emerging from Eastern Europe: Slawomir Mrozek, the Polish playwright, and Tadeusz Rozewicz, the Polish writer.

Can words really communicate? Can they kill? This is the terrain of Slawomir Mrozek. Three marooned characters, Fat, Medium and Thin, are stuck on a raft in the middle of the ocean. How will they survive? Can Thin be persuaded to 'sacrifice' himself to keep the other two alive? This was *Out at Sea,* and a year later I directed the same playwright's *Charlie,* a truly absurd comedy. The *Hindustan Times* critic, Kavita Nagpal, wrote at the time, 'Charlie is the unknown quantity stalked by an old man who goes to an occulist for glasses so that he is sure to recognize Charlie when he finds him. So if there is no Charlie, he has to be created, and if he is there he should be shot. Pablo Bartholomew, Rajeev Saigal and Ram Rahman gave superb performances under the expert direction of Feisal Alkazi. The painted banner-like set and stylized acting produced a peculiar rhythm, the pace of which the players never let flag.'

Years later, exactly two days after the Emergency was declared, we performed *Striptease* by the same author. Of this production, Kavita wrote, 'Two babus (the play has been rendered in Hindi by Rajeev Bhargava) arrive at an unknown destination.

'Even as they discuss internal freedom and the rights of the individual, a red-gloved hand emerges from within the décor and each man is made to strip down to bare underpants. With handcuffs as reward the two receive an added bonus: the presentation of dunce caps covering the eyes. They are alive. They know the idea of freedom. But they are "blinded" to it by the Hand.'

Harold Pinter also drew my interest and Alok Nath and Mona Chawla played the leads in my production of the *The*

Lover in Hindi. The play opens on what we imagine is a husband and wife at breakfast. Within a couple of lines Pinter pulls the rug from under our feet as the 'husband' asks: 'Is your lover coming today?' And when she replies yes, he says he will return home late! In the very next sequence she is dressed seductively and opens the door to her 'lover', played by the same actor who has just played her 'husband'! What is real, what fantasy?

Jean Genet's classic, *The Maids*, posed a completely different challenge. As suggested by the author in his introduction to the play, the three women characters, and there are only three, are all to be played by men. And that's how I decided to do it: three young virile men in black vests and black trousers 'play-acting' as it were, the maids. The story is simple. In the absence of the wealthy Madame whose house they work in, the two maids, Solange and Claire, 'enact' the power play between Madame and her maids, playing each role in turn. So my production had three men playing three women who in turn roleplay boss and employee!

Gayatri Sinha wrote in the *Indian Express* at the time, 'Alkazi's beautifully conceived stage, bits of white lace and satin contrasted against black, is eloquent, as are the superb compositions in which the sisters represent the interplay between the characters. Alkazi deserves credit for achieving the right degree of stylization and highlighting the clarity and beauty of Genet's language.'

A few years later a young American playwright, Wendy Kesselman, gave me a manuscript of her first play, *Blood Bond*, that was based on the same incident in France in the 1940s and that had inspired Genet to write *The Maids*. It tells the story of the two sisters, Claire and Solange, and how they are mistreated by Madame and her daughter whom they finally hack to pieces. But unlike Genet's rendering of the same story, Kesselmann's is in a quasi realistic style. The violence of Madame is evident in that she never directly addresses Claire and Solange through the entire play. Shonali Bose, who has gone on to become a major film director (with successes like *The Sky is Pink* and *Margarita with a Stra*w to her credit), played Claire in my production, originally presented by the Miranda House Dramatic Society and subsequently performed under the Ruchika banner.

And of course there was Eugene Ionesco's *Rhinoceros* that examines and explores the herd-like mentality of man, when holding your opinion that may run counter to the mass, can be both challenging and difficult.

In a small French town square the populace is alarmed when a rhinoceros is seen thundering down the roads. Soon this 'Rhinoceritis' has grabbed the entire population and it is only Berenger (the protagonist played by Alok Nath) who can hold out against the onslaught. Bina Aggarwal, noted film editor and director of the Trivandrum Film Festival for years, acted opposite Alok and a tiny walk-on part was played by a young college student who went on to establish a major bank in India! Koko De transformed himself on stage into a rhinoceros before the audience's eyes. Powerful stuff and an apt allegory for our times.

In their own way, I feel these plays influenced the course of Delhi theatre, bringing the style and content of the Absurd tradition to audiences in the capital. Not that I was alone in presenting the Absurdists. My colleague Arun Kuckreja did an outstanding production of Beckett's *Happy Days* with Sohaila Kapoor and a group called Non-Group presented a wonderful version of Beckett's *Endgame*.

Eighteen

Turning Twenty-one

On the cold January morning of my twenty-first birthday I was rudely awakenedly by the sound of an insistent doorbell. Downstairs on the doorstep stood my good friend Pablo Bartholomew and my cousin Ayesha Sayani. They were both grinning, holding a large chocolate cake in their hands that simply read 'Aargh!' All of my friends were aware that I suffered from a Peter Pan complex, the idea of growing up was anathema to me.

Pablo and Ayesha were dating at the time and my two great friends Rajeev and Tani were close to matrimony. Other friends would marry in a couple of years. Everyone around me was growing up! Ruchika Theatre Group was already four years and many productions old. I had played the existential anti-hero of Jean Paul Sartre's *No Exit*, the central character in Mohan Rakesh's *Aadhe Adhure*, the father in Arthur Miller's *All My Sons*. I was through with college. I was on the threshold of having to decide what to do next. It was time for me to grow up too.

My next step surprised me. On a two-month-long vacation in the US that summer, that was my aunt Candy's graduation gift to me, I decided to enroll for a Masters in Social Work at Delhi University. My family was baffled—why not the Film

Institute or a career in advertising? I wasn't sure why, but I was sure that it was the next step I would take. It was a big step for the family. My mother had never completed school, my father had never completed college, my sister had gone directly to the NSD after she finished school, so my decision to pursue an MA was something really new and out of the way for them.

Our family was once again at a moment of transition. My father had resigned from the NSD and he knew that he wanted to disengage from theatre for some time. He wrote one of his rare letters to me at the time: 'For the first time in fifteen years, I shall not be returning to the NSD. In previous years I used to plan for the new academic year with relish and a sense of excitement. But that is now a phase of my life which I have left behind me. I shall miss it to some extent but honestly I do not have much regret. In many ways one has to learn to be detached from one's work even while one is deeply committed to it. The theatre is a dangerous activity, full of temptations for the ego, it encourages one's narcissism and one's sense of vanity. One is working all the time with living human beings, and moulding them to one's own vision and the danger is of going into a self-indulgent space. It requires an innate humility to realize how little one knows.'

My mother had completed her term at the Kunika Gallery, established another gallery in the Black Partridge, the Haryana arts and crafts emporium on Baba Kharak Singh Marg, and was ready to do something new. In 1977, both my parents, now in their early fifties, decided to open a gallery together, Art Heritage. And they were lucky to find ideal premises in the basement of Triveni Kala Sangam, right at the heart of the cultural hub of Mandi House. Here in the serene, highly aesthetic building of Joseph Stein and under the benign yet watchful eye of Sundari Shridharani, Triveni's founder-director, they found a perfect location. Along with art and sculpture they chose to include ceramics and photography as well. And to support all their exhibitions with an excellent 'season' catalogue that included specially commissioned articles on each of the artists exhibiting, and often an overview of the season by my father. Years later my father was to write of the gallery: 'Art Heritage is not a "commercial" gallery in the accepted sense of the term. With its well-documented and impeccably presented exhibitions, it seeks to serve the perceptive connoisseur, art historian and serious student of art, whose interests go deeper than passing fads and fashion, into gaining an understanding and appreciation of art that is likely to endure.'

The very first show that opened Art Heritage was of a beautiful collection of antique large urn-like containers in which opium had been shipped to China from Gujarat in the nineteenth century. They were amazing large ceramic containers in shades of ochres and russet browns enlivend with lion-like decorations on some, filigree on others. The patina of age had lent them a certain grace. My mother called upon Koko and me to design the display. Handling these jars, I could sense the ghosts of my grandmother Kulsumbai's ancestors hovering around me. Had any one of these jars actually been filled in Talaja, the family estate, when opium was the most lucrative cash crop? Using bamboos and diffused lighting, Koko and I created a stunning display of the containers that numbered more than eighty.

Over the next thirty years I was called on to display almost all of the ceramic shows at the gallery, from master potter Devi Prasad to ceramic stylist Kristine Michael, from Gouri Khosla's exquisite sculptures to Daroz's stunningly beautiful large-scale doorways and urns, from the classicist B.R. Pandit to his innovative son, Abhay. It was an exciting way to marry my theatrical skills of lighting and design with my fascination for art.

The top artists of the time—M.F. Husain, K.G. Subramanyam,

Tyeb Mehta, Somnath Hore, Akbar Padamsee, Gulam Mohammed Sheikh, Dhruv Mistry, Gieve Patel, Nalini Malani along with several emerging voices, regularly exhibited at the gallery. Several big names like Laxma Goud and Surya Prakash had had their first shows with my mother at Kunika, and now they were in the hands of not one, but two experts in the art scene. They were aware of my parents' first-hand knowledge and experience in handling and projecting contemporary art ever since the late 1940s. Rekha Roddwitiya, a leading artist today and student at the time, recalls her first meeting with my father in London.

'I received this phone call on a public telephone that was in the corridors of the Royal College of Art. I heard this very crisp voice—very to the point—wanting to meet me in my studio. I had no idea of what Mr Alkazi looked like in the pre smartphone and social media era, and was slightly taken aback when I encountered this extremely well-dressed man in a three-piece suit (my father always wore one too), immaculate in manners and with no power games on display. Perhaps there was a mutual comprehension of genuineness of intention, and belief and faith in common grounds, that allowed us to immediately strike up an empathy and forge a connection.

'After five minutes of quiet viewing, Mr Alkazi asked me about my future plans as I was at the end of my post-graduate course. I had turned down a prestigious solo show and was returning to begin my practice as a full-time artist in the city of Baroda. He asked me how much money I would need. I stated a figure to which he replied that Art Heritage would like to extend an offer of a contract (I was never asked to sign any papers ever), providing me the said remuneration for a period of one year. He stated that the gallery would in that same year, host my solo show and recover the stipend from the sales. I must have looked a little alarmed because he clarified that this was a professional dealing that he was entering in with me. What followed was a three-year contract and many solo shows over the years. It provided me the freedom to be a full-time artist and Mr Alkazi personally put in great effort to popularize my art in India and abroad. His faith in me was immense.

'Perhaps what I treasure the most is the care with which he structured his relationship with me, and the dignity he accorded our friendship. He protected me as a young woman artist in ways that I hold most precious. He arranged for me on multiple occasions to stay with Mrs Alkazi at her residence, on my visits to Delhi. Those visits unfolded such unique and beautiful interludes with Mrs Alkazi where she would share her personal time with me on the patch of lawn where we would talk of many things.

'Mr Alkazi taught me so much in those quiet conversations we shared at Triveni over tea and biscuits. He spoke with passion about the values of documentation and archiving—about the need for critical writing, autonomy in the arts, and for artists to hone their communication skills with greater focus. He felt very strongly about quality art education and research about ethical practices that should guide collectors and collections, about the need for collective engagement within the arts, about independent cinema and experimental theatre and greater inter-disciplinary practices, about more opportunities for Indian artists to travel and be exposed to varied cultures...'

Rekha was only one of the many young artists who blossomed under this mentoring by both my parents.

My mother was a seasoned gallerist with over ten years of experience. Young art students would flock to her for encouragement and direction. Visitors to the gallery were often surprised when she would appear at their elbow ready to show them around, make them more comfortable around art. Krishen Khanna described her well: 'Roshen was an extremely gentle, extremely kind, at the same time a very determined person.'

Within five years of setting up the gallery, my father was invited by the Museum of Modern Art (MOMA) in Oxford to curate an exhibition of contemporary Indian art there. His collaborators were the Director of MOMA, Oxford, David Elliot, and old India hand, Victor Musgrave. It was the first major showcasing of Indian art abroad.

About twenty years later, in the 1990s, my father returned to the stage, first directing three productions for the NSD Repertory Company and then establishing a new drama school, Living Theatre, strikingly similar to the one he had run at the Theatre Unit forty years earlier. With the students there he directed nine productions, revisiting three of his favourite scripts— Shakespeare's *Julius Caesar*, Lorca's *The House of Bernada Alla* and Chekhov's *Three Sisters*. He combined these with the premieres of new plays by the reigning playwrights at the time, Girish Karnad's retelling of the poet reformer Basavanna's life in *Rakt Kalyan* and the second part of Mahesh Elkunchwar's *Virasat*. They were perfect textbook productions, mounted with all his attention to detail and my mother's impeccable costuming. But they were plays of another age, an age that had gone by and the new actors couldn't match the well-honed talents of Naseeruddin Shah, Om Puri, Rohini Hattangadi, Uttara Baokar, Surekha Sikri, Manohar Singh and numerous others who had brought his productions to international levels in 1976.

My father divided his time between India and abroad over the next several years. Thirty years had passed since 1947 and in those years he had had minimal contact with his parents and family members. He now plunged into getting to know them all over again. And they embraced him with open arms. His family had a strong tradition of the young men leaving home, going away and making their way in the world, never to return. My grandfather, Ubba, had left Saudi at the age of sixteen to make his fortunes in India, my father's eldest brother, Ali, left at age fifteen and was never heard of again while my father's youngest brother, Basil, only met my father thrice in his lifetime. Similarly my father had kept a distance for thirty years. So his return to the family fold was much celebrated. He was in a way a prodigal son. A prodigal son who had achieved great success and won many laurels in the country he called home: India. He had already been awarded the top civil honours: the Padma Shri, the Padma Bhushan, and he would go on to also be awarded the Padma Vibhushan

Through long-distance phone calls he and my mother chartered the course of the gallery over the next thirty years. Every three or four months, my mother would change into Western clothes at midnight, rather like Cinderella, and leave for Kuwait where they had set up home together. Two of my father's sisters, one of his brothers and several nieces and nephews lived in Kuwait, so it was family time for my parents. They had lunch everyday with my father's sister, Lulu, who lived in the same building, and served as the fulcrum of the family. Members who now lived in Kyoto and Ibiza, London and Saudi, Canada and Turkey, US and India congregated regularly at her table, very much like in my mother's family. The Alkazi family came together as never before and many of my cousins were greatly supported by the liberal mindset of Uncle Ebrahim and Aunt Roshen. If my father said anything was right, it was right and had to be followed. After all he was the eldest brother!

Years later, my parents got trapped in Kuwait during the Iraqi invasion. Amal and I lost contact with them for more than two weeks. Till they arrived back in Delhi, travelling while

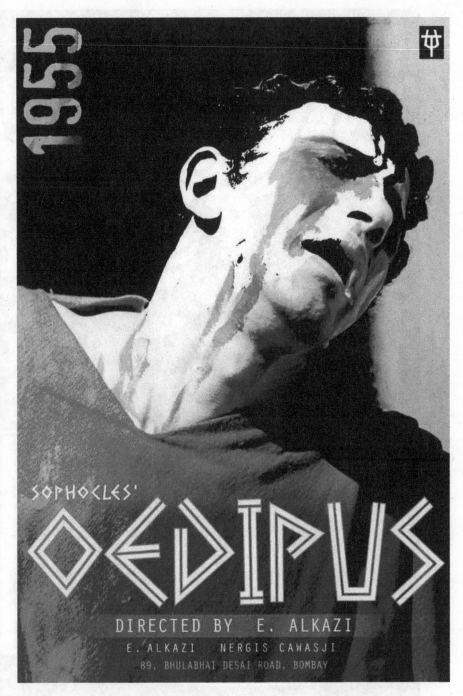

1955

SOPHOCLES'

OEDIPUS

DIRECTED BY   E. ALKAZI

E. ALKAZI   NERGIS CAWASJI
89, BHULABHAI DESAI ROAD, BOMBAY

Poster of *Oedipus Rex*, 1955, with Ebrahim Alkazi in lead role

All images courtesy Alkazi Theatre Archives. All productions on pgs 1-14 directed by

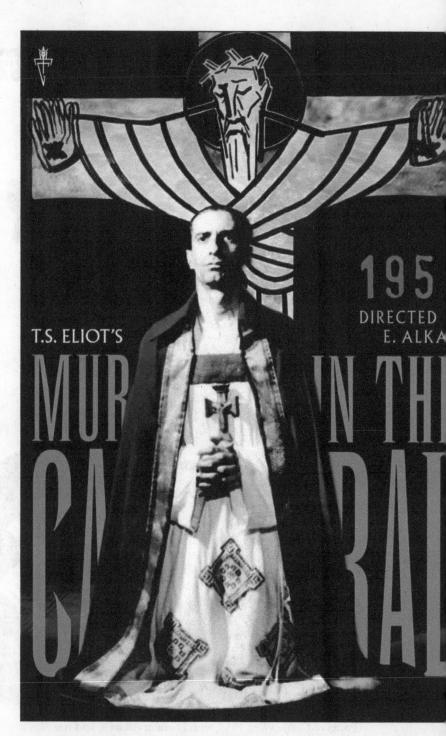

Poster of *Murder in the Cathedral*, 1953, with Minoo Chhoi as Thomas Becket.
Painting in background by M.F. Husain

Scene from Ibsen's *Ghosts* with Usha Amin, Ebrahim Alkazi and Sylvester da Cunha, 1952

Scene from *Oedipus Rex* with Ebrahim Alkazi as Oedipus, 1954

JEAN ANOUIH'S

Antigone

DIRECTED BY E. ALKAZI

Kusum Behl & M.Chitnis

Theatre Unit, School of Dramatic Art
89, Bhulabhai Desai Road, Bombay

1955

Poster of *Antigone*, with Kusum Behl as Antigone, 1955

Scene from *Antigone* with Kusum Behl as Antigone, M. Chitnis as Creon, 1955

Scene from *Eurydice*, 1959, with Kusum Behl as Eurydice and Zul Vellani as Orpheus

Scene from *Macbeth*, 1956, with Ebrahim Alkazi as Macbeth

Scene from
Medea, 1961,
with Usha Amin
as Medea, Kersy
Katrak as Jason,
Feisal Alkazi
as boy

Poster of *Medea*, 1961, with Usha Amin as Medea

Scene from *Eury*
1959

Ebrahim Alkazi as Jean in *Miss Julie* (above), and (right) Alaknanda Samarth as Miss Juli

Scene from *Hedda Gabler*, 1958, with Hima Devi as Hedda Gabler

Scene f
Yerma,
with U
Amin a
Yerma

Scene from *Tartuffe*, 1960, with
Ebrahim Alkazi as Tartuffe

Scene from *Andha Yug*, 1963, w
Meena Pethe as Gandhari

Scene from *King Lear*, 1964, with Anjali Chitnis as Regan and
Meena Williams as Goneril

Scene from *King Lear* with Om Shivpuri as King Lear

Scene from *Tughlaq* by Girish Karnad, 1972, with Manohar Singh as Tughlaq

Scene from *Sultan Razia*, 1974, with Rohini Hattangadi as Razia and Naseeruddin Shah as Jamaluddin Yakut

Scene from *Tughlaq*, 1972, with Manohar Singh as Tughlaq and Uttara Baokar as stepmother

Zohra Sehgal as Birjees in
Din ke Andhere Mein, 1992

Swaroopa Ghosh as Aai in
Virasat 1 and II, 1992

Seema Biswas as Mumtaz in *Din ke Andhere Mein*, 1992

Feisal Alkazi and Mona Chawla in *A Month in the Country*, 1982

Walter Peter and Seema Diwan with baby Mowgli in
Yeh Bhi Jungle, Woh Bhi Jungle, 1997

All productions on pgs 15-16 directed by Feisal Alkazi

Armaan Alkazi and Nandini Sra in *A Qu*
Desire, 2013 (left); Keshav Anand and She
Italia in *The Crucible*, 1987 (top, right), a
(below) Radhika Alkazi and Sanjiv Desai
Goodbye Forever, 2013

sitting on the floor in a cargo plane, the only Indian flight that left Kuwait thanks to I.K. Gujral. On the actual night of the invasion my mother had got up at two a.m. to write a poem that had formed in her mind, uncannily about being trapped.

Certainly my parents shared a completely unique relationship. For the first fourteen years of their marriage they had grown together, educated themselves, built their reputations and created a family. In the next fourteen years, after my father's move to Delhi, their relationship showed signs of strain though my mother doggedly and very bravely soldiered on, working alongside my father as costume designer for all his plays at NSD. Once he resigned, she proved to be the backbone of the family, establishing Art Heritage along with him and restoring some semblance of a home together in Kuwait.

Three journeys I made in my undergrad days to different corners of India really excited me and created a wanderlust. In the very first year of college I travelled with five of my friends and a driver, so seven of us squeezed into an Ambassador car to Pushkar in Rajasthan. Rajeev and Tani, Yusuf and his fiancèe Fatima, Aseem Chabra and I explored the completely rural cattle fair over three days. This was long before Pushkar became a tourist destination. Milling crowds of tall moustachioed Rajasthani men with their camels on sale, dressed entirely in white but with colourful turbans accompanied by large groups of dazzlingly dressed Rajasthani women. The evening entertainments were truly rustic—powerful voices rose in song, the rhythm provided by unusual instruments, the khadtaal, the ektara, the jews harp, the surnai...

The very next year I travelled with my father, Uma and the wonderful actor Manohar Singh, who played Tughlaq in my father's production, on a road trip across Himachal Pradesh, culminating at the Dussera Mela in Kulu. I watched entranced as processions of men high on bhang made their way down the steep mountain paths carrying their local deities in palanquins to participate in a massive Rath Yatra in Kulu. Musicians playing long trumpets and S-shaped harsinghas led the processions.

And in one of my Christmas breaks, my parents, Nissar, Amal and I went to spend a week in Goa renting a room in a fisherman's house on the Colva beach. Again, this was years before this beach with its white sand became an international tourist destination. Our stay was really basic, without any frills. My mother cooked in clay utensils over an open wood stove. We slept on the floor. And there was no toilet! So every morning each family member by turn would disappear into the nearby forest, armed with a lota and a stick to keep the eager pigs away.

Rajasthan, Himachal Pradesh, Goa, a peep into the diversity of India. The beginnings of an understanding of our rich rural traditions and a life far from the cities I knew. Each one of those trips was a breakaway from the regular and now even monotonous up-down of Bombay-Delhi. Over the next few years I travelled with my friends to Belur, Halebidu, Shravanbelgola, Ajanta, Ellora, Ajmer, Jaipur, Kolkata, Mussoorie, Shimla and even Bhutan.

My horizons were opening up to an Indian reality way beyond and completely different to what I was familiar with. I decided that in the future my career must include regular travel and working with people in different parts of our country. And luckily that has been possible as I have worked for over thirty years in Jaipur, for a month every year, I have been in and out of Srinagar over seven years and in Chennai, three-month-long projects have drawn me to the city. Bangalore, Hyderabad, Guwahati, Thiruvananthapuram, Mumbai, Pune, Kolkata, Dehradun, Chandigarh, Leh are other places that I have enjoyed working, everywhere with the local population.

One particular image lingers in my mind from a trip to the Chisti dargah in Ajmer with my mother and my cousin Alexander in the late 1980s. We were staying in the vicinity of the dargah in the house of one of the khadims. Every morning a huge cauldron of kheer would be ready. This kheer had been paid for by a believer who had returned to the dargah to make a shukrana, a thanksgiving visit, because his mannat (wish) had come true. This was the traditional way of thanking the Sufi saint. We could witness at dawn the ceremony by which it would be distributed across the city. The degchi in which it was cooked was at least fifteen feet wide, a gift from Emperor Jahangir.

It was an amazing sight to look down into this huge cauldron at sunrise, the kheer having slowly cooked through the night. It was daybreak, and the kheer was still steaming, vapour rising from its yellow surface as it had been flavoured with saffron. As the sun slowly emerged, twelve men, their bodies bandaged from head to foot, entered this steaming liquid and passed it out in a bucket relay! It was then distributed through the city, available at every crossroads.

A truly medieval sight that set my heart racing. I felt I had stepped back several centuries. There was so much more to discover.

Nineteen

A Theatre of Questioning and Dissent

The phone rang early one morning. The voice at the other end was well spoken, authoritative and deep. 'This is L.K. Advani, has one of your productions been banned by the government? Can you give me the details, I want to bring it up in Parliament this morning.'

Dissent and questioning the powers that be have always been an essential part of the theatrewallah's *raison d'etre*. And perhaps in the case of Ruchika, even more so, as we have never shied away from controversial subjects.

The play in question was I.S. Johar's *Bhutto*, dramatized from the book by Pran Chopra, *If I Am Assassinated*, and directed by Arun Kuckreja. The play depicts Bhutto's last hours before his assassination and the villain of the piece is General Zia ul Haq. As Zia was to visit Delhi coincidently on the day we were staging it, the Congress government got cold feet and tried to ban its performance. We were not ones to step down without a fight and so we appealed. Reading through the script in the open court, the judge ruled against us.

We decided to go ahead with the dress rehearsal of the production and informed the press of what had happened. Aware of the judgement and the consequences they would have to face, the hall authorities locked the auditorium doors, so we sneaked the press in up the back stairs and they watched from the wings. The next day this incident made headlines, and we were happy and vindicated.

Something similar happened to us during the Emergency years. Two of my productions for Ruchika came to a shuddering stop after the opening performances. The police arrived and suggested that we do no more shows at that time.

Slawomir Mrozek's *Striptease* in a Hindi translation shows us two suited men locked in a room receiving and carrying out the orders from a female hand, even as they mouth sentiments of being free. They are forced to undress, dunce caps are placed on their heads, they are handcuffed together, and are finally seen walking towards their own death. The play was staged two days after the Emergency was declared and at a time when the 'hand' had just become the Congress election symbol!

Eugene Ionesco's *Rhinoceros* is the classic allegory about the crowd morphing into rhinoceroses as their ideology changes. It was originally written as a comment on those French who had sided with the Nazi's during the occupation of France in World War II. The message of the play in the Emergency years was clear.

For the very first Women's Day rally in the capital in 1980, I was coopted at the last minute to direct a street play with my Ruchika actors on the Mathura rape case. A young woman's rape while in custody and the subsequent release of the two policemen guilty of raping her was the trigger. The girl's name was Mathura.

Working swiftly, as we were short of time, we created a powerful street play, *Balaatkaar*, performing thirteen shows in seven days, including one show on the pavement outside the Supreme Court. It was among the pressure points that attracted media attention and resulted in more stringent anti-rape laws being passed.

Another street play, *Roshni*, that I worked on with the Manushi Collective, explored the socialization of a young woman from birth to the time she protests against being forced into an arranged marriage. With an all-woman cast and a delightful set of sardonic songs, it was both a crowd pleaser and still very provocative.

It went on to be performed over 100 times and was subsequently published by Manushi and received productions all over India. Interestingly, the main actress in my production, Prabha, had witnessed my first street play, *Balaatkaar*, from her balcony window several years earlier. An amazing coincidence.

In more recent times, *The Diary of Anne Frank*, *The Women*, *Attempts on Her Life*, *Fatal Accidents of Birth*, *The Dark Road*, *Love in a Time of Oppression* and Charles Dickens' *A Tale of Two Cities* have explored different facets of international oppression and the need for a voice, even a single voice of protest to rise against the tide, to bear witness and be heard.

The Diary of Anne Frank was the last play I directed in the last millennium and in my Director's Note I optimistically wrote that I hoped all such oppression wouldn't travel with us into the twenty-first century. How wrong I was. Exploring a similar theme was the true story of a young Hungarian girl, Magda, in *Love in a Time of Oppression*. She travelled alone across Nazi-Europe in the 1940s to pick up a forged travel document for her lover, who was Jewish.

The Women by Ariel Dorfman, originally known as *Widows*, narrates the true-life stories of thousands of Chilean women during the horrific years of the Pinochet regime, where entire villages were left without fathers, husbands or sons. In the play they rise in revolt against the regime.

On the night before the premiere of this production I was invited to talk about the play on NDTV's ten p.m. show.

Pinochet had been arrested that very day in the UK and would soon be extradited to face trial in Chile. Our play was amazingly timely. The montage of this news item featured the women who led the agitation against him. I was speechless, disturbed. Here were the women about whom Ariel Dorfman had written. The reality of the events of the play struck me for the first time. In describing this to the cast the next day while giving them a 'pep talk' just before the show, I broke down and wept. There was suddenly an onerous responsibility placed on our shoulders to do justice to these women, it was this fact that had overwhelmed me.

The Dark Road was dramatized by me from a powerful novel by the Chinese dissident author, Ma Jian. From 1980 to 2015, for over thirty-five years, China implemented its one-child policy where 'family planning refugees' would flee the big towns, often living on small boats on the polluted Yangtze. Moving constantly, they were afraid of being caught by officials who would inject distemper into the pregnant woman's uterus to abort the second or third child. Once aborted, the foetus could not even be buried but was incinerated. Horrific, but true. My hour-long play in my characteristic style of actors performing their roles and also narrating, in third person, their own stories, was a dramatization of just one section of the nightmarish novel's 'storyline'.

Interestingly, in so many of the plays I have described above, the central character is a woman and it is she who leads the movement for change and to establish justice once again, whatever part of the world she may belong to: Germany or Hungary, Chile or China or India. I truly believe that when change comes to the world, it will be spearheaded by women, not men.

Several decades earlier I was witness to one of the first collective protests by artists against communal violence. I vividly remember one particular night, after the communal riots in

Ahmedabad in 1969. My mother and I along with Tyeb, Sakina and Yusuf were at a show of a French new wave film at the DAVP auditorium at ITO. The Delhi Film Society, begun by Vijaya Mulay, regularly screened outstanding films every month and my introduction to Bergman, Kurosawa and Satyajit Ray began here.

On the screen a handwritten slide appeared that for those who needed to know, the Lalit Kala Akademi was allowing the artists an all-night vigil at their galleries at Rabindra Bhavan. We rushed out, abandoning the cinema classic, to help mould our own history.

When we arrived at the LK galleries, the first-floor space was electric, with artists furiously working on the spot, putting paint to canvas to mount a show by the following evening. This was to raise money for the riot victims. I recall Husain with his three-feet long brush as he created an iconic image on the waiting empty canvas. I remember the young intense Ramachandran painting an elongated figure of Gandhi splattered with blood.

Over the next years and decades, and culminating in Sahmat (1990) and Artists Unite Against Hatred (2015), the visual artist has always raised his voice (and often had it silenced) against the Indian state. Many artists have boldly questioned the powers that be in their work. In the 1970s, at the art gallery run by my mother, Kunika, Krishen Khanna's large canvases in ochres, reds and blacks capturing the death of Che Guevara with a gaggle of generals grouped around a table was as much an iconic image of the period, as were Vivan Sundaram's strange abstractions of Indira Gandhi's face. In the late 1980s he also created haunting images of the 1984 violence against Sikhs in the capital. The serene landscapes with peasants working and celebrating in a quasi Soviet style that many artists had churned out soon after Independence had turned into the disgruntled industrial workers of Gieve Patel's and Sudhir Patwardhan's work by the mid 80s.

Twenty

Engaging with the Violence of Our Times

Sitting on the rooftop of the Nanaksar Gurudwara in east Delhi, I surveyed the scene around me. It was as though I was at a refugee camp just after Partition. Except that it was November 1984, days after the terrible violence that erupted across Delhi against the Sikh community following the assassination of Indira Gandhi.

Families were devastated, their household objects, whatever they had been able to salvage, lay in piles around them, scattered on durries spread across the vast terrace. I and the entire staff of Ankur, the NGO that I headed at the time, got to work with these victims of violence, some of us consoling older members, organizing group activities for the children, distributing food, while others sat hearing stories, writing FIRs. The testimonies we were recording were deeply disturbing. Many men had been pulled out of their homes, burning tyres placed around their necks and left to die. Several women had had rapes as horrific as that of Nirbhaya years later. Family members had been witness to all of this violence. It was a time of extreme trauma.

The news of the prime minister's assassination on 31 October 1984 had come by lunchtime from Lalaji who ran the local tea shop. I gathered the staff of Ankur together and told them to get home as soon as possible. 'There will be riots, worse than Partition,' were my prophetic words, 'Don't come to the office till we ring you.'

An eerie silence engulfed the city that evening and for the next two days. Our Sikh neighbours smashed their own nameplates, scared of being targeted, the Sardar-run taxi stand in our colony was burnt and neighbourhood watch committees came up at night in Greater Kailash II, where we were then living. And then news of what was happening to poor Sikh families began to trickle in.

All of us volunteers were part of a group of citizens who had spontaneously come together as Nagrik Ekta Manch. It was an ecletic group: artists and theatre workers, activitists and college students, business people and housewives. Over the next thirty years I would see many of these faces repeatedly, even if I didn't know their names, at rallies and marches celebrating Safdar Hashmi, against communal violence, for gender justice. In 1984 we had come together to reach out to those affected while the government stood by, a passive spectator. Delhi was almost a ghost city as we drove through it every morning, smoke and flames billowing across the sky.

Some of the volunteers with Nagrik Ekta Manch refused to sign the FIRs, worried that they would jeopardize their subsequent careers. The fault lines in the intelligentsia were already beginning to show.

Many of the activists of the late 1970s and 80s had emerged during the crucible of the Emergency. Among the several women who linked hands with me to establish Ankur in 1980 were Pramila Lewis, the first to be arrested in the Emergency, and the formidable gender activist and spokesperson, Kamla Bhasin.

Through the following decades as we rooted ourselves

in gender and environmental issues, the numbers grew, even though much of the core remained. 'Narmada Bachao' was as much a rallying point as was the murder of Safdar Hashmi, the demolition of Babri Masjid and more recently, the outburst of anger against the Nirbhaya case. Though we often meet and despair about our dark times, the fact that the young of today have rallied and are seeking to build a new India on their own terms is a vindication of what we fought for, stood for and represented. 'Raasta hai lamba, bhai, manzil hai door' was a song we often sang and that still resonates for all of us.

1984 was only one of my brushes with victims of violence. Years later, from 2004 to 2011, I worked with a group of young people in Srinagar whose fathers had been killed by terrorists. I remember how alarmed I was on my first night in Kashmir when the Zabarwan mountains that surround the city reverberated with the sound of machine gun fire. Every night it was the same, while in the day Srinagar had barricades and soldiers hidden behind sandbags every kilometre. But surprisingly over the next seven years as I returned repeatedly to work in Kashmir, I got used to it. The major part of my work in the Valley was in promoting resilience.

It is amazing how quickly we, as human beings, adjust to the 'new normal' whether it is violence or lynching, pollution or the wearing of masks outdoors or using air filters at home. We begin to skip over those pages in the newspaper that make us uncomfortable or withdraw from news-watching altogether. Many of my friends are happy leading this ostrich-like existence, insulated from the world by air conditioning and spending the day with the diversions of Netflix. Reality is kept at arm's distance.

In recent years as the levels of violence escalate across the world, the idea of resilence has gained prominence in the professional social work field. It is used to describe a child or adult who is able to cope with extremely difficult life circumstances, whether on the street, in the orphanage or on the battleground of Kashmir. A child who can rise above adversity is called resilient.

There is much said about the negative consequences of abusive care or severe material deprivation. And yet many 'victims' do well despite early childhood trauma. So the question for a social worker is: how do some succeed despite their circumstances? What learnings can be extrapolated from their stories?

If we think of a person's development as moving down a path, what happens next is certainly influenced but not solely determined by what happened earlier. People are never passive bystanders in the process of their own development. Resilence is an outcome of access to supportive and protective services.

Change can come at the most basic level through supportive relationships. In daily life each one of us plays a variety of social roles, wears a number of different hats. Meeting for a family lunch, playing football with friends, rehearsing for a play, building something together... Reciprocity, routine and ritual all help to keep people together. Every individual needs a secure base that can console us at a time of distress. To go beyond being an 'orphan at risk', the person needs to excel or just be involved in any activity or role. Every relationship is a reflection of caring and love and results in a boost of self-worth.

Mental health professionals suggest that the wider the range of social roles we play, the better is our mental health. Aren't we all brothers and children, cousins and uncles, friends and colleagues?

Over the past twenty-five years, it is the Kashmir valley that has experienced some of the worst violence the world has ever seen. Kidnapping, rape, arson and of course bombing has turned the garden paradise into a living hell. In such a setting where geography and history combined to produce a rich tapestry of a syncretic culture born of myriad influences, what role can and must education play? How do we bring the pluralistic past alive to the young child who has grown up in an atmosphere of increasing violence and fundamentalism? How do we generate values of tolerance and non-violence in a generation starved of peace in their lives?

With this in mind, Creative Learning for Change, an NGO in Delhi I headed, designed an in-depth educational programme reiterating and reinforcing the vitality of 'Kashmiriyat' and of living in a part of India proud of its own past. We covered topics such as the history, heritage, the natural beauty, crafts and the culture of Srinagar. The project was designed as a child-centred experiential learning experience, participative and workshop-oriented. Its final outcome was a well attended exhibition and finally eighteen months later, a publication.

In yet another tragic episode, I accompanied my uncle Alyque Padamsee on a hair-raising trip to a small village near Ganga Nagar in Rajasthan. Just a few days earlier a young Dalit Sardar boy had stolen ten paisa from the local temple. The upper-caste men of the village gathered together as a lynch mob, stripped his mother naked, covered her with black paint and paraded her through the village on a donkey before beating her to death. The village watched, silent. It sounded like it was almost out of the medieval period except that this happened in Rajasthan in the opening years of this century—barbaric, callous, inhuman. Incensed by a tiny news item he read in the paper, Alyque decided to seek justice from Bhairon Singh Shekhawat, the then chief minister of Rajasthan. I accompanied him on this mission. We first visited the family in the silent aggressive village and then got them to accompany us to the CM who promised to place the two children in a residential school at the state's expense and also help the father in his search for justice.

My Masters in Social Work programme in Delhi University (1977–79) brought me in touch with many aspects of an Indian reality that my early years in south Bombay and in south Delhi had hidden away from me. It is easy in our country to live one's entire life immune to the lives of others. And that is a shame and perhaps even a disgrace.

Dealing with the extreme poor whom Indira Gandhi had just moved out of slums in Delhi to resettlement colonies on its outskirts in the Emergency years was a revelation. Stable lives, safe occupations, livelihoods a walk away from your residence had all been disrupted forever by an executive fiat. People's lives were fractured and I witnessed even more fracturing and the bitterness and despair that goes with it over my many years in the practice of professional social work.

I have never shied away from the seedier parts of our society and the violence that increasingly engulfs the world around us. I feel it is essential to get out there and do something, engage in a real way with the injustice we see and try to make a difference, however small it may be. 'Silence is complicity,' said Mahasweta Devi, and I believe she was completely right.

My own work as a counsellor at Sanjivini, a walk-in counselling centre, for over thirty-five years, has brought me in touch with the other violence of our lives: emotional violence and the toll it takes on many. Individuals turn to Sanjivini because of the lack of support that they have grown up with and as a result they lack the tools to comprehend how to get over the damage they have experienced in their lives. Sanjivini is a great mirror to our times. Over almost four decades the changing fabric and issues of our society are constantly reflected here, from the distraught parents of the dowry death victims of the 1980s to the selfie-

and Tinder-obsessed generation of today. Working intensively with individuals over a period of months, walking along with them in their attempts to understand and better cope with childhood trauma, sexuality, relationship issues, drug and alcohol dependence and even attempted suicide is always challenging. Just 'being there' for someone as a counsellor, being completely non-judgmental and accepting makes all the difference as people feel they are being heard for the first time.

For a period of five years, starting in 2002, I was also a Master Trainer in HIV/AIDS prevention work for the United Nations system. Travelling across India, to train groups as diverse as commercial sex workers, AIDS activists and hospital personnel was a rich learning experience. It was a window into a world unknown to me. We have yet to comprehend the many layers of sexual contact and sexuality in our country and working on this project started me on a journey. The tremendous violence and exploitation both female and male sex workers are subjected to and the courage and determination that NGOs display in dealing with issues of stigmatization, advocacy and support is amazing. Anjali Gopalan of NAZ India was inspirational and became a close friend. Other grassroots organizations, VAMP (Vaishya Aids Mukti Parishad) and Sangama, fill me with optimism.

Many years later in the 1990s, my wife Radhika's passionate involvement in making the world a better place for children and adults with special needs has also had a huge impact on me. It has been a humbling process working with severely disabled people as they struggle to reach out to the world around them. And to find acceptance. Over the course of directing thirty documentaries and producing five plays with people with disabilities, I have often wondered—what is normal? Who is able-bodied? Of course all of these experiences have found an immediate echo in my theatre work.

Twenty-one

Theatre at Another Turning Point

I remember the theatre activist Safdar Hashmi clearly, sitting on his own occasionally, but most often surrounded by a group of his friends in the Sri Ram Centre canteen. Lanky, bespectacled, charismatic with a lopsided grin, writing furiously on a paper, brushing his hair out of his eyes. Safdar had a tremendous ability with words, bringing language to life with a turn of a phrase, rhyming verse, pointed metaphor. He was to become an icon of street theatre in India.

Sri Ram Centre was still a new institution in the 1980s, barely ten years old. This one-of-a-kind concrete monolith rose above the cultural hub of Mandi House. It had two separate performing spaces, a proscenium theatre and a 'black box' basement theatre. And an excellent Hindi theatre bookshop and cafe which served delectable parathas, mint chutney and other delicacies. Much of Delhi's theatre crowd gathered here on a daily basis: N.K. Sharma, M.K. Raina, the recently established group of ex-NSD students, Sambhav, and we ourselves, members of Ruchika Theatre Group. We virtually colonized the SRC basement theatre for over fourteen years with our frequent productions. The space was eminently affordable, we could accommodate approximately eighty to a hundred people (the perfect size of an audience) and the empty space lent itself to experimentation. Chai and cigarettes in a rehearsal break was de rigeur and that's how many of us met. Conversations flowed easily between the tables in the cafe.

The draconian Emergency of the 1970s and the horrific pogrom against the Sikhs in 1984 brought many theatre workers together, conscious of the need to loudly voice our protest, dissent and rising concern on the failure of the State to deliver, though it was very sucessful at stifling dissent.

Regular proscenium theatre in Delhi was largely out of sync with social concerns at the time. The focus on using folk elements in urban theatre had started and for many theatre workers this trend towards the 'folk' was seen as being regressive. A completely new middle-class audience was flocking to see comedies in Punjabi at Sapru House, full of sexual innuendo. Similarly in Mumbai, commercial theatre in Marathi, Gujarati and English held sway, with a limited experimental theatre movement in Marathi and Hindi often working out of new and more affordable performance spaces.

It was at this time in Delhi that street theatre emerged as a form. With almost no investment of money and rounding up audiences in public spaces with the loud beating of a drum, short pithy hard-hitting scripts began to be performed in several mohallas across the city. They centered on the issues of the day. While some groups like Theatre Union with Anuradha Kapoor, Maya Rao and Manohar Khushalani among others were articulating their voices against dowry and dowry deaths, others like Safdar and Jan Natya Manch (Janam) produced plays in solidarity with workers, reflecting their concerns.

Jan Natya Manch had been created by a group of young people barely out of college in April 1973, who had literally been thrown out of the IPTA office in Shankar Market because they were seen as being too subversive.

After the Janata Party replaced the Congress post the Emergency, Janam was already into creating street theatre. Within days their iconic script, *Machine,* came to be written and performed.

The background of their work was an indepth understanding of the reality of workers' lives and their issues, even as they articulated the CPI and CPI(M) party position.

Dressed in black kurtas worn over jeans, a small tight cast of ten or twelve enacted various characters: a cop, a worker, all played in broad strokes. Choreographed action led to dramatic stage pictures performed with an audience on all sides. The comical banter between street magician (madari) and his assistant (jamura) was a device often used in the Janam plays.

Twenty-two other original plays emerged over the next ten years, each of them a valid experiment in form and content. Many of these were written by Safdar. He exemplified a new force in Indian theatre: young, idealistic, committed to expressing the truth of our times in a completely new performance space, the street.

And then this talented young man was killed on the first day of 1989, when he was only thirty-four. The government in power at the time strongly objected to the content of his plays and used goons to kill Safdar. His death resulted in a public outcry and the establishment of Sahmat (Safdar Hashmi Memorial Trust) which for over twenty-five years has brought together like-minded people from across India to celebrate Safdar's life and legacy.

Another playwright who captured our tortured times and shot into prominence in the same period was Marathi playwright Mahesh Elkunchwar. I recall seeing Satyadev Dubey's production of *Aarakt Khsan* by Mahesh in a Hindi translation at Chhabildas in Mumbai in 1978. Dubey was now leading the Theatre Unit and went on to direct over a hundred plays in his long career.

Just as Janam had moved out of the proscenium and into the street, Chhabildas was an attempt to move theatre out of a formal auditorium and into the midst of the audience. Both the form and content of theatre changed automatically.

Situated in one of the most middle-class crowded areas of Bombay-Dadar, overlooking a congested bridge on one side, and a market on the other, the Chhabildas theatre had no green rooms, no toilet facilities and poor acoustics.

As Vijay Tendulkar said, the audience psychology in this kind of intimate theatre as against a red-seated, air-conditioned auditorium, was congenial to the kinds of plays done there.

When the Marathi group, Rangayan, split in 1972, a new group, Awishkar, was started by Arvind and Sulabha Deshpande, Vijay Tendulkar and others. In 1974 they rented Chhabildas to stage their plays and hold rehearsals. Soon they opened their doors to everyone. For over a decade this makeshift theatre, a part of the 'General Education Society's Chhabildas Lallubhai High School for Boys', was the epicenter of experimental Marathi and Hindi theatre. The number of amateur groups in Mumbai surged from twelve to fifty between 1974 and 1978.

Aarakt Kshan (or *Rakt Pushp*, Mahesh's original title) explores the loneliness of a married woman and had four powerhouse performances. Mahesh's earlier plays on callous college brutality in *Holi* and incest in *Vasankand* had already showcased his talent. But his best was yet to come.

I remember the premiere production of *Wada Chirebandi* in Mumbai in the mid 1980s with Vijaya Mehta (who also directed it) in one of the key roles. She played Aai, the powerless matriarch around whom four generations of the Deshpande family disintegrate. It was a turning point in Marathi theatre, and Elkunchwar replaced Vijay Tendulkar as the reigning playwright. He followed this play with another two plays focusing on the travails of this family. Few plays have captured the swift decline of rural India since the 1970s better than this trilogy by Mahesh Elkunchwar.

Over the years several stellar directors have attempted these scripts: my father, Satyadev Dubey, Shyamanand Jalan and more recently, Anuradha Kapoor, who directed the entire trilogy for the NSD Repertory Company.

Vijaya, as the long-suffering mother of a Brahmin family, sat centre stage throughout the two-hour play as the story of her four children and their ancestral homestead unfolded around her. Her eldest son Bhasker has stayed on in the village, not done too well and is married to a traditional wife, while his younger brother Sudhir has moved away to Bombay and is married to the upwardly mobile Anjali. The third child, a daughter, Prabha, yearns for an independence she can never attain, and finally there is Chandu, constantly ignored, physically injured, always at the receiving end.

While in the first play the siblings come together after their father's death, the second one opens with the outsiders from Mumbai returning for their nephew Parag's wedding. A sour and immoral young man, resentful of never having been taken to Mumbai by his uncle Sudhir, Parag is rebellious and arrogant. Abhay, his cousin, has migrated to America and though he achieves material success, feels empty and disillusioned by the end of the trilogy. Ranju, Parag's sister, longs for the glamour of the Bombay film world, and finally runs away but is brought back to the village. Parag's wife, strong-willed Nandini, emerges as the contemporary Indian woman willing even to accept her husband's affair with a widow in the village. Gradually she turns into the fulcrum of the family.

Four generations in the throes of change, ten characters battling with it, living in an old crumbling mansion. In the last part of the trilogy the village has turned into a barren desert. In fact, it is nearly non-existent. Dead carcasses of animals, the wait for the water tanker, no water even for the last rites of the dead. Only four characters remain. Abhay returns from Sweden on the occasion of the death of Aai. Parag returns from Kashi, bringing Chandu, who he has seen standing in a row of beggars in Kashi, for 'the house belongs to him too'. Even in such dire circumstances, human values still prevail. The rest is a desert.

In Elkunchwar's own words, 'This play is about the inner space of these four characters. At one level, it is about the devastation unleashed by us and of the resultant barren desert—a desert of the spiritual, political, social, environmental, and all other kinds, and also the devastation of the four people caught in it.'

There is no criticism in Mahesh's gaze—no attempt at satire, no attempt to put the playwright's viewpoint into the mouth of one of the characters. In play after play, Mahesh strips bare different aspects of contemporary reality. One such script is *Dharmaputra* in which he deals with the theme of child abuse.

This play, that I directed in 2002, portrays the horrifying contemporary reality in which over-anxious parents caught between traditional expectations and modern pop-psychology brutalize, terrorize and finally sacrifice their child.

Mahesh plays with language and imagery: the two times table, can two threes really be seven? Is maths a certainty? Can language be honestly used to communicate? Is psychology an exact science? Are there no limits to love?

'What happens if you misread,' the woman asks early in the play, 'misread a book, a situation, a life...' and the answer, 'God punishes you, yes, God punishes you.' Not a benevolent, caring god—but a malevolent one, looking for retribution, wanting to punish, to teach a lesson.

As man and woman exchange roles in the play each playing the child by turn, Mahesh takes them through the posture of parenting: over-concerned, over-anxious, overbearing. The child's expression, his attempt to grow free as a tree is questioned, as is his exploration of his own body, his sexuality. 'Take your hands out of your pocket. That's filthy, I was told right in my childhood. God punishes this. Vulgar, filthy. That is all you ever have on your mind!'

The tremendous repression of sexual desire, the violence and manipulation in relationships, the recourse to pop psychology and science as saviours, the use of emotional blackmail and guilt as weapons in the Indian family... this is the territory Mahesh explores in *Dharmaputra*. In our world children are cheap, they are malleable, they have no rights and therefore no power.

English theatre also went through a radical change in the 1970s and 80s, looking to express Indian themes and preoccupations, though the language of performance was English. The age of Indian actors playing British or American characters called Tom or Mary in artificial accents in a box set was coming to an end.

It was in 1970 that Alyque directed Girish Karnad's *Tughlaq* in English with Kabir Bedi in the lead role. This production opened with the well-built Kabir in a scant loincloth with his back to the audience, dressing, transforming himself from Tughlaq the man to become Tughlaq, the king. It was the first of many Indian English plays that Alyque was to direct, including Gurucharan Das' revolutionary *Meera*, Tendulkar's *Gidhade*, Mahesh Dattani's *Final Solutions* and *Tara* and several others. English theatre on Indian themes by our own playwrights had finally arrived on the main stage.

In the same decade, Alyque directed India's first rock opera, *Jesus Christ Superstar* which ran for several shows and created several 'stars'. He followed this musical with *Cabaret, Man of La*

Mancha, and of course *Evita*. Each production was as much a comment on the prevailing political reality as it was a wonderful piece of musical theatre. Sharon Prabhakar, who went on to marry Alyque, starred in many of these musicals.

But that was only one side of the coin. In the same decade he brought us an outstanding production of Harold Pinter's Comedy of Menace, *The Birthday Party*. Here was theatre stripped to the basics, presented to an audience of less than thirty-five each evening and showcasing outstanding performances in a haunting Theatre of the Absurd piece. I sat rivetted, literally sitting with my back to the wall, as I watched the dress rehearsal in my grandparents' home, Kulsum Terrace, where the play was performed every evening for over a month. Vijay Krishna, Bomi Kapadia, Homi Daruwalla were in the cast and were to appear in many of Alyque's productions over the years, along with the other regulars, Sabira Merchant, Gerson da Cunha and Farrokh Mehta.

Arthur Miller, who reaches out to squeeze the audience's conscience in every play, was an all-time favourite of Alyque's. *The Crucible*, *All My Sons* (in English and Hindi) and *A View from the Bridge* were directed by him and every ten years he would bring back *Death of a Salesman* with himself in the lead role and a revamped cast. The tragic figure of a lean and tall Alyque bowed down, a suitcase grasped in each hand, remains the lasting image as he played Willy Loman in every production of the classic.

This particular script touches a raw nerve whenever it is performed as it narrates the travails of an ageing door-to-door salesman and his wife and two sons. That it was originally written and staged in the 1950s becomes irrelevant as the theme is universal and timeless.

But to other classics like *Romeo and Juliet* and *Julius Caesar*,

Alyque gave a contemporary twist. Luke Kenny of MTV played an energetic Mercutio in one, while Usha Katrak played Caesar in the other, almost like Indira Gandhi.

Making English theatre accessible, popular and relevant to middle-class audiences as Bombay metamorphosed into Mumbai was Alyque's lasting contribution. He could with ease create compelling contemporary pieces as he could reinterpret the classics. Working on an intimate scale and also on largescale flamboyant productions were both a part of his audience appeal.

Safdar Hashmi, Mahesh Elkunchwar, Alyque Padamsee: three individuals who widened the scope, subject matter and audience for theatre in the 1970s and 1980s ensuring that it would never again look the same.

Twenty-two

Different Ways of Discovering

Seventeen young people in the their late teens lie fast asleep in various postures on the large carpet in our drawing room. Some are curled up into a foetal position, others sleep with their limbs thrown out, almost kicking their sleeping companions. First-time moustaches, tousled hair, open mouths, gentle snoring all capture the abandon of youth.

It was in this way that a bunch of very talented young people grew up, virtually in my house, for almost all of ten years. They were a part of the Music Theatre Workshop (MTW), a wonderful young people's performance company started by Barry John, my mentor, along with the talented musical composer, Param Vir. In 1982 Barry handed over the mantle of the drama part of the work to me, and along with Param Vir, I moulded its growth over the next six years.

The plays we presented were usually created by the members themselves and went through an amazing scripting process. Dissension, debate, improvisation, heated late-night discussion and extensive rewriting and reworking were intrinsic to the process. For us the process was certainly as important as the product.

Besura Desh (1982) is a parable set in an imaginary country where the concept of harmony between nature and man, between one man and another, does not exist. It depicts a society where the rich and the powerful live on top of the sewer pipes in which the poor live, and environmental destruction is around the corner. The plot follows the exciting adventures of two street performers who decide that the time is ripe for change. They plunge into conflict with the ruling class, leading to their imprisonment and finally to a winsome alliance with the people of the forest to restore harmony.

Rehearsals always brought new experiences—meeting people involved in the Chipko movement (an ecological movement in the Himalayas), experimenting with new skills in mime, dance and singing, discussing the tribal lifestyle with social anthropologists, creating poetry out of traffic noise, viewing films on ecology, imagining themselves imprisoned for years on end, designing a set made of sewage pipes, listening to the sound patterns on a construction site, hunting out literature dealing with the issue of exploitation, and finally blending all of this into a musical that was truly their own.

Fallout (1983) told the story of the building of a nuclear bomb by a modern-day Abhimanyu. In the process of doing so he faces the same dilemma that his namesake from the Mahabharat had faced aeons earlier. All the events in the play, from the finding of a U234 container in a junkyard to the building of a bomb by a seventeen-year-old, were based on actual events gleaned from newspaper reports. For us the bomb served as a symbol for the prevailing violent culture of our times, whether it was in the marketing of 'Superguns' as toys for kids or the self destructive competition in the school system, or the armament-dealing world of adults in the play. A song from the play went:

> So burn out the beautiful hopes in your head.
> Put them away, let them die
> And when all your tomorrows just go up in flames

Then look away and sigh
Forget all the pictures of pain that you see
Yours is not to reason why.

Azaadi (1985) came next, a close look at the genesis of communalism in India from the national movement onwards. As the 1984 violence in Delhi had deeply disturbed us, we felt the need to explore and express our concerns. The play took the form of a collage juxtaposing contemporary and past events, culminating in a song which asked whether the freedom struggle was over or just beginning:

We live in the silence after the scream
The stillness after the dying
Here in the dark you question what comes next
You wonder which way you'll go
Azaadi
The burning of the sun
The shining of a distant star
in your eyes.

The separation of 'us' from 'them', political interference, communal history were all reflected in a production that deeply disturbed its audience. Performed in an arena style, the production used puppets, phad painting with slogan writing and stylized movement to dramatic effect.

The plays grew out of their own concerns, the lyrics and scripts were written entirely by them and Param Vir and I only helped to shape the final outcome.

From this crucible of talent emerged many formidable voices, leaders in the cultural arena today, such as Pankaj Rishi Kumar and Avijit Mukul Kishore, both outstanding documentary filmmakers with much to say and highly original ways to say it, Jagan Shah and Jatinder Singh Marwaha who have moved way beyond their original discipline, architecture, and the activist couple, Ashwini Rao and Rupal Oza, in New York along with the fine actor-cum-therapist Siddharth Chakravarti in Seattle. Siddhartha Mukerjee, the author and oncologist and above all thinker extraordinaire, as well as Shuddhabrata Sengupta of the Raqs Media Collective, a critic/curator/impresario in the arts, were a part of the group that included several others. Mentoring and nurturing these talented individuals from the ages of fifteen to their early twenties, was a joy and a celebration for me.

Looking back on the MTW experience, I felt it was important not only in that young people were selecting, researching and writing their own material, but that everything they wrote reflected the close link between self and society. India in the early 1980s was in the throes of a vast political change. The tyrannical overbearing image of Indira Gandhi was open to question. The Durga ma image that was created for her after the liberation of Bangladesh in 1971 was now a decade old. The Emergency had opened our eyes to the need for the intelligentsia to question and even challenge the State. Democracy and civil liberties were something that we could not take for granted. And the battle was ongoing. New political forces, Dalit and OBC on the one hand and right wing on the other, were beginning to gain momentum.

All of this got reflected in the young people's plays.

Support for the MTW work came in a great measure from the Max Mueller Bhavan and the British Council. Param Vir was a master at gaining their support and we rehearsed for years on Sunday mornings in the MMB library and got British Council funding to bring over musicians to work with us on our large-scale musical productions. I had changed the population of MTW dramatically, bringing in children from a range of different social backgrounds, not only the children of university professors, bringing in girls and choosing to work in Hindi often. My own experience of working with the urban poor in Ankur, of involvement in the women's movement and the nascent environmental movement, along with production of plays like Mahasweta Devi's *1084 ki Ma* had both widened and deepened my understanding of the Indian reality.

Faced with a generation ten or twelve years younger than myself and their relentless questioning of what they experienced, read and rallied against, pushed me to confront several issues which many of my peers—all well into their careers—had brushed under the carpet. Many of my Ruchika colleagues had gone into the corporate sectors—hospitality, trade, export; others into academic careers while some had ventured into full-time careers in theatre, television and film, more often behind the camera.

These intensly creative years encouraged many of the MTW members to move into careers in the arts. Till today, thirty years later, several of them still work regularly with me or keep in touch. MTW is 'family' to them and our home remains the adda for many impromptu parties.

My career gained an entirely new dimension through one of the last projects I did with them. They were all grown up, ready to take flight, to move across India and the world to train for their own professional careers. And then there was the Mehrauli project.

Mehrauli is a small urban village in Delhi today and architecturally still the capital's most interesting area. It was the hub of the city in the 1100s and over the subsequent centuries has added onto its architectural legacy, starting with the resplendent, graceful Qutub Minar, the tallest brick tower in the world, that overshadows the Quwwat-ul-Islam mosque. This mosque, made up of pillars from several religious structures that possibly existed here earlier, has a beautiful qibla screen gracefully decorated with the geometry, calligraphy and arabesque that mark Islamic architecture around the world. Close by is the madrassa established by Allaudin Khilji, the Alai Darwaza built by him and Sultan Altamash's tomb.

In the immediate vicinity are the wonderful stepwell, Rajon ki Baoli, the tomb of Akbar's foster brother Adam Khan and Zafar Mahal, where the last Mughal emperor stayed when he travelled to Mehrauli every year to celebrate the multi-faith Phool Walon ke Sair. All in all, an area of Delhi redolent with history. And then there were the new challenges of this 'urban village' that was in the process of being engulfed by the metropolis.

I had just completed a four-month project in which the students, staff and some of us from Ankur had been led through Meharuli by Meera Chatterjee and Narayani Gupta and had created an invigorating heritage education project. Ritu Menon (of Kali for Women, now Women Unlimited) asked me to make a film about this project. As I stuttered, 'But I have never...', 'Oh, just go ahead, you have seen so many films, surely you can make one yourself,' was Ritu's reply. At the time she headed the Educational Division of the newly established INTACH, the Indian National Trust for Art and Cultural Heritage.

I decided that instead of trying to capture something of the educational process that had just got over, I should record a new group of young people as they experienced their first brush with the environment of the past and its interplay with contemporary urban issues. Working with a small camera team, I introduced the MTW group to Mehrauli. This poem by Shuddhabrata Sengupta, written on site at a stepwell, captures the essence of our experience:

Time curves back and forth
Like a punkah

And spidery questions crawl
On the stones of Zafar Mahal

Arches and doorways
Sandstone and marble
And holes in the wall
Whisper an unfinished story

Does the forgotten mosque call the faithful to prayer?
Does the drunk in the gutter spy on the
Princess in the garden?
Do the broken pillars dream of being whole?

Does chisel strike marble?
Do dynasties crumble
Do Emperors reign
And craftsmen work once again?

The story stands still like Zafar Mahal
Interrupted
History is a sly old snake
Coiled in the crevice of an Emperor's tomb.

The film turned out marvellously and Doordarshan, the only TV channel at the time, screened it on a Sunday night at nine p.m., just after the weekly Hindi movie. Phone calls and letters poured in from educationists around the country, celebrating the project and wanting to know how to carry out similar activities themselves. Ritu said, 'Well, now that you have done the film, write the book.' And that was precisely what I did.

Now in its second edition, this book, *Exploring an Environment: Discovering the Urban Reality*, helped me to lay out a format and showed me the way forward, shaping much of my career over the next thirty years. I ran similar projects in

Jaipur (1990 onwards), then in Kashmir (2004–11) both with my colleague Priti Jain, and most recently, I have initiated a similar heritage education project in Hyderabad (2019–20).

The intangible heritage of a city, its unique local culture, is a very new area of inquiry. For it to continue, to be refreshed and rejuvenated, it must first be thoroughly understood. In our country 80 per cent of the cities are historical, with a majority of them being built in the late eighteenth century. While our major cities today—Kolkata, Mumbai, Chennai and Bangalore—were put into place by the British, there are many others—Srinagar, Varanasi, Delhi—with much older histories. The urban settlement has taken many different forms in India. For the repository of a culture is finally its people. Heritage has to be embedded in the people's way of life if it is to flourish. While certain individuals and certain art forms can only cater to a select few, culture at its widest and most vibrant must 'belong' to the people from where it has emerged, for it to have significance, to have life.

Delving into the myriad aspects of what constitutes the heritage of a city and gives it its unique character has been a journey of discovery. Jaipur, where I ran my second Heritage Education project, has become a second home to me over the past thirty-plus years. I enjoy its wide avenues and old buildings, its peacocks and its changing seasons. To wake up in the morning in a colonial property and have a large peacock leap onto your window sill with its characteristic cry, is sheer joy.

To most of the world, Jaipur is seen as being exotic, picturesque, mysterious, enchanting, a name redolent with history and culture. But today this city with its rich past is bursting at the seams as it struggles to renew itself, keep alive its fast-disappearing culture and lifestyle. Malls replace Maniharon ka Rasta, MTV replaces the Kalbelia dance, cement replaces lime plaster... yet both must co-exist. But what do students of today really know of their own legacy? Of the history of the city they live in? Its lifestyle and language, its architectural heritage, its fabulous recipes and community celebrations? Keeping pace with the fast-changing world of today and tomorrow has its own cost.

Every city has a story to tell. A story of how it began, why it began, how it developed and grew, what it has become today and what it 'hopes' for its future. And Jaipur has one of the most fascinating stories among the cities of India.

I found Srinagar equally intriguing when I began work there in 2004. With its characteristic architecture of wood and brick that have aged over the centuries, the many bridges over the Jhelum, for Srinagar was a riverine culture, the unique Sufi shrines with their pagoda-like structures, the singular 'dub' balconies and khatamband ceilings in residences and above all the scenic beauty of the Valley charmed me.

Located at the crossroads of four very different civilizations, each of which had a tremendous impact on local history, Kashmir also met three other empires—the empires of religion— Hinduism, Buddhism and Islam. So as we uncover the layers of Kashmiri history we see a tapestry made up of very different strands.

During the heritage education workshops we conducted in the Valley, each participant got a feel of the oral history of Srinagar, visited old houses, monuments, bridges and toured the city. They described the street on which they lived, carried out research on crafts, collected local legends and created short plays around Srinagar's history. This culminated in a large public exhibition attended by hundreds of children and a festival of films for children. Many children had never seen a film on the large screen ever!

While my Mehrauli experience was encapsulated in a film and a book, Kashmir saw the writing of two books, one called *Discovering Kashmir* on the project Priti Jain and I had headed, and the other on the traditional architecture of Srinagar, commissioned by INTACH and Roli Books.

More recently, beginning in 2018, I have initiated a project entitled BIG (Before It Goes) to document the varied unique local celebrations that are held annually in distant parts of our country. With three members of MTW, Pankaj, Mukul and Jatinder, working alongside me, and a young talented photographer, Nikhil Roshen, on board we hope to create a window into understanding lesser documented local traditions of India.

Thirty-seven years later the spirit of MTW lives on!

Twenty-three

The Right Script

Searching for and finding just the right script that will excite and challenge my actors, my audience and most importantly myself has been a round the year process for me for over forty years. If I read a play and feel that I know how to direct it, I usually don't choose it!

From the very beginning, impatient with the limited themes and restricted horizons of British and American authors, I worked a lot from translation. Looking back at the huge range of plays I have directed, and they number more than 300 full-length productions, I realized that I have extensively directed texts that were originally in Polish, Hebrew, Swedish, Norwegian, Russian, French, Greek, Spanish, Arabic, Chinese, Japanese, leave alone Marathi, Bengali, Hindi, Rajasthani and of course English.

Setsuko, Himiko, Tajomaru, Natalya, Shipuchkin, Jean, Berenger, Krogstad, Mrs Alving, Lakshmi, Saroj, Sadhana, Sujata, Vrati, Manoj, Waghmare, instead of Tom, Dick, and Harry are the names of the characters in my plays.

I have adapted from real-life events, novels, short stories, scripted from improvisation and have also written original plays. Keeping a finger on the pulse of society and the issues it is constantly debating and articulating is for me the task of drama.

A trilogy of plays that I directed between 2007–2011 reflected issues relevant to the fast-transforming social landscape of Delhi. The challenge was to create a series of scripts that would immediately mirror the concerns of the audience I drew. *People Like Us*, *Choices* and *After Dark* were the three plays.

What happens to three grown up sisters living together in Defence Colony, when they come to the realization that their father molested them as children, even as the middle sister battles a sexual harassment case in office? Ironically, the compensation money she gets goes to finance an operation for the father who molested them. This was the plot of *People Like Us*.

In *Choices*, Ayesha returns from her highly placed career in the UN to the family property in Civil Lines in Old Delhi, that her grandmother has left her as an inheritance The dead grandmother, the living granddaughter and the mother trapped between the two must come to terms with the choices they have made in their lives.

What happens when a young woman battling issues of gender discrimination at the workplace begins dating a young man who is new to Delhi? He belongs to conservative small-town Shimla, while she is a rebel who has built an independent life for herself. Can their two worlds ever connect? Or will they collide? Juxtaposed with her story is the story of middle-aged Shiela, a housewife from Lajpat Nagar. Her husband walks out on her and yet she is resilient enough to liberate herself from a lifetime of drudgery and being a persona non grata. Meanwhile the young woman grows increasingly anxious as her date transforms into a stalker. This was the plot of *After Dark*. Very much the stuff of Delhi newpaper headlines.

Aakritiyan (images), a play that we evolved completely through improvisations in 1982, followed the events of six months in 1947, pre- and post-Partition. Since most of the actors in Ruchika belonged to families that had migrated to Delhi during Partition, the play built on the individual stories of their own families. Along with the family interviews that formed the backbone of the play, we also collectively read Bhisham Sahni's *Tamas*, Chaman Nahal's *Azadi* and Khushwant Singh's *Train to Pakistan* to give us a thorough grounding in the reality of those years.

Journalist Pamela Philipose interviewed me about the production at that time. 'An event that took over one million lives cannot disappear from popular consciousness. Razor-sharp shards of memory have worked their way into the collective psyche of two nations. And long after the event, images recollected in relative tranquillity breathe new life into an old experience. The Partition cannot be forgotten, and indeed should not be forgotten—it is the closest the Indian subcontinent has got to the gas chambers of Auschwitz,' I told her.

During the first show, many in the audience broke down and wept. The experience gave me a clue as to why so few people have attempted the theme of Partition on the stage. Somehow, we still have to come to terms with it.

Another issue that exercises me and that I want to better understand through my plays is the senseless violence of the young. We read their stories daily in our newspaper, we discuss them vehemently and offer opinions, and then we completely forget till reality slaps us in the face once again. *A Matter of Life and Death* (2008) revisited the famous American trial of the 1930s where two affluent young men, Leopold and Loeb, killed a classmate to commit the 'perfect' murder. A major lawyer of the time, Clarence Darrow, defended them and they got a life sentence. The play raises crucial questions of morality, class and justice. *Chaal* (2010) was an adaptation of the novel and film *The Talented Mr Ripley*, and had a maniacal Pranay Manchanda in the lead role. This story of a cold-blooded conman is disturbing because the author gets us to empathize with him.

From the 1980s I have consciously sought out women playwrights as they bring a refreshing perspective. In a world in which we increasingly look upon women as beauty objects—to be devoured, beaten, raped and yanked out of their culture, we need to re-examine our ways of looking, our ways of understanding.

I have had a chance to work with several leading American women playwrights. Marsha Norman's *Night Mother* that argues the case for suicide was a trailblazer. And I had the privilege of having one of the first-ever Skype conversations with the playwright organized by the USIS. Wendy Kesselman's *Blood Bond* was offered to me while still in manuscript form. Wendy Wasserstein's *The Heidi Chronicles*, the iconic play about a group of women as they come of age in the Women's Movement, was directed by me for Jesus and Mary College. Rose Leiman Goldemberg's *Letters Home* (1986–87), a dramatization of Sylvia Plath's letters to her mother leading up to her suicide, was one of my finest productions and had Smita Vats playing Sylvia Plath to Mona Chawla as her mother.

At the end of 2019 we were fortunate to get the rights from Pulitzer prize winner Lynn Nottage to adapt her powerful play *Ruined* (*Barbaad*) that is set in a brothel located between the armed forces, extremists and the landless tribals.

Other women playwrights whose work I have directed include Shelagh Stephenson's *The Memory of Water*, Olwen Wymark's outstanding study of schizophrenia, *Find Me,* and Velina Hasu Houston's play about five Japanese women, *Tea*.

After the horrific atomic bombs were dropped on Hiroshima and Nagasaki, bringing an end to Word War II, Japan was defeated and one lakh women married American GIs and moved to America. *Tea* is about how life has treated five of these women over the years. The starting point is the suicide by the central character, Himiko. The play deals with the clash of cultures, the contained, petite, cute, well-behaved Orientals, very much like traditional Indian women, and the brash, bullying American. Their continuing search for the elusive American dream, full of glamour and ripe with opportunity, is the subject of the play.

It talks of all our stories of migration, belongingness, acceptance and loneliness. Infused with lyricism and deft, light touches, this play has been performed internationally to great acclaim. During rehearsals we discussed why we chose to do this play now. Someone said it's about the Iraq war, someone else said it's about displacement and someone else connected it with her own life and how she feels at home in New York and a misfit in Delhi.

Even more challenging than *Tea* were five monologues by France Rame and Dario Fo that I brought to the stage in the 1980s and revived later. Marvellously realized by the highly talented Mona Chawla, the monologues explored the world of women—from household drudgery to being the mother of a terrorist!

Of course there have been several women authors of our own country whom I have had the privilege of working with and adapting: Mahasweta Devi (*Hazar Chaurasi ki Ma*) Kusum Ansal (*Rekha Kriti*) and Nasima Aziz (*Women Without Men*).

And then my constant search for relevant scripts pushed me towards writing original plays. Even though I have been directing for the past forty years, my first foray into playwriting took me twelve years to complete. Being a student of history, the Mughal Empress Noor Jahan had always intrigued me. Four hundred years ago, this young girl, abandoned as a child by parents who were political refugees, rose to become Empress of Mughal India. She was a widow with a child, and yet she married Emperor

Jahangir and became his twentieth wife. Both a businesswoman and a connoisseur of art, and perhaps also a conniving bitch.

What moulded this woman who rose like a phoenix from the ashes of a brutal first marriage? How did she hold such power in a patriarchal society where all women were in purdah? Virtually ruling all of India as her husband was lost in a miasma of drugs and alcohol. And who proved to be her nemesis?

The resonances and echoes of today that I attempted in this script posed the real challenge. Deciding to see the entire story through the eyes of a eunuch, confidante of both Noor and her niece Mumtaz Mahal, gave the play a very unique gendered lens.

I worked on the script steadily over the years, battling with the contrary pulls of real history and artistic license. When it was completely ready I decided to open it far away. Just in case it was a failure, I could bury my ambitions as a playwright on distant shores. But I was happily surprised. An invitation from the US by a new group, EnActe Arts, gave me the required push. *Noor* opened in English, for ten shows in San Francisco and San Jose in the summer of 2013. In Delhi it opened in a wonderful Urdu translation by Mr Javed, a well-known professor and author of several radio plays, four years later. Luckily for me it was an unqualified success and encouraged me to write more.

Since 1987, I have enjoyed reading all the fresh new translations of Tagore that appeared every year. Eloquent, evocative writing— poetic, emotional, suffused with sadness. Poetry, drama, stories, novels, novellas, articles, and in all of them the same woman seemed to appear: loving yet distant, obviously his muse. Who was this woman, I wondered. Krishna Kripalani's wonderful biography of Tagore provided the answer. Robi's sister-in-law, Kadambari, had married his elder brother, Jyotirindranath, at the age of eleven. With just a year's age difference between the brother and sister-in-law, the two developed a strong bond over the years. For the longest time, she was his only reader, friend and confidante in a house full of more than a hundred people. I was fascinated.

My play explored the strong bond between the two which is not talked about openly. The fact that Kadambari committed suicide four months after Tagore's marriage indicates the depth of their bond and I drew 80 per cent of my text from the prose, poetry and music of Tagore. It seeks to explore their relationship through the medium of Tagore own words.

Blending these together seamlessly was the major challenge I faced and then I searched for a production style that would do justice to Tagore's characters, situations, the period and the poetry. Apart from the three main characters, Kadambari, her husband and Tagore's brother Jyoti, and Tagore himself, the rest of the cast are acapella (unaccompanied) singers and narrators of the story.

A Quiet Desire opens with a young Robi, Jyoti and Kadambari enjoying a summer together in Chandanagar. The striking age gap between Kadambari and Jyoti and her close relationship with Robi is evident within the first few minutes. We follow the three in a boat on the Padma river, where Robi's songs and poetry melt into one another, creating an air of suspended animation and beauty. As the play progresses, we see Robi's increasing fame as a poet making him drift away from Kadambari, once his sole admirer, critic and inspiration. The growing distance with Robi and her own husband's indifference, drive Kadambari into severe depression leading to her suicide.

The play is suffused with melancholia and loneliness, themes intrinsic to Tagore's work. His deep understanding of a woman's psyche in a fast-changing world is the central theme of this play. Poetic narration and his own songs in Bengali help to expand this theme.

Through all these plays women emerge as resilient, strong people who fight their own battles. For us in Ruchika, it is important that theatre as an art form raises pertinent questions about our day and age. Theatre is really the forum of debate, discussion and ideas. That's how it becomes significant to the actors, the director and ultimately to the audience.

Choosing the right content for the children's theatre that I direct alongside my adult theatre work has also posed an immense challenge. Too much of what is written for children to perform is still about princesses waiting to be rescued from their fate by brave princes, or curses surrounding a helpless maiden. In one verson of *Cinderella* that I directed, the young Cinderella stopped midway while escaping from the prince at midnight, whipped off one of her silver shoes and left it on the steps of the palace, saying, 'Bring me that, prince!'

In another *Cinderella* I directed years later, Cinderella was a karate champion! *Alladin* of course is excellent material as is the *Panchatantra* (which I have directed fourteen times!) as they are both stories of living by your wits in the real world and of being street smart.

Alibaba and the 40 Thieves was adapted by me, and set in an upwardly mobile family in Gurgaon, where Ali's brother Kasim owns several malls, fleets of cars and a number of 'aspirational' pet dogs! And then by the mid 1990s new scripts, many of them gender sensitive or reinterpretations of classical stories, began to be published.

Rudyard Kipling's *Jungle Book* was directed by me for NSD's Theatre in Education Company as it is the ultimate coming-of-age story. We retitled it *Yeh bhi Jungle, Woh bhi Jungle.*

Mowgli experiences every important transition of adolescence: the breaking of rules, attraction to a delinquent subculture, asserting his manhood and finally, a search for his identity.

Fear, friendship, fun, drama and comedy were the ingredients of our production, which was based entirely on Kipling's original *Jungle Book* and not the one adapted by Disney.

Kipling's view of the jungle is anti-colonial in the extreme. By the time he began writing, a very clear colonial forest policy was in place in our country. Existing jungles were to be cleared, and in their place manmade forests of cheap timber were planted. Wood that could be used for building railway tracks, build ships and for export abroad. By contrast Kipling's jungle emphasizes that this is the animals' home, and has space for every animal. Rules and regulations and a jungle law govern all transactions; here 'man' is the jungle's greatest threat for he hunts animals for pleasure, and razes entire forests to the ground. In fact Kipling's view seems like the in-ecological view of the 1990s (and remember the *Jungle Book* appeared in 1893). Nature knows best, and man really can't interfere with it without causing damage to himself. It is in this delicately balanced ecosystem that Mowgli must grow into a young man. His educational process is one of understanding the jungle, 'every scratch of a bat's claws meant as much to him as the work of his office means to a businessman.' And what he cannot learn from Bhalloo and Bagheera, he must learn from actual experience. He must respect the boundaries of others and truly believe 'we be of one blood, you and I', for to transgress them is to court disaster, for one cannot destroy a part without destroying the whole. These lessons, learnt during a carefree childhood, hold good for Mowgli through a gawky adolescence, and finally as he transits into adulthood, responsibility and identity.

He must pay the debts of childhood, come to terms with adulthood and seek his own path. But even as he walks alone, he is secure in the knowledge he has gained from those who nurtured him. For a time comes in every person's life when he must cast off the slough and move forward.

Twenty-four

My Mother's End

My mother spent the last three years of her life in hospital. She had an immune condition that required her to be in a more or less sterile environment. But her adjustment to the reality of hospitalization was amazing and even inspirational.

We worked hard as a family to create a 'normalcy' around her changed living condition. The nursing home was close to our respective homes, and Amal and I filled her room with her paintings, her bedroom curtains, even her food came daily from home. I visited her at least five days a week, often coordinating my timings to eat lunch or drink tea with her. Two of her friends came once a week to spend the entire day, chit-chatting over a Chinese lunch. She had her bed repositioned so she could enjoy the large tree that leaned towards her window. Her bedside table always held the latest novel and next to the TV were a bunch of films she was yet to see. Her driver reported to her every morning and she was ready with a list of errands for him. Her tailor would come by to fashion yet another of her innumerable self-designed kaftans. Artists and actors, old friends and even older family retainers made the time to visit her as she had for them in her lifetime. Till the last day she was dictating material for her third book on Indian costume. Even though her body was slowly giving way, her mind was ablaze with activity.

Nephews, nieces, in-laws, grandchildren leave alone my wife, sister, brother-in-law and father were there regularly. In her last days M.F. Husain dropped by and the hospital was agog with the visit of 'Mr Madhuri Dixit', as he was known at the time. Husain had been an ardent admirer of the film star Madhuri Dixit and had painted her on many occasions, hence the name! Three days before he died veteran film actor Amrish Puri called to speak to my mother in his deep baritone voice. He had been one of my father's earliest students in his Bombay days. Amrish, a fabulous actor on the stage had gained fame and notoriety by his performance as the villain Mogambo in the megahit, *Mr India*.

My mother died as she had lived, surrounded by family. My last image of her was her with an oxygen mask on her face, raising her hand to give me a thumbs up sign.

I was not overwhelmed with grief at her passing. I was of course sad but I was also quietly relieved that she had gone painlessly and swiftly. She had made it clear through her life that she should not be put on any machine in order to live and we all assiduously followed her instruction. The day after her funeral I rejoined the final rehearsals of a massive children's play I was directing for a Delhi school. The show was only three days away and I knew that was what she would have wanted me to do. The show must go on.

I had interacted with my mother every single day of my life and since moving to our new flat in 1992, my mother had stayed every night under our roof until she shifted to hospital.

She was a woman of habit and ritual. Early in the morning after her bed tea that was to be served sharp at seven with the tea made just so, the doily and the tea cosy placed just so... she would walk down to her house ten minutes away and spend time in her garden watching the birds and interacting with her plants. Surrounded by foliage and flowers, just sitting and listening to the chirping of birds or seeing them in the birdbath made her happy. My mother was very close to nature. Mid morning would see her at her desk in the India International Centre library working on her new book, the third volume in a series on Indian costume, and soon after lunch she would move to Art Heritage, the gallery she had set up in the Triveni Kala Sangam basement. Here, as she had done for over thirty years, she nurtured the talents of several young artists, while still presenting the 'greats' in Indian Art. I helped out occasionally designing the display of a ceramic or sculpture show. For many of my friends she was their friend too—she was Roshen to them—eager to find out about their lives, their thoughts, their aspirations. Ever willing to take them around the gallery, to explain contemporary art or even to share a recipe. She quietly encouraged everyone along—no advice, always a suggestion. Her insatiable curiosity about life, about people, their joys, hurts and sorrows are the foremost memory of all who surrounded her.

Many of my friends wept uncontrollably at her funeral, including the usually impassive Pablo Bartholomew. Everyone who acted with me had looked forward eagerly to her detailed feedback after the opening night of my new productions and she often saw my plays more than once. After all her career in the theatre had begun with her brother, Sultan Padamsee, when she was sixteen and she died at eighty-five—a career of sixty-nine years. And a life quietly lived, dignified, yet full of passion.

Throughout her life she was constantly reaching out to the last person—to those neglected or in need of care or understanding. My mother worked in Bombay in the early 1960s with terminally ill children on the hospital ward—playing with them, telling them stories, cheering them up in their last hours. In Delhi she worked with the Okhla Centre for the Mentally Challenged and when my wife Radhika started an NGO for children with disability, my mother was its greatest supporter, always eager to know and learn something new about disability. In her last days in hospital I remember her proudly showing me a list of the people she had sponsored to have cataract operations.

In the late 1980s, deciding to write a follow up to her initial book on Ancient Indian costume, my mother began work on the next volume. Some of her research required that she study miniatures of the same period housed in collections at the Topkapi Museum in Istanbul and the Hermitage in St Petersburg. My mother took me along to assist her. We sat in the backrooms of these outstanding museums handling twelfth-century miniatures, my mother talking notes while I copied out details from them. It was a fascinating task and sharpened my abilities as both artist and costume designer.

My own career as a costume designer had started while I was still a child—fashioning masks, headgear and costumes for Barry John's productions, first for kids and then, while still in college, for his productions of *Hamlet* and *The Trojan Women*. Years later I was to work as costume designer on two mega serials directed by my sister: *Mullah Nasruddin* and *Raj se Swaraj*. Along with these projects I also design the costumes for all of my own plays. Right from researching the clothes of a particular period and the prevalent colours, to finalizing the silhouette to be created and the appropriate 'look' for each character is a joyous voyage of discovery in each play.

Locating the actual fabric I want to use, its exact shade of colour, it's fall, how to cut the garment and how to use accessory and detail to create just the right garment for each character has become second nature to me. And the speed at which I can do it alarms many! Sharing the evolving costume design for a play with the actors is an intrinsic part of my directorial process. My work as a costume designer has been both a continuation of my mother's legacy in this field and is also an ongoing tribute to her.

One of my mother's lifelong dreams was fulfilled in the last ten years of her life. She had always been keen to have a second home in the mountains, having spent many of her childhood summer holidays along with Miss Murphy and some of the school students at a holiday home in Bhowali near Nainital in the Himalayas.

As luck would have it, my mother-in-law bought a plot on a mountainside in Bhowali, overlooking a reserve forest, and built a beautiful cottage there. Using it as a base and with my father-in-law Sadhan's unstinting support, my mother went in search of where she had stayed as a child over half a century earlier, and located it! She decided this was the sign she was looking for and buying the plot adjacent to my mother-in-law's, had a house built. She gifted this house, even before it was completed, to my wife, and so we now have two homes adjacent to one another in the cool climes of the Himalayas. Here as the mist obliterates the mountains and the excited chatter of many birds fill the sky, we can sit and relax far from the hectic pace of the city.

An air of grace pervaded every action of my mother's, a grace expressed in relationships, in the setting of a table, in an arrangement of flowers, in the fall of a costume—she embodied elegance. To the last her clothes expressed this refinement— weeks before her passing she had a new kaftan tailored for her eighty-fifth birthday, perfect down to the last trimming, the buttons at the throat.

The fine art of food was another quiet passion. Herself an excellent cook, she never failed to enjoy a new dish without putting down the recipe and the name of the person she got it from in brackets. It was as though she wanted to fondly remember the person who had introduced her to the dish, when she herself cooked it. Even cooking was personalized.

She died as she had lived, with great dignity. Many at her funeral were perplexed at her cremation—was she a Muslim or was she really a Parsi? a friend asked me. My mother believed in an abstract god, beyond religion. She did not visit a mosque, temple or church in her lifetime. She was a woman who embodied the value of what it is to be truly 'humane'.

Till today, when faced with a dilemma, I ask myself the question: 'What would my mother have done in this situation?'

All of the values I embody in my personal life and in my professional work in education, theatre and as a counsellor, I owe entirely to my mother. It is the greatest privilege of my life to have been her son.

Twenty-five

The Family Endures

Love came late into my life. Having started my theatre career at seventeen, and a professional career in social work when I was only twenty-one, left me with little time for romantic involvements. Many of my own emotional needs, as with several others in Ruchika, were met within the group itself. And then of course there were 'friends with benefits'. We were 'that' generation.

By the time I was thirty-two, my mother began to worry that I may remain a bachelor! In one of her birthday cards to me, she wrote: 'The deeper one is involved emotionally with other human beings, the more one's relationship with them stirs one in the very depths of one's being, sending a thousand ripples that reach out and enlarge one's perception of life.

'I know that you are now thinking "Ah, mummy is leading up to speaking to me about my getting married". I will not deny that this thought is there, but not in the way you think, my dearest. It is there because I want you to know what it is to share your life with another human being, to experience the wonder of seeing from another's point of view and so expanding your own. To share your dreams and thoughts and so come to understand your own and another's mystery. And more than anything else to know that you can build a place you can return to, where your children can grow and you can share with them all you know and understand—just as I have shared with you and Amal in what have been some of my most treasured moments of life.

'I cannot bear to think that when I am gone—you will come to a home where you will find no one waiting for you. As you grow older you will find all your friends will have made their own homes and will not have the time they may now have, to spend with you and to work alone is a barren exercise if not fed by life and yes, love. So think about it, darling, and choose someone soon—all the girls of your age group, the best ones will soon be gone!'

In an interview that I gave to *The Times of India* in 1985, I wrote: 'There are two important qualities which I personally admire in women. One is the quality of intelligence, along with an independence of spirit. She must be her own person and have the courage to continue being that in all circumstances. She must have her own point of view and be able to hold her own. Though, I must clarify that I don't mean the steamroller kind of person. This is the woman who has the intellectual ability of probing and questions the situations and circumstances that life keeps throwing up.

'The second quality is style. This definitely excludes any reference to physical attributes. Besides being very limiting, it makes a woman a kind of commodity, the kind that beauty pageants make them out to be. Physical attributes are merely outward manifestations. Style, for me, is an individual way of doing things. Not following trends or set patterns and norms.

'Style always comes along with substance. In fact it is the style with which you carry off your substance which is important. When a woman has the perfect combination of these two, it will reflect in her entire personality.'

'Also my kind of woman would always be evolving, be innovative, keep growing, stay alive, which is more than mere survival. It means keeping her interest in life alive always. She must avoid stagnation at all costs.'

Radhika, arrestingly attractive, compassionate and intellectually alive, first met me when I was twenty-seven to do a story on the Music Theatre Workshop. She was a journalist at the time. We only began dating five years later and within six months we decided to marry. As she often says, we were bound to hit it off as both our mothers had scrambled eggs on toast for breakfast! Of course that was one of many reasons, but a shared perspective on life, our concerns, the values we wanted to live by and a deep lasting love were the real reasons. It has been a marvellous companionship of over thirty years with lots of participation in demonstrations and marches for a multitude of causes, a lot of growing together and that final cement: a director and his leading lady. There is no better time of day for me than sharing a cup of tea and conversation with her every morning.

Her ability to constantly be well turned out, to listen with complete empathy, to get passionately involved in causes have been a learning for me. We have travelled the world soaking up new experiences, and bringing up our kids together has been a wonderful rollercoaster ride with occasional low times and many high times.

Undeniably, Radhika has been my closest and constant companion since marriage but before that for years it was my cousin Rhea along with a few select others. What exactly creates that 'chemistry' to be able to bond without borders is a million-dollar question.

To grow with someone alongside you through your life is an incredible experience. And for Rhea and me it has been just that. Bearing witness to another person's life and being available to them whenever they have needed a compassionate shoulder and vice versa has been an important part of my life, and one I have always done horizontally—with people of my own age. To be your naked self, warts and all and also to be able to discuss the most disturbing and intimate secrets is both a responsibility and a privilege. And that I am often privy to as a counsellor, but that is with a stranger and in a professional context.

Interestingly the two actresses, Paro Anand and Meera Jain, who I overtook to play the Baroness Gudrun von Grubelstein in Barry John's production of *Trudi and the Minstrel* when I was fifteen, became and remain my closest friends. Paro played my pet troll in this production and Meera my pet dragon! So the arrogant baroness, her dragon and her troll: a weird collection of formidable villains all together and altogether different to one another as people. With them I have with ease shared many parts of my life that are hidden to others.

My sister Amal has been my staunchest supporter through life other than my wife. Amal has always looked out for me, kept me in her protective shadow, as every elder sister should. And Nissar has been her perfect companion. Their exciting avant garde theatre work of many years has been followed by a complete immersion into furthering my father's formidable legacy. As families, we are very close and her children and grandchildren often invite themselves over to our place for dinner and a chat.

A close circle of friends: the ever-dependable Sunil Arora, my 'lights' man and much more and his delightful wife Meenakshi, always ready with an acerbic retort to my non-stop gabbling, Paro, the children's book writer and her husband Keshav, excellent actor and most compassionate human being, and the talented duo of Mona and Nona Chawla. These six friends along with Radhika and myself form a tight group, meeting at least once a month over the past ten years. For Rhea, as she lives in faraway LA, we have an annual meeting of families, three or four intense days of catching up every year, basking in each others's company.

Fatherhood has been one of the most fulfilling experiences of my life. I remember when my older son Zaen was born, I requested the nurses at the nursing home where Radhika had delivered him, to wake me up early the next morning and teach me how to bathe him. They burst into laughter. I couldn't understand the reason why. They said in their seventeen years working at the nursing home, no father had made such a request! But I had my way.

I actively involved myself in every aspect of Zaen's development and did a lot of carrying, bottle-feeding and burping! With Armaan, our second son, it was the same. I remember how after two years of almost no speech, he asked me a question one night. I was lying in bed, so was he with his head tucked under my arm while I read him a bedtime story. 'Daddy, yeh toh chuha hai' (this is a mouse) was the first sentence he uttered. I fell out of bed onto the floor.

Radhika and I worked hard at bringing up our kids gender neutral. Their initial jublas (baby dresses) were all yellow, no pinks and blues. And we strongly believed that they should be aesthetically attuned to an Indian sensibility, so instead of the usual Disney characters that are printed, embroidered and embossed on every children's garment and bit of nursery furniture, Radhika embroidered elephants and peacocks onto their baby clothes.

My close attention to fatherhood, its joys and responsibilities was an obvious reaction to my own father not being around for many of my childhood years. Luckily for me my father-in-law, the warm and friendly Sadhan Mullick, compensated tremendously for my absentee father. He was always around as he lived next door, sitting with me at the table for lunch, enquiring with great interest on my latest assignment, encouraging and supporting my burgeoning interest in TV production. He himself had been head of Doordarshan and had set up the TV section of the Film Institute of India in Pune before he retired. He was inspirational to me, almost a role model. He had a joyful, happy-go-lucky attitude towards life that endeared him to people.

My father was aware of Sadhan's influence on me, and at the memorial meeting we organized after Sadhan's death, he spoke of how lucky I had been to have him as a father-in-law, as he made up for many of the gaps he himself had left in my growing-up years.

Both Zaen and Armaan have matured beautifully into caring, kind and compassionate men and have been lucky to find life companions engrossed in the same questions that they grapple with in their careers. It's been an exciting journey for Radhika and me as we exposed them to issues, causes, ideologies close to our hearts from the very beginning. We also encouraged them to always be around and participate as equals when our friends and colleagues were over. Through their childhood we travelled for a month every year as a family, exposing our kids to all parts of India, many parts of Asia, Europe and of course England. Having spent a good deal of my formative years in the south, I didn't want the kids to grow up with the notion that north India was the only India and everyone else was a 'madrassi'! There is no better education than travel. And the family tradition of acting and direction continues with them, rounded off by Sadhan's push for them to turn into avid football players.

My mother brought to our children all the experience she had gained working with young children over the years. A cupboard full of toys, retelling the story of Ramayan with wooden figurines, involving them in the viewing of art and encouraging their first attempts at writing put them firmly in touch with their own creativity. With my mother-in-law, Mohini Mullick, a double doctorate and professor of philosophy for years at the Kanpur IIT, they have engaged with the world of ideas, debate and vigorous discussion. They also equally enjoy her masterful cooking and her beautiful cottage-like home in the hills.

But it is Radhika's amazing ability to relate to even the last person with compassion and warmth that has given them tremendously humane qualities,

Mumbai and often Kulsum Terrace itself, still remains the family's gathering place and at least once a year, most of us cousins, including those living abroad, get together for two or three days to celebrate a birthday, whether the person is alive or dead! Often sitting around that age-old horseshoe table!

Over the last few years we have redone our house in Delhi, remodelling every floor, letting in light, keeping out sound as we live on a busy road, greening as we go. Andhra stone in shades of russet browns and pale yellows, deep streaks of grey and maroon line the floor leading to our signature spiral staircase, the site of many TV shoots. In the living room three paintings of women by Husain, Souza and Krishen Khanna face each other, on the staircase there are three striking tree studies by Zaen in black and white. Our bedroom is bathed in light and I spend much of the day writing in a rattan chair, occasionally looking out at the activities on the road. Next to me is a sunburst design Portuguese cupboard in shades of white and grey that often has a huge vase of cut flowers on it. The rest of our first floor is a large open plan kitchen/living space designed by Armaan, visually striking and highly functional. On the second floor Zaen and his partner of fifteen years, Naina, have done up their book-lined flat with sparkling white floors and in their own style.

Right on top is Teesri Manzil, our rehearsal cum small

informal performance space with a sprung wooden floor, excellent for movement. A simple grid of inexpensive theatre lighting is in place as is a perfect acoustic. This large area opens up to a wonderful rooftop garden, created and tended to by Radhika. Thirteen types of vegetables and a vast array of flowers attract hosts of butterflies and bees.

It is to Teesri Manzil that my actors aged 16–70 arrive almost every evening for rehearsal. And twice a week my young actors aged 8–14 come for a workshop. This space often doubles up as a party venue or to host the family for a Sunday lunch.

Many family traditions must be nurtured, if they are to endure. Radhika and I have created our own tradition of the family eating together with her parents and my mother every night. A family that eats together, stays together. My mother had continued the Sunday family lunch tradition for many years and now that she is no more, my sister does the same. Unwinding and chatting with members of our two families, and there are sixteen of us, over a delicious leisurely lunch of recipes taken from my mother's recipe book, is an event everyone looks forward to. Three generations come together sharing thoughts and activities. Occasionally we even follow up this 'fat lunch' with a 'thick' sleep and some of us then head off to the movies! Shades of Kulsum Terrace and the carrying on of a family tradition that is now almost a hundred years old.

Epilogue

Last Act

My father died in August 2020 during the Covid-19 pandemic that paralyzed the world. He was ninety-four and went quietly without any pain having led a life in which he was much celebrated, won several laurels and enriched the lives of thousands with his pioneering work in theatre and art. The last years of his life were spent under the caring, eagle eye of my sister and brother-in-law and a wonderful team of caretakers led by his devoted low-key servant of over thirty years, Jeevan. It was Jeevan's father Dewan Singh who had opened the door to my mother on that traumatic night in 1963 when my parents separated.

Despite their separation my parents had been the closest friends, intellectual companions, professional colleagues for over sixty-five years. This poem by my mother captured something of their turbulent relationship.

Mosaic

Man—wife
Deep note—long drawn
Strong thread—hold fast
Love filled—calm thoughts

Work done
Hate shrilled—lust filled
Undone
Two minds—entwined
Root bound
Dig deep—heart beat
Sound on.

My father had been devasted by my mother's death in 2007. We found a large collection of her poems, in her own handwriting. My father took them home and read through them and was deeply disturbed. Perhaps he realized the kind of loneliness and sorrow that she had lived with. Within a couple of years of her going he also lost his constant companion of the past fifty-odd years, Uma Anand, who had battled cancer for several years.

My father was suddenly alone, perhaps for the first time in his life. He had grown up in the midst of a bustling, closely knit family in Pune, then moved to Bombay for college where the very welcoming Padamsee family engulfed him for twenty years. Even when he split the Theatre Group the family still doted on him, enjoying his excellent sense of humour and delighting second-hand in his achievements. He was, after all, Sultan's closest friend and had been part of the family since he was eighteen.

For the rest of his life two women, my mother and Uma, had always been at his side. My mother definitely the more independent and wilful.

Since his departure from NSD, my father and she had spent over thirty years working every day to build the reputation of the gallery. Each year, they would travel to Kuwait together, where they shared a home. If ever he was alone in Kuwait, he had only to call upon two of his sisters and his favourite niece, who stayed in the same building. It was incumbent on him to have lunch daily with one of his sisters, and his doting younger brother was only a phone call away. Otherwise in Delhi, London and New York which he visited every year, Uma had always been with him.

When my parents separated, it did create a distance between father and son. I remember my mother advising Alyque when he divorced Pearl, 'You can divorce your partner but you can never divorce your children.' Easily said but almost impossible to do. Any couple who separate are acutely aware that their children will grow closer to the parent they live with. I had spent my initial years as a child with both my parents and in the Vithal Court years, my father had been a vital presence in my life. But from the age of nine I had lived exclusively with my mother, as did my sister. As mentioned earlier in this book, Amal had the advantage of seeing my father every day, as she was a student at NSD. But though my mother valiantly strove to keep father and son together, I never had the same rapport with him as I did with her, all through my growing up years.

Now that I am a father to two sons myself I know the importance of being available all the time, to be at your child's side through all the ups and downs that mark the fortunes of every family. Being a father cannot happen over two hours on a Sunday afternoon.

For him and for all the family I was always the outspoken son, the one who talked back. When I was barely twenty and my father attended one of my plays with Uma, I bluntly told him the next day that he should either have come alone or with my mother. He stayed away for fifteen years! But I knew he was extremely proud of my achievements in theatre and in social work, never failing to admire me behind my back.

Certainly in many ways, such as the expression of myself through theatre, I am very much my father's son. Many who have watched my plays regularly see the close link in my work, particularly in the aesthetics of the stage and the high emotional content, that echoes my father's directorial style. Those first eight years at Vithal Court with the rehearsals in full swing were the best theatre education I could get. During my adolescent years I would walk down from my school to NSD after lunch and sit in on my father's rehearsals, learning and absorbing like a sponge.

Did I ever resent Uma's integral role in my father's life? No. She was his steady companion, homemaker, intellectually alive. And she never tried to reach out to either me or my sister, to build an independent relationship with Alkazi's children, something I respected her for. Before she died she sent a message through my father to me asking me to come and see her, and I went. Already completely bedridden and on oxygen, she told me to look after my father once she had gone, and that he would need me to be around.

So there he was after Uma's death, alone. He was already eighty-three and age had set in.

My father bravely soldiered on running Art Heritage and building an institution, the Alkazi Foundation for the Arts, around his collection of nineteenth-century photographs. But the gallery now lacked the warmth and informality of my mother's touch. And the art scene had completely changed. I remember accompanying my father to one of the first editions of the India Art Fair in its early years when it was housed in a strange pavilion in the midst of Pragati Maidan in Delhi. People hurried up to my father, genuflecting and bowing low, but he was not impressed by what he saw.

'Art has found a suitable place, hasn't it, Feisal?' he said in a caustic tone on our way out, 'On one side there is an exhibition of defence missiles, on the other tractors and farm machinery: No need to say more.'

On another occasion I accompanied him to a five-star hotel where he was to release a book on an eminent artist. He was disturbed by the fact that the function had been organized in a bar with the book release happening on the minuscule dance floor. Big money had entered the art world and art was beginning to be seen as an investment rather than as an aesthetic experience. This was no longer a world he recognized or related to, it was no longer a world he wished to belong to. He felt almost out of place in the changed scenario and focused much more on creating the impressive series of exhibitions and publications emanating from his collection of nineteenth-century photography. His grandson Rahaab Allana was groomed by him to take over and proved to be more than equal to the task as he was able to navigate the new world of social media and international collaboration with ease and finesse.

My father was the last survivor of those who had gathered at the horseshoe-shaped dining table seventy-seven years earlier to establish the Theatre Group. With his going an age has ended forever.

Acknowledgements

Thanks to all those family members and friends who were ready to talk with me about what happened along the way to growing up. I certainly hope this book is the first step to recalling memories long buried that will add to a second edition, if there is one!

Special thanks to my cousin Ayesha Sayani for giving me open access to the long video interviews she had done with my mother Roshen, my aunt Candy and uncle Alyque, and family friends Khorshed Ezekiel and Gerson da Cunha. Special thanks also to my sister Amal for spending enormous amounts of time organizing our family photo archives.

I would also like to thank Hamza, my administrative assistant, for making sense of the scrawl of my handwriting and typing out revision after revision. And finally to my wonderfully discreet editor, Renuka Chatterjee, who first floated the idea to me at a Diwali party, catching me totally unawares and rather startled. And then increasingly excited and overjoyed as I began writing. Renuka walked the path with me, subtly suggesting how to tighten and improve my manuscript over an eighteen month period. Many thanks.